the Majesty of JESUS CHRIST

the Majesty of JESUS CHRIST

BURKE REES

CFI
An imprint of Cedar Fort, Inc.
Springville, Utah

This is not an official publication of The Church of Jesus Christ of Latter-day Saints. The opinions and views expressed herein belong solely to the author and do not necessarily represent the opinions or views of Cedar Fort, Inc. Permission for the use of sources, graphics, and photos is also solely the responsibility of the author.

Paperback ISBN 13: 978-1-4621-5017-5
eBook ISBN 13: 978-1-4621-5018-2

Published by CFI, an imprint of Cedar Fort, Inc.
2373 W. 700 S., Suite 100, Springville, UT 84663
Distributed by Cedar Fort, Inc., www.cedarfort.com

Library of Congress Cataloging Number: 2025943173

Cover design by Shawnda Craig

Edited and Typeset by Liz Kazandzhy

Printed in the United States of America

10 9 8 7 6 5 4 3 2 1

Printed on acid-free paper

To Toni, my amazing wife. Thank you for showing me what it means to be a true disciple of Jesus Christ.

Contents

Foreword

Around 600 BC, Nephi saw in vision the Bible going forth among the nations of the earth. He was told by an angel that originally the Bible contained the fulness of the gospel including the covenants the Lord makes with His obedient followers. Then, troubling, Nephi saw that a "great and abominable church" removed from the Bible many plain and precious truths as well as many covenants (see 1 Nephi 13:1–29). Nephi called this church "great" because of its worldwide influence and "abominable" precisely because it removed many plain and precious gospel truths including gospel covenants.

The Prophet Joseph Smith wrote, "From sundry revelations which have been received, it was apparent that many important points touching the salvation of men, had been taken away from the Bible, or lost before it was compiled." Also: "I believe the Bible as it read when it came from the pen of the original writers. Ignorant translators, careless transcribers, or designing and corrupt priests have committed many errors."[1]

Some of the gospel truths that were removed from the Bible diminish the majesty of Jesus Christ. Although all of Christendom reveres Jesus Christ, without the benefit of scriptures that have come forth in our dispensation as part of the Restoration of the gospel, no

1. *Teachings of the Prophet Joseph Smith*, sel. Joseph Fielding Smith (1976), 61, 327.

one would understand His full majesty. One of the beautiful truths removed from the Bible has to do with the very nature of God.

History tells us that shortly after Christ's Ascension to heaven, the early Christians suffered great persecution. At first, the Jews were the chief persecutors. They were fearful that this new Christianity might supplant Judaism. Then the Roman emperors attempted to totally obliterate and stamp out Christianity. During this period of great persecution, the ancient Apostles (except John) were killed.

But then there came to the throne Constantine the Great who was friendly to the Christians. Though he was a pagan, he made Christianity the state church. Constantine found that there was great division among the Christians; they were not sure of their theology. Seeing that there was division among them, he called a convention to define Christian theology.

The main point of contention in that convention was the Christian theology of God and the Godhead. Having no prophets or apostles to teach and guide them, that convention and others that followed issued creeds. In part, those creeds declared that God was without body, parts, and passions and that "God the Father is incomprehensible. God the Son is incomprehensible. The Holy Ghost is incomprehensible."[2]

Now compare those decrees to the truth taught by Jesus: "This is life eternal, that they might know thee the only true God, and Jesus Christ, whom thou hast sent" (John 17:3). Christ taught that it is life eternal to know God. The creeds of Christianity teach that God is incomprehensible. If God is incomprehensible, and as it is life eternal to know Him, then there can be no life eternal, for we cannot know the incomprehensible.

In 1831 the Lord told Joseph Smith that "every man walketh in his own way, and after the image of his own god" and that a primary purpose of the Restoration of the gospel was so "man might speak in the name of God the Lord, even the Savior of the world" (Doctrine and Covenants 1:16, 20). So it appears that the true identity of God, and the relationship between the Father, the Son, and the Holy Ghost, was removed from the Bible by the great and abominable church.

---

2. Hugh B. Brown, *Continuing the Quest* (Deseret Book, 1961), 382.

When God the Father and His Son, Jesus Christ, appeared to the boy prophet Joseph Smith in 1820, They told him to join none of the sects of his day and declared "all their creeds were an abomination in his sight" (Joseph Smith—History 1:19). The experience of Joseph Smith in a few moments in a grove on a spring day in 1820 brought more light and knowledge and understanding of the personality and reality and substance of God and His Beloved Son than men had arrived at during centuries of speculation. With that sure understanding, the Prophet Joseph boldly challenged the creeds of Christianity with this declaration: "The Father has a body of flesh and bones as tangible as man's; the Son also; but the Holy Ghost has not a body of flesh and bones, but is a personage of Spirit" (Doctrine and Covenants 130:22).

Just as Nephi saw the loss of many plain and precious truths being removed from the Bible, he also saw in vision the latter-day Restoration of those truths. Nephi writes that God "will bring forth unto them, in mine own power, much of my gospel, which shall be plain and precious. . . . I beheld other books, which came forth by the power of the Lamb . . . [which] shall make known the plain and precious things which have been taken away . . . and shall make known to all kindreds, tongues, and people, that the Lamb of God is the Son of the Eternal Father, and the Savior of the world; and that all men must come unto him, or they cannot be saved" (1 Nephi 13:34–40). Those other books that Nephi saw in vision, which would restore the plain and precious truths of the Lord, are the Book of Mormon, the Doctrine and Covenants, and the Pearl of Great Price. Perhaps other books may come forth by the power of the Lord in the future. The majesty of Jesus Christ is more gloriously manifest because of the Book of Mormon and other Restoration scriptures.

Our understanding of the majesty of Jesus Christ becomes richer and deeper because of Restoration scripture that has come forth from modern prophets. In order to better portray and appreciate the full majesty of Jesus Christ, I unapologetically and liberally use the truths given to us in modern-day revelation and scripture. Without Restoration scripture, we simply miss the full mighty majesty of Jesus Christ.

The Majesty of Premortal Jesus

Our appreciation and understanding of Jesus Christ and His mission here on earth is greatly enhanced when our perspectives are not bound by His birth in Bethlehem and His death on Calvary. Mortal life does not stand alone. Life is better understood when it is related to the premortality that went before and the immortality that will come after.

Small tidbits of truth are found in the Bible that help us realize that there was a premortal life. But those truths are oblique and difficult to find. Many people are familiar with Jeremiah 1:5: "Before I formed thee in the belly I knew thee; and before thou camest forth out of the womb I sanctified thee, and I ordained thee a prophet unto the nations." That scripture is a powerful witness that there was life before earth, that God knew us, and that He ordained at least some of us to perform important missions during mortality. We learn the same from the teaching of Paul: "He hath chosen us in him before the foundation of the world" (Ephesians. 1:4). Peter tells us that Jesus Christ was foreordained before the foundations of the world (see 1 Peter 1:20).

The Lord asked Job some intriguing questions, and through those questions, we learn that we watched the Creation of this earth and shouted for joy when it was complete. "Where wast thou when I laid the foundations of the earth? . . . When the morning stars sang together, and all the sons of God shouted for joy" (Job 38:4, 7)? We were in a premortal existence watching the Creation.

Ecclesiastes 12:7 teaches us that when we die, our spirits will return unto God. The inference is clear: We lived with God prior to mortality.

The psalmist declared that "all of you are children of the most High" (Psalm 82:6). Paul corroborated this truth when he wrote, "We have had fathers of our flesh which corrected us, and we gave them reverence; shall we not much rather be in subjection unto the Father of spirits, and live" (Hebrews 12:9).

The healing of a man born blind by Jesus presupposes a knowledge of a premortal life. We read, "And as Jesus passed by, he saw a man which was blind from his birth. And his disciples asked him, saying, Master, who did sin, this man, or his parents, that he was born blind" (John 9:1–2). Birth deformities can indeed be caused by parental abuse and disobedience. The taking of drugs while pregnant can and has caused birth deformities. Immorality can lead to disease, which can cause blindness in an unborn child. But how can an unborn child cause his own blindness? Can an unborn child sin, which would cause the blindness? The question is a manifestation that the disciples understood premortality. Can premortal sin cause one to be born blind? In this particular instance, Jesus replied, "Neither hath this man sinned, nor his parents; but that the works of God should be made manifest in him" (John 9:3). The Savior proceeded to heal the blind man.

The Gospel of John begins with these words, which are a great witness of a premortal life: "In the beginning was the Word, and the Word was with God, and the Word was God. . . . And the Word was made flesh, and dwelt among us, (and we beheld his glory, the glory as of the only begotten of the Father,) full of grace and truth" (John 1:1, 14).

Jude tells us that "the angels which kept not their first estate, but left their own habitation, he hath reserved in everlasting chains under darkness unto the judgment of the great day" (Jude 1:6). Further, John the Revelator writes, "And there was war in heaven: Michael and his angels fought against the dragon; and the dragon fought and his angels, And prevailed not; neither was their place found any more in heaven" (Revelation 12:7–8). Those two scriptures simply can't be understood without a knowledge of a premortal life and some of the events that occurred there.

There is considerable evidence from apocryphal writings and the Dead Sea Scrolls that suggests that a premortal existence was taught in the early Church. Josephus wrote of the Essenes, who believed in a premortal existence.[3] As Joseph Fielding McConkie concluded after referencing some of the ancient Jewish and Christian texts, "The doctrines of premortal existence, heavenly councils, and foreordinations were all a part of the theology of the ancient saints."[4] It seems that the doctrine of premortality is one plain and precious truth that was removed from the Bible.

Spirit Creation in Premortality

Latter-day revelation provides a wealth of information regarding premortality. In the book of Moses, we learn that God created all people in the heavens before the earth was formed. We read, "I the Lord God, had created all the children of men; and not yet a man to till the ground; for in heaven created I them; and there was not yet flesh upon the earth" (Moses 3:5). Again, "I am God; I made the world, and men before they were in the flesh" (Moses 6:51). We now clearly know that all of us lived with God, our Eternal Father, in a premortal world. All men and women who have ever lived or who will yet live were born as spirit children to our Father in Heaven. "Man was also in the beginning with God" (Doctrine and Covenants 93:29). We also learn that Jesus Christ was the Firstborn of the spirits (see Doctrine and Covenants 93:21). We know that God created both male and female spirits; gender was determined prior to one's mortal birth.[5]

---

3. See Flavius Josephus, *The Antiquities of the Jews* (Alpha Editions, 2021), 15:371; *The Jewish War* (Penguin Classics, 1984), 2:154–56.

4. *Apocryphal Writings and the Latter-day Saints* (Greg Kofford Books, 2007), 183–84.

5. "The Family: A Proclamation to the World," Gospel Library.

We are not given any detailed account of the spirit creation. This spirit creation happened untold ages before we came to this earth. Abraham described the sons and daughters of God as *intelligences*. The term *intelligence* is also used as a synonym for *spirit element*. The sons and daughters of God were organized intelligences or spirit bodies born from spirit element (see Doctrine and Covenants 93:29; 131:7–8; Abraham 3:22). In a literal sense God is the Father of our spirits. In Athens, Paul declared, "Forasmuch then as we are the offspring of God" (Acts 17:29). This understanding gives us greater appreciation when we talk about the brotherhood and sisterhood of humankind. Not only have we all descended from Adam, but all of us have the same heavenly parentage. We address Him such—our Heavenly Father—in our prayers. Today, we are striving to become acquainted with Him. In reality, we have merely forgotten what we knew while living with Him.

How long did we live with our Father in Heaven in this premortal sphere? We are not told, but it was likely eons of time. During that time, spirits progressed and grew in wisdom and power through their diligence and obedience (see Doctrine and Covenants 130:19).

Abraham received a vision of the premortal world and he tells us, "There stood one among them that was like unto God" (Abraham 3:24). Abraham said Jesus was "like unto God"! Jesus had yet to pass through a mortal probation, to overcome the world, to attain a resurrection, and to return to His Father with His own glorious and tangible body to enjoy eternal progeny. In those important aspects, Jesus was not like God. But Jesus was like Him in intelligence, in knowledge and understanding, in the possession of truth, in conformity to divine law, and therefore in power. Jesus was like Him in plan and purpose, in desires for righteousness, in a willingness to serve His brethren. Jesus was like Him as a guide and a light to all others.

Jesus Christ Was the Great Creator

Jesus Christ's diligence and obedience far surpassed what any other spirit exhibited. So much so that we learn that Christ, under the direction of the Father, became the Creator. "Worlds without number have I created; and I also created them for mine own purpose; and by the Son I created them, which is mine Only Begotten" (Moses

1:33). Jesus Christ was and is the Lord God Omnipotent, the great Creator—"that by him, and through him, and of him, the worlds are and were created" (Doctrine and Covenants 76:24). John testified, "All things were made by him; and without him was not any thing made that was made" (John 1:3).

Our world is just a small orb in the vast space of the universe where trillions of worlds exist. The mortal mind cannot fully comprehend the vastness of all the creations. As a young boy, I often would sleep outside under the stars during the summer. I enjoyed looking up at the night sky with its myriad of stars. Recently, the Hubble Satellite and the James Webb Space Telescope have given us a deeper look into the universe, and scientists have concluded that it is even bigger than we originally thought. Today's astronomers tell us that the Milky Way Galaxy has roughly 100 billion stars! We simply cannot fathom the vastness of that number. Traveling at the speed of light—roughly 186,000 miles per second—it takes only eight minutes to travel from our sun to Earth. To travel across the Milky Way Galaxy at that same speed would require more than 100,000 years! Yet if we were sufficiently distant from the Milky Way, it would be seen as but one bright dot among countless bright dots in space. Such immensity!

When Moses was shown a portion of all the Lord's creations, he exclaimed, "I know that man is nothing, which thing I never had supposed" (Moses 1:10). In comparison to the might and majesty of God, we are, comparatively speaking, nothing. Given our relative nothingness, the psalmist wrote, "When I consider thy heavens, the work of thy fingers, the moon and the stars, which thou hast ordained; What is man, that thou art mindful of him? and the son of man, that thou visitest him?" (Psalm 8:3–4)? If we have visions of just this life, we would be filled with hopelessness precisely because of our nothingness.

The Prophet Joseph taught in his King Follett discourse, delivered in April 1844, that Elohim, our Eternal Father in Heaven, was the savior in His world:

> God himself was once as we are now, and is an exalted man and sits enthroned in yonder heavens. God himself the Father of us all, dwelt on an earth the same as Jesus Christ himself did. Scriptures inform us that Jesus said, As the Father hath power in himself, even so hath the Son power—to do what? Why, what the Father did.

> The answer is obvious—in a manner, to lay down his body and take it up again. Jesus, what are you going to do? To lay down my life, as my Father did, and take it up again.[6]

So Elohim experienced mortality, then became a God as he lived the gospel faithfully, and then had spirit children, including Jesus Christ. Then who made Elohim's world? How do we reconcile God's declaration that Christ made all the worlds when Jesus did not create the world on which Elohim lived? Our finite minds cannot comprehend such things. God speaks to man simplistically (basic math) rather than providing all the intricate details (calculus) precisely because of our finite minds. It is reasonable to my mind that God is simply telling us that all creations that man can see or even fathom were all created by Jesus Christ. God wants us to know that Christ was unlike any other of His spirit children! Rather than being bogged down by the unfathomable, let us simply stand in awe at the majesty of Jesus Christ being the Creator of all that we know.

Heavenly Father's Plan of Happiness

One can only imagine that we were happy as we lived with God. Over time, we understood that we could never attain complete joy or realize our complete potential without becoming like our Father in Heaven. We wanted to be like Him. He desired the same for us.

There were three distinguishing features that made us different from our Father in Heaven. First, He has a glorified, resurrected, immortal body of flesh and bones (see Doctrine and Covenants 130:22). We had just spirit bodies. Latter-day revelation reveals that a person will receive a fulness of joy only when their eternal spirit is joined with an immortal body of flesh and bones (see Doctrine and Covenants 93:32–34). Second, God is perfect and holy in every good attribute. We lacked perfection in those attributes. We needed an environment where opposition existed so we could prove ourselves, or demonstrate who we really are or who we could become by our consistent choices. Third, our Father in Heaven has the power to beget children

6. Discourse, 7 April 1844, as Published in *Times and Seasons*, 614, josephsmithpapers.org.

throughout all eternity. All of us are His children. In that premortal world, we simply did not have that power.

Our Father in Heaven had a plan for us to eliminate those three differences and become like Him. It is called the plan of salvation or the plan of happiness. Jesus Christ did not present a plan in the heavenly councils that was adopted in preference to a less desirable plan presented by Lucifer, as is so often mistakenly taught. Our Father in Heaven is the author of the plan of salvation. As the Prophet taught, "God himself finding he was in the midst of spirits and glory, because he was more intelligent, saw proper to institute laws whereby the rest could have a privilege to advance like himself. He has power to institute laws to instruct the weaker intelligences, that they may be exalted with himself."[7]

The Lord's plan called for the creation of a world to allow His spirit children to come and receive bodies. Our mortal bodies are incredibly inferior to the body of our Father in Heaven, but they are a prerequisite to obtaining such a body. The plan would have our mortal bodies die so that we might be resurrected with immortal bodies. One's resurrected body will never be subject to disease, pain, or affliction and will never again die.

That plan called for a world in which an environment of opposites existed. We were taught that we would experience trials and afflictions, including pain, sorrow, and disappointment. We learned that those trials would be for our good (see Doctrine and Covenants 122:7) and would help us develop godlike attributes as we responded to them with faith. The Lord would place a veil over our memories of the premortal life so we could exercise our agency to choose good or evil without being influenced by the memory of living with our Heavenly Father.

God's plan also provides a way for us to have children and a family throughout eternity, just like our Father in Heaven. But eternal procreation is such an honor and privilege that a specific path would have to be followed in mortality to obtain such a blessing.

---

7. *Teachings of the Prophet Joseph Smith*, sel. Joseph Fielding Smith (1976), 354.

The Need for a Savior

Dependent only upon our own abilities, we would fail in two spectacular ways. First, when we come to this world, we do indeed receive bodies of flesh and bones, but they are mortal, subject to death. Death is the common lot of all humankind, no matter one's wealth or status. Death is a certainty. Contrary to how the world thinks, death is part of the Lord's merciful plan (see 2 Nephi 9:6). When death occurs, none of us, by our own strength, would ever have the power to raise our bodies from the grave and transform our bodies from mortal, corruptible bodies to immortal, incorruptible bodies. Death is part of the Lord's merciful plan precisely because He made it possible for us to rise from the dead—to resurrect.

Second, we would fail because all of us would sin. Living in a fallen world with intense opposition, we would simply all sin to some degree or another. Paul taught, "All have sinned, and come short of the glory of God" (Romans 3:23). He also taught, "The wages of sin is death" (Romans 6:23). This death is not the death of the body. It refers to spiritual death, meaning being cut off from the presence of the Lord. In our day, the Lord has declared, "I the Lord cannot look upon sin with the least degree of allowance" (Doctrine and Covenants 1:31). Sin would prevent us from returning to our Father in Heaven and becoming like Christ! Thus, left to our own devices and powers, physical death and sin prevent us from ever returning to and becoming like our Father in Heaven.

The Lord's plan had a way to overcome physical death and sin: a Savior, or Redeemer. The Lord's plan would work only because of this Savior. This Savior needed to have power over death and the power of the Resurrection. The designated Savior would be given that power because His birth would be unique. The Savior would be given those powers by virtue of the fact that God Himself—having such powers—would sire the Savior. Since God would sire only the Savior, the Savior would be known as the Only Begotten of the Father (see John 1:14). With a mortal mother, the Savior could die. With God as His father, the Savior would have the power to withstand death indefinitely and have power over the grave once He did die.[8] While ministering on earth, Jesus declared, "Therefore doth my Father love me, because I lay down my life, that I might take it again. No man taketh it from me, but I lay it down of myself. I have power to lay it down, and I have power to take it again" (John 10:17–18).

For the plan of salvation to work, this Savior needed to save us from our sins, for the punishment for sin was banishment from God. In order to have the power to redeem us from sin, the Savior needed to live a sinless life! Who could we trust for such an assignment?

Noble and Great Spirits

Abraham tells us, "Now the Lord had shown unto me, Abraham, the intelligences that were organized before the world was; and among all these there were many of the noble and great ones" (Abraham 3:22). Abraham continues: "And God saw these souls that they were good, and he stood in the midst of them, and he said: These I will make my rulers; and he said unto me: Abraham, thou art one of them; thou wast chosen before thou wast born" (Abraham 3:23). I pondered at great length what those spirit children, including Abraham, did to become noble and great. It is obvious from that scripture that not everyone became noble and great.

The answer came to me while reading the words of Alma: "The Lord God ordained priests, after his holy order . . . to teach these things unto the people . . . this is the manner after which they were ordained—being called and prepared from the foundation of the world according to the foreknowledge of God, on account of their exceeding faith and good works; in the first place being left to choose good or evil; therefore they having chosen good, and exercising exceedingly great faith, are called with a holy calling" (Alma 13:1–3). Some spirit children of God became noble and great precisely because they chose good over evil and exercised great faith.

Choosing good over evil denotes that we had agency in the premortal world. In order to have agency, there must be four elements present: (1) laws must exist that can be obeyed or disobeyed; (2) opposites must exist—good and evil, virtue and vice, and each force vying

8. James E. Talmage, *Jesus the Christ* (1916), 22.

for the attention of the individual; (3) there must be an awareness of those opposites; and (4) the individual must have the power to act in accordance with their own wishes, to follow that path they want to follow. Alma clearly taught that the noble spirits chose to do good. It is well to remember President Dallin H. Oaks's masterful discourse "Good, Better, Best," delivered at the October 2007 general conference. He taught, "As we consider various choices, we should remember that it is not enough that something is good. Other choices are better, and still others are best."[9] It is reasonable to assume that those spirits who became noble and great were not content with doing good but consistently chose the best paths.

Jesus Christ Was Chosen to Be the Savior

The question posed in Abraham 3:27 is the source of confusion regarding volunteerism in the premortal heavens: "And the Lord said: Whom shall I send?" That question was asked as God contemplated who should be the Savior. One needs to understand the setting or context to fully appreciate that question. I submit that it was not asked in a Grand Council or in some grand sacrament meeting for all spirits of the heavens to hear and to which they could respond.

When Abraham recounts his version of the Creation, he always uses the plural "Gods" who created the earth (see Abraham 4). Abraham consistently teaches that God our Father counseled with other gods during the Creation. Even in the Genesis account, we read, "Let *us* make man in *our* image, after *our* likeness" (Genesis 1:26; emphasis added). The obvious reference to "us" and "our" would be the gods. I submit that the question "Whom shall I send?" was posed in a council of gods. Elohim, our Father in Heaven, along with the full council of gods, looked upon all the faithful and noble children and chose the greatest spirit—indeed His Firstborn—to be His Only Begotten Son, to be our Savior and Redeemer. Can anyone doubt that the call came to him in a private interview?

The government of God is on display in The Church of Jesus Christ of Latter-day Saints. The government of God on earth is patterned after the government of God in the heavens. Parley P. Pratt wrote what

9. Dallin H. Oaks, "Good, Better, Best," *Ensign* or *Liahona*, Nov. 2007, 104.

he called a "Proclamation" in the *Millennial Star* in 1843. It reads in part as follows: "The legislative, judicial, and executive power is vested in Him (the Lord). He reveals the laws, and he elects, chooses, or appoints the officers; and holds the right to reprove, to correct, or even to remove them at pleasure. Hence the necessity of a constant intercourse by direct revelation between him and His Church."[10]

Elder John A. Widtsoe wrote, "By the spirit of revelation, the Priesthood governs the Church of Christ. Under this government, the Priesthood has power to instruct, rebuke and bless, as needed for the welfare of individuals, but only as authorized by the officers of the Church. And the government so obtained is perfect. It is freed from the dross of personal desire, and the uncertainty of self-assumed authority."[11]

When I served in a stake presidency and we needed to select a new bishop or an elders quorum president, we did not go to the ward and ask in a sacrament or priesthood meeting for volunteers who would be willing to serve in those capacities. We called someone as moved upon by revelation. When the Brethren come to organize or reorganize a stake presidency, they do not ask for volunteers. They call someone as directed by revelation. In other words, God calls them.

God directs His kingdom by calling and ordaining those who He would have preside. Surely those same principles operated in the premortal world. To think that God would call righteous, noble men and women who had shown exceedingly great faith to be great leaders in this mortal world, and then rely upon some volunteer to assume the greatest role on earth, a role that makes the plan of salvation work, is simply not congruent with how God governs. As President Joseph Fielding Smith taught:

> It is reasonable to believe that there was a Church organization there. The heavenly beings were living in a perfectly arranged society. Every person knew his place. Priesthood, without any question, had been conferred and the leaders were chosen to officiate.

---

10. Quoted in Harold B. Lee, *Stand Ye in Holy Places* (Deseret Book, 1974), 150–51.

11. John A. Widtsoe, *Priesthood and Church Government* (Deseret Book, 1950), 48.

> Ordinances pertaining to that pre-existence were required and the love of God prevailed. Under such conditions it was natural for our Father to discern and choose those who were most worthy and evaluate the talents of each individual. He knew not only what each of us *could* do, but what each of us *would* do when put to the test and when responsibility was given us. Then, when the time came for our habitation on mortal earth, all things were prepared and the servants of the Lord chosen and ordained to their respective missions.[12]

Abraham tells us that the Lord foreordained the great and noble spirits to be His rulers on this earth. He did so in order to carry forward His purposes among all people and nations. Those foreordinations designated certain individuals to perform missions that the Lord knew they had the talents and capacities to do. Alma taught the great truth that every person who would hold the Melchizedek Priesthood was foreordained to receive that priesthood because of their noble stature in the premortal world. Similarly, all women who would serve in God's kingdom on earth by divine investiture of priesthood authority were also foreordained. One can learn of his or her foreordained mission to some degree by receiving a patriarchal blessing. The Prophet Joseph taught, "Every man who has a calling to minister to the inhabitants of the world was ordained to that very purpose."[13]

Restoration scripture includes many instances of specific foreordination. Christ was foreordained to be the Son of God and the Savior of the world (see Moses 4:1–4; Abraham 3:27). Mary, the mother of Jesus, was foreordained for her sacred mission (see 1 Nephi 11:18–20). John the Baptist received a premortal commission to prepare the way for the first coming of the Savior (see 1 Nephi 10:7–10). The Lord's Twelve Apostles were chosen in the premortal world (see 1 Nephi 11:29, 34–36). Joseph, who was sold into Egypt, spoke prophetically of Moses and Joseph Smith and their foreordained missions long before they were born in this world (see 2 Nephi 3). The mission of Columbus to bring the American nations to the knowledge of the Old World was foreordained (see 1 Nephi 13:12). The Founding Fathers

12. Joseph Fielding Smith, *The Way to Perfection* (Deseret Book, 1984), 50–51.

13. *Teachings of the Prophet Joseph Smith*, 365.

of the American nation and the establishment of the Constitution were foreordained in the premortal world to accomplish that great work (see Doctrine and Covenants 101:80). Perhaps the same could be said regarding the great statesmen of the ages, the great artists, the great scientists, the great inventors, the leaders of nations, or even the technological wizards of today

Foreordination does not destroy agency. The Lord foreordains individuals to perform certain missions. If the individual chooses wisely and measures up to the standards expected by the Lord, the foreordained mission will be accomplished (see 1 Nephi 3:7). However, we are taught that "there are many called, but few are chosen" (Doctrine and Covenants 121:34). In other words, in the premortal life, many were called or foreordained to perform missions on this earth. One becomes chosen when one performs the mission for which he or she was foreordained. Sadly, the Lord notes that "few are chosen." The scripture continues, "And why are they not chosen? Because their hearts are set so much upon the things of this world, and aspire to the honors of men" (Doctrine and Covenants 121:34–35). The Lord also warns, "There is a possibility that man may fall from grace and depart from the living God; Therefore . . . take heed and pray always . . . even let those who are sanctified take heed also" (Doctrine and Covenants 20:32–34).

Jesus Christ was asked to condescend below all things by coming to this fallen world where He would suffer great temptations, pain of body, hunger, thirst, and fatigue, a world in which He would be rejected by most men, a world that would not shower Him with glory as He enjoyed in premortality, and a world that would ultimately kill Him. He was to suffer all these things without crushing all of His enemies, which He had the power to do. Always meek and humble, always eager to please His Father, Jesus majestically and simply responded, "Here am I, send me. . . . Thy will be done, and the glory be thine forever" (Moses 4:1–2). In essence, one who is called as a bishop, a stake president, an Apostle, or any other calling says the same thing. They willingly submit to the demands of the calling.

It is reasonable to assume that the Father informed all His spirit children in a Grand Council that He had called our eldest brother to fulfill the role of Savior and asked for our sustaining vote. Endowed with the divine power of agency, we could choose to follow the Father's plan and accept the chosen Savior, or to reject the goodness and grace offered by the plan. All who have or will live upon this earth sustained the plan. I have become convinced that we accepted the plan of happiness primarily because we had great hope and faith in Jesus Christ that He would fulfill His mission to be our Savior.

Christ Defeated Lucifer's Rebellion

In that Grand Council, one who held great authority and position, who the scriptures have referred to as "a son of the morning" (Isaiah 14:12–20), no doubt a mighty personage, not only objected to the call being extended to Jesus Christ but also objected to the plan of salvation. He showed no faith in his eldest brother. It appears from the scriptures that sufficient time was given to this spirit son to expound on his alternative plan and to convince us to follow him. However, make no mistake—the Father did not seriously consider the plan, for He knew it was fatally flawed. Lucifer, who has been called the "father of lies," told the great first lie that we know of: that he could save us all, "that one soul shall not be lost" (Moses 4:1). He knew his plan would not lead us back to God or help us become like Him. He didn't want to pay the heavy price to redeem us. His plan would have made us subject to him, thus giving him glory in some perverted way, but none of us would have become like our Father, the sole object and purpose of the plan of salvation.

When the Father announced that His plan would continue as outlined, with Jesus Christ being our Savior, Lucifer rebelled in outright apostasy. So John tells us of the "war in heaven" (Revelation 12:7). It was a war between following God or following Lucifer who wanted to take God's place. Lucifer turned "a third part of the hosts of heaven" away from God. Because of their rebellion against God, by the power of Jesus Christ they were cast out of heaven! Lucifer became Satan (see Doctrine and Covenants 29:36–39). Satan and his followers lost all opportunity to have physical bodies and to be saved by the plan of salvation. He and his followers now "maketh war with the saints in this life" (Doctrine and Covenants 76:29).

Isaiah saw this war in heaven and lamented, "How art thou fallen from heaven, O Lucifer, son of the morning! how art thou cut down to the ground, which didst weaken the nations! For thou hast said in thine heart, I will ascend into heaven, I will exalt my throne above the stars of God; I will sit also upon the mount of the congregation, in the sides of the north: I will ascend above the heights of the clouds; I will be like the most High. Yet thou shalt be brought down to hell" (Isaiah 14:12–15). We are told that "the heavens wept over him" (Doctrine and Covenants 76:26).

Faith in Jesus Christ in Premortality

As previously noted, Alma taught that for those who received the promise of priesthood, it was "on account of their *exceeding faith* and good works" (Alma 13:3; emphasis added). When I was a Primary child, my teachers told me we came to earth to learn to live by faith. That just isn't true! Alma clearly taught that some became noble and great and received priesthood promises because they exercised exceeding faith in the premortal world! Exceeding faith in what? We lived with God, so faith in His existence was not required. They showed exceeding faith in Jesus Christ (i.e., that He would come to earth and fulfill His mission as the Savior). How did one show exceeding faith? By not standing on the sidelines and watching. Rather, one actively fought alongside Jesus Christ to trumpet the plan of salvation when there were other forces shouting that the Lord's plan of salvation should be scrapped.

The difference between Jesus and Lucifer was this: Jesus was willing to submit to the Father. Everything that we read about Jesus Christ, coupled with our own experience in relation to the effect of the Spirit of God upon the heart, leads me to the conclusion that if Jesus had proposed a plan that would not have been accepted by the Father, He would not have rebelled against the Father nor against the chosen Redeemer. How different it was with Lucifer! Because he could not have his way, he was determined to wreck everything. He was not one with the Father. If he had been, that rebellion would not have occurred.

Now, with the decree issued that Jesus should redeem and save humankind—that His Atonement would enable men to return to and become like their Father in Heaven—the Messiah "verily was foreordained" (1 Peter 1:20) and became "the Lamb slain from the foundation of the world" (Revelation 13:8).

With Christ having been chosen as our Savior and Redeemer, our Father in Heaven then gave Him the commission to build this earth whereon we would dwell. Perhaps some of the noble and great assisted in that effort, for we read, "*We* will go down, for there is space there, and *we* will take of these materials, and *we* will make an earth whereon these may dwell" (Abraham 3:24–25). We do know that "all the sons of God shouted for joy" (Job 38:7) when the creation of this earth was complete.

Jesus Christ Is Jehovah

As the Savior, it fell upon Christ to deal with all humankind. From the beginning, all revelation that came from God came from Jesus Christ. On rare occasions, our Father in Heaven would introduce Jesus Christ. Jesus Christ was the God of the Old Testament, even Jehovah! Jesus Himself declared to His critics that He was Jehovah and they attempted to stone Him for what they considered blasphemy.

Modern revelation clearly teaches that Jehovah is the premortal Jesus Christ. "The Lord Omnipotent . . . shall come down from heaven among the children of men, and shall dwell in a tabernacle of clay . . . he shall be called Jesus Christ, the Son of God . . . the Creator of all things; and his mother shall be called Mary" (Mosiah 3:5–8). When Jesus appeared to the Nephite nation, He testified, "I am Jesus Christ, whom the prophets testified shall come into the world . . . I am the God of Israel" (3 Nephi 11:10), and then He taught, "I am he that gave the law, and I am he who covenanted with my people Israel" (3 Nephi 15:5).

The prophet Nephi further testified, "The God of our fathers, who were led out of Egypt, out of bondage . . . yea, the God of Abraham, and of Isaac, and the God of Jacob, yieldeth himself . . . into the hands of wicked men, to be lifted up . . . and to be crucified . . . and to be buried in a sepulchre" (1 Nephi 19:10).

When the Lord appeared to the Prophet Joseph in the Kirtland Temple, Joseph recorded that the Lord Jehovah proclaimed, "I am he who was slain; I am your advocate with the Father" (Doctrine and Covenants 110:3–4). Knowing that Jesus Christ is Jehovah only enhances our appreciation of His majesty. Because of the truths removed from the Bible, the world at large does not have a correct understanding that Jehovah and Jesus Christ are one and the same. No wonder Nephi called the forces who removed such precious truths "abominable."

We gain valuable insight regarding the likeness of our spirits when Jesus Christ, as Jehovah, appeared to the brother of Jared thousands of years before His birth in a manger in Bethlehem. After appearing, Christ declared, "Behold, this body, which ye now behold, is the body of my spirit . . . as I appear unto thee to be in the spirit will I appear unto my people in the flesh" (Ether 3:16). "Our spirit beings were men and women appearing in all respects as mortal persons do, excepting only that their spirit bodies were made of a more pure and refined substance than the elements from which mortal bodies are made."[14] "All spirit is matter," the Prophet said, "but it is more fine or pure, and can only be discerned by purer eyes" (Doctrine and Covenants 131:7).

The intent of the Lord's plan of salvation or plan of happiness is to have His children become like Him. It will work only because of a Savior. Jesus Christ was called and foreordained to be the Savior of the world. The Savior would overcome physical death and sin, which we were powerless to do. His great work to save us from physical death and from sin is called the Atonement. The Atonement was the Savior's mission.

14. Bruce R. McConkie, *Mormon Doctrine*, 2nd ed. (1966), 589.

Jesus of Nazareth Is the Chosen Savior

Some years ago, I had a gentleman tell me that he attended theological school, desiring to become a priest. On the first day of one of his classes, the professor asked the students how many believed that Jesus was the Son of God. He was surprised to learn that one-third of them didn't. Then he was stunned when the professor said it was his objective to convince the entire class that Jesus was *not* the Christ—that He was just a great teacher. That day is when he started serious reflection on his faith in his church and his direction to become a priest. He eventually left the theological school, found the missionaries, and was baptized into The Church of Jesus Christ of Latter-day Saints. He rejoiced when he learned so much more about Jesus Christ than he had ever learned in his schooling.

If Jesus of Nazareth is not the Son of God, then His birth, life, and death would be of no great consequence, for He would be just another mortal who passed through this existence. His mission—to overcome death and sin—could only be accomplished if He is the Son of God. Rescuing us from those deaths is the central part of the plan of salvation and constitutes the doctrine of the Atonement.

Elder Bruce C. Hafen has written:

> There are many opinions regarding Jesus Christ. The Jews disclaim him. The Unitarians regard Him only as a great teacher. The heathen nations, by the millions, have never heard of him. The intellectual may rationalize Him out of existence. The unbelievers may scoff. Nevertheless, all the various attitudes and beliefs do not change the unalterable truth that Jesus Christ lives today and that He is literally, biologically the Son of God in the flesh. He is the Savior and Redeemer for all humankind.[15]

Jesus of Nazareth was the promised Son of God, our Savior and Redeemer. Testimonies to this effect are numerous in the four Gospels. John wrote, "But these are written, that ye might believe that Jesus is the Christ, the Son of God; and that believing ye might have life through his name" (John 20:31).

At one point in His ministry, Jesus asked His disciples, "Whom do men say that I the Son of man am? And they said, Some say that thou art John the Baptist: some, Elias; and others, Jeremias, or one of the prophets. He saith unto them, But whom say ye that I am?" (Matthew 16:13–15). That is *the* question for each of us. It's interesting how Satan works to keep men from accepting saving truths. When Christ ministered among men, the vast majority did not accept Him as the Son of God, the promised Messiah and Savior. But they did accept Him as a righteous man. Some thought He was Elias who was to come and restore all things; others thought He was John the Baptist; others thought He was Jeremiah or one of the many other ancient prophets. None thought Jesus to be some evil man. Satan, by having the people think of Jesus as a good man, just *not* the Son of God, kept them from the truth that would have exalted them. Even the Pharisees and the other Jewish leaders came to know He was the promised Savior, but they rejected Him for their own purposes.

Similarly, many in the world today teach that Jesus was a great teacher, or even a great prophet, but they refuse to accept Him as the Son of God. Some have even gone so far as to teach that the Bible does not contain strong testimonies from Jesus Himself that He was the Son of God.

---

15. Bruce C. Hafen, *The Broken Heart* (Deseret Book, 2008), 198.

Witnesses from Ancient Prophets

Because Christ's mission is so essential for the eternal happiness of all humankind, Adam and all subsequent prophets prophesied of Christ and taught the plan of salvation whereby all of God's children could return to Him. Adam, the first man, knew of Christ and His sacrifice for humankind. That is one of the plain and precious truths removed from the Bible but gratefully restored by revelation to the Prophet Joseph (see Moses 5:6–10; 6:53–62). The great prophet Enoch saw the Messiah and His Resurrection (see Moses 7:47, 62). The prophet Abinadi asked, "Did not Moses prophesy unto them concerning the coming of the Messiah, and that God should redeem his people? Yea, and even all the prophets who have prophesied ever since the world began—have they not spoken more or less concerning these things?" (Mosiah 13:33). Another ancient prophet testified, "Abraham saw of his coming, and was filled with gladness and did rejoice" (Helaman 8:17). Isaiah is known for his prophecies regarding the Savior. He told of His birth by a virgin (see Isaiah 7:14). Other notable scriptures from him include Isaiah 9:6–7 and Isaiah 53. Peter testified, "To him give all the prophets witness" (Acts 10:43). The Book of Mormon prophet Jacob testified, "None of the prophets have written, nor prophesied, save they have spoken concerning this Christ" (Jacob 7:11). Indeed, in all four quarters of the earth wherever prophets dwelled and people had the gospel, they talked of Christ, rejoiced in Christ, preached of Christ, and prophesied of Christ so people would know to what source they may look for a remission of their sins (see 2 Nephi 25:26).

The witnesses from the Book of Mormon prophets are more plentiful and powerful. Some of those prophecies were so specific that they constitute a veritable witness that Jesus of Nazareth is the promised Messiah. The first Book of Mormon prophet, Lehi, knew the Savior would come 600 years from the time he left Jerusalem (see 1 Nephi 10:4). Nephi saw in vision His birth, His ministry, the choosing of the Twelve Apostles, His miracles, and His Crucifixion (see 1 Nephi 12:13–34; 2 Nephi 25:12–14). Abinadi gave an eloquent testimony of the ministry, death, and Resurrection of Christ (see Mosiah 13:5–13).

King Benjamin eloquently taught:

> The Lord Omnipotent who reigneth . . . shall come down from heaven among the children of men, and shall dwell in a tabernacle of clay, and shall go forth amongst men, working mighty miracles, such as healing the sick, raising the dead, causing the lame to walk, the blind to receive their sight, and the deaf to hear, and curing all manner of diseases. And he shall cast out devils . . . And lo, he shall suffer temptations, and pain of body, hunger, thirst, and fatigue, even more than man can suffer, except it be unto death; for behold, blood cometh from every pore, so great shall be his anguish for the wickedness and the abominations of his people. And he shall be called Jesus Christ, the Son of God . . . the Creator of all things from the beginning; and his mother shall be called Mary. (Mosiah 3:5–8)

Can one get more specific than that? King Benjamin's testimony clearly states that Jesus, born of Mary, is the Son of God.

Alma corroborates the testimonies of Nephi and King Benjamin. He testified, "The time is not far distant that the Redeemer liveth and cometh among his people. . . . And behold, he shall be born of Mary . . . she being a virgin. . . . And he shall go forth, suffering pains and afflictions and temptations of every kind. . . . And he will take upon him death, that he may loose the bands of death . . . and he will take upon him their infirmities" (Alma 7:7–12).

Witnesses from Angels and Christ's Peers

Was Jesus of Nazareth the promised Messiah? There are numerous witnesses found in the four Gospels. The first witness comes from the angel Gabriel who told Mary, "Thou shalt conceive in thy womb, and bring forth a son, and shalt call his name JESUS. He shall be great; and shall be called the Son of the Highest; and the Lord God shall give unto him the throne of his father David" (Luke 1:31–32). "The Son of the Highest" clearly means that God the Father shall be the father. The phrase "the throne of his father David" was the symbol of all Jewish hope for triumph, hope, freedom, and deliverance. In unmistakable words that a faithful Jew would clearly understand, Mary was told that her son was to be the Savior of the world!

Gabriel gave a second testimony to Joseph and told him that Mary had conceived by the power of God and that his Son would be the

Savior—one who would save people from their sins (see Matthew 1:20–21).

When Mary visited Elizabeth before the birth of Jesus, Elizabeth testified that Mary was the "mother of my Lord" (Luke 1:43).

The angels testified to the shepherds "unto you is born this day in the city of David a Saviour, which is Christ the Lord" (Luke 2:11).

When the Christ child was presented at the temple, both Simeon and Anna testified the child was the Lord's salvation, a light unto the world, and that He would bring redemption (see Luke 2:25–38).

When the Wise Men came, they inquired at Herod's court, "Where is the child that is born the Messiah?" and when they saw the young child, they fell down and worshipped him (see Matthew 2:2–11).

John the Baptist gives us a powerful witness: "In the beginning . . . the word was with the Son, and the Son was with God, and the Son was of God. The same was in the beginning with God . . . which was the true light, which lighteth every man who cometh into the world; Even the Son of God . . . He was born, not of blood, nor of the will of the flesh, nor of the will of man, but of God. And the same was made flesh, and dwelt among us, and we beheld his glory, the glory of the Only Begotten of the Father, full of grace and truth" (Joseph Smith Translation, John 1:1–14 [in the Bible appendix]). A short while later, as he was with two of his disciples, Jesus walked nearby. John the Baptist again testified, "Behold the Lamb of God" (John 1:36). He who was foreordained to be the forerunner of Christ again bore testimony to his disciples that Jesus was the Savior (see John 3:26–36).

At the baptism of Jesus, the Father's voice was heard from heaven bearing record that Jesus was His Son (see Matthew 3:17; Mark 1:11; Luke 3:22).

One of the first disciples to follow Jesus was Andrew. Andrew did what every new convert desires to do: He sought out family members so they too could rejoice in gospel truths. The record tells us he approached his brother Peter with this testimony: "We have found the Messias" (John 1:41). Peter later testified, "We believe and are sure that thou art that Christ, the Son of the living God" (John 6:69).

Philip was another early convert who approached his friend Nathanael with the same testimony; that is, he had found the Messiah about whom Moses and the other prophets had written (see John 1:45). Nathanael then goes to see Jesus, and after some conversation, Nathanael proclaims, "Thou art the Son of God; thou art the King of Israel" (John 1:49).

The Samaritan woman who was taught by Jesus at the well rushed to her family and friends and testified that she had listened to a man who was the Christ. They, in turn, approached Jesus and asked Him to abide with them. He did so and preached the gospel. Afterward, they bore witness, "We have heard him ourselves, and know that this is indeed the Christ, the Saviour of the world" (John 4:42).

Just after His masterful Bread of Life testimony, when many decided to no longer be disciples of Jesus because He wouldn't be their political savior, Peter declared, "Lord . . . thou hast the words of eternal life. And we believe and are sure that thou art that Christ, the Son of the living God" (John 6:68–69). At a later time, Peter again testified, "Thou art the Christ, the Son of the living God" (Matthew 16:16). Peter's testimony had come to him by revelation—not by reason, not by logic, not by man. It had come by revelation through the Holy Ghost. "No man can say that Jesus is the Lord, but by the Holy Ghost" (1 Corinthians 12:3).

Martha, a faithful disciple, proclaimed while talking with Jesus, "Lord: I believe that thou art the Christ, the Son of God, which should come into the world" (John 11:27).

Near Jericho, a blind man named Bartimaeus cried out, "Jesus, thou Son of David, have mercy on me." As people clamored for him to keep his peace, he cried out even more fervently, "Thou Son of David, have mercy on me" (Mark 10:47–48). The *Son of David* is another name for Jesus Christ. It was well known among the Jews that the promised Messiah would be a descendant of King David. The Jews mistakenly thought that the Son of David would reign with power like King David had done.

On a special Sunday, which we now call Palm Sunday, great multitudes spread their garments, palm fronds, and other foliage to make a path for Jesus. They were thrilled that He had arrived, riding on a donkey. Talmage writes that the donkey had been designated in literature as the ancient symbol of Jewish royalty.[16] Moved and directed by the Holy Ghost, the multitudes praised Him as the Holy One of Israel. All their praise was clearly messianic in nature. They accepted Him as their King, one who offered the gospel of peace and who would save them in the eternities. (see Matthew 21:7–11; Mark 11:7–10; Luke 19:37–38; John 12:13).

While Christ was in the temple healing the blind and the lame, children cried out, "Hosanna to the Son of David" (Matthew 21:15), which all Jews knew was a title referencing the Christ.

On a number of occasions, even the devils of Satan bore witness that Jesus was the Christ. In every case, Jesus silenced the demons. He wanted no such testimony; only a testimony given by the Holy Ghost is acceptable to the Lord.

When Jesus ascended to heaven after His forty-day ministry subsequent to His Resurrection, the angels proclaimed, "Ye men of Galilee, why stand ye gazing up into heaven? this same Jesus, which is taken up from you into heaven, shall so come in like manner as ye have seen him go into heaven" (Acts 1:11). Jesus will indeed return in great glory; it will be His Second Coming.

Jesus Christ's Own Witness of Himself

An even greater witness that Jesus is the Son of God, the promised Messiah, the Savior of the world, comes from the lips of Jesus Himself. Over my lifetime, I have had a few discussions with people who asserted that Jesus never claimed He was the Son of God. I was dumbfounded at their ignorance. Jesus proclaimed Himself as the promised Messiah many times. He was crucified by evil men for His steadfast testimony.

After Jesus had cleansed the temple the first time, the leading Jews approached Him and demanded a sign that proved He had the authority to cleanse the temple. He responded, "Destroy this temple, and in three days I will raise it up" (John 2:19). The sign proving He had authority to cleanse the temple was the same sign that would boldly testify that He was the Son of God—that of His Resurrection. Despite their false pretensions, they knew exactly what He meant.

16. James E. Talmage, *Jesus the Christ* (1916), 517.

His testimony was not forgotten. Three years later, a false witness, hoping to see Him crucified, would testify, "We heard him say, I will destroy this temple that is made with hands, and within three days I will build another made without hands" (Mark 14:58). A scoffer, glad that Jesus was on the cross, said, "Thou that destroyest the temple, and buildest it in three days, Save thyself, and come down from the cross" (Mark 15:29–30). While His body lay in the tomb, some Jewish leaders approached Pilate with this request: "We remember that that deceiver said, while he was yet alive, After three days I will rise again" (Matthew 27:63). They understood His testimony: I am the Savior; I am the Lord of this temple; I have the power of the Resurrection; I am the promised Messiah; this gives me the authority to cleanse the temple.

Jesus gave a powerful testimony to Nicodemus: "For God so loved the world, that he gave his only begotten Son, that whosoever believeth in him should not perish, but have everlasting life. For God sent not his Son into the world to condemn the world; but that the world through him might be saved. He that believeth on him is not condemned: but he that believeth not is condemned already, because he hath not believed in the name of the only begotten Son of God, which before was preached by the mouth of the holy prophets; *for they testified of me*" (Joseph Smith Translation, John 3:16–18 [in John 3:18, footnote *c*]; emphasis added). Jesus minced no words; His testimony was plain and beyond debate.

To the Samaritan woman at the well, Jesus testified, "Whosoever drinketh of this water shall thirst again: But whosoever drinketh of the water that I shall give him shall never thirst; but the water that I shall give him shall be in him a well of water springing up into everlasting life. . . . The woman saith unto him, I know that Messias cometh, which is called Christ: when he is come, he will tell us all things. Jesus saith unto her, I that speak unto thee am he" (John 4:13–14, 25–26).

In His hometown of Nazareth, Jesus went to the synagogue to worship with His family, friends, and associates. In that day, whenever some great rabbi, famed preacher, or distinguished stranger was in town, it was the custom to invite him to preach to the people. Given His recent fame as a result of His earlier ministry, it was not surprising that Jesus was asked to preach. He read the first two verses of Isaiah chapter 61, a passage widely recognized as a messianic prophecy: "The Spirit of the Lord is upon me, because he hath anointed me to preach the gospel to the poor; he hath sent me to heal the brokenhearted, to preach deliverance to the captives, and recovering of sight to the blind, to set at liberty them that are bruised, To preach the acceptable year of the Lord" (Luke 4:18–19). After reading that messianic prophecy, He then gave this certain testimony: "This day is this scripture fulfilled in your ears" (Luke 4:21). The audience was aghast that, in their estimation, Joseph's son should proclaim Himself to be the promised Savior. His testimony fell on stony ground. It was too much for their faithless hearts. They cast Him out of the synagogue and attempted to kill Him for His "blasphemous" claim. But the governor of the universe simply passed through their midst unharmed (see Luke 4:15–30).

Another witness from Christ is found in these words: "And Jesus, walking by the sea of Galilee, saw two brethren, Simon called Peter, and Andrew his brother, casting a net into the sea; for they were fishers. And he saith unto them, I am he of whom it is written by the prophets; follow me, and I will make you fishers of men" (Joseph Smith Translation, Matthew 4:18–19 [in Matthew 4:19, footnote *a*]).

He also bore strong witness of His divinity when He healed the man with palsy. Before the healing occurred, Jesus said to the man, "Thy sins be forgiven thee." The faithless in the crowd murmured in their hearts that only God could forgive sins. In essence, Jesus said to His detractors, "You are right that only God can forgive sins, and I *am* God. I have power to heal men from their sins *and* from their physical deformities" (see Mark 2:1–12; Matthew 9:1–8; Luke 5:17–26).

Jesus testified to the Pharisees that He as Jehovah gave the law to Moses: "Then said the Pharisees unto him, Why will ye not receive us with our baptism, seeing that we keep the whole law? But Jesus said unto them, If ye had kept the law, ye would have received me, for I am he who gave the law" (Joseph Smith Translation, Matthew 9:16 [in Matthew 9:16, footnote *a*]). He gave the law as Jehovah!

Jesus provided another powerful witness of His divine sonship in John 5. Jesus had healed an impotent man on the Sabbath and was roundly condemned by the Jewish leaders for breaking the Sabbath as they defined it. But Jesus testified that He didn't break the Sabbath as

God the Father defined it. Jesus testified that everything He did had the blessing of the Father. He then testified that He had power over life and death, He would redeem the dead, and as the Redeemer of all humankind, He would judge all men—all powers that only the Savior could possess. The record tells us that the "Jews sought the more to kill him, because he . . . said also that God was his Father" (John 5:18).

Jesus invoked the law of witnesses (see 2 Corinthians 13:1). He reminded His disciples that John the Baptist, whom they revered as a prophet, had given witness that He was the Lamb of God. He told them that God the Father had testified of Him at His baptism. He testified that His own works were a testimony that He was the Messiah. He then added a final external witness: the scriptures (see John 5:31–47).

When Jesus was again condemned by the Jewish leaders for breaking the Sabbath, He testified that He as Jehovah made the Sabbath day; that He was the Lord of the Sabbath (see Matthew 12:1–8; Mark 2:23–28; Luke 6:1–5).

John the Baptist had given powerful testimony that Jesus was the promised Messiah. There was no question in John's mind, but some of his disciples still looked to John as the prophet they should follow despite John's testimony. As a last remaining hope for them, John sent some disciples who weren't fully converted to Jesus to obtain their own witness. They asked the question that is the core of all religion: Is Jesus the Christ? Jesus's response was not one of words but of miracles. Who but the Son of God could cause the blind to receive sight, the deaf to hear, the lame to walk, the leper to be cleaned, the dead to live again? (See Luke 7:18–23; Matthew 11:2–5.)

There seems to be no doubt that all who heard Jesus understood His testimony that He was the Son of God, for we read, "Then came certain men unto him, accusing him, saying, Why do ye receive sinners, seeing thou makest thyself the Son of God" (Joseph Smith Translation, Mark 3:28 [in Mark 3:28, footnote *a*]). The Jews of that day heard what He said and knew what the words meant; for them, it was a matter of believing or disbelieving. The same is true today. But then as part of His answer, Jesus proclaimed, "All manner of sin and blasphemy shall be forgiven unto men who receive me and repent"

(Joseph Smith Translation, Matthew 12:31 [in Matthew 12:31, footnote *a*]). Only the Savior can forgive men of their sins.

After witnessing another miracle, that of casting out a devil from a man and then curing him of his blindness and dumbness, the wicked Pharisees demanded of Jesus another sign that He was the Son of God. They apparently wanted something more wondrous and glorious. Jesus rebuked them and then said, "There shall no sign be given to it, but the sign of the prophet Jonas: For as Jonas was three days and three nights in the whale's belly; so shall the Son of man be three days and three nights in the heart of the earth" (Matthew 12:39–40). For the Pharisees of all ages, there is only one sign to prove the divinity of Jesus Christ: His resurrection. Only the Son of God could burst the bands of death. The Resurrection bears witness that Jesus is the Redeemer.

Just a side note regarding the title *Son of Man*. Adam was taught, "In the language of Adam, Man of Holiness is his name, and the name of his Only Begotten is the Son of Man, even Jesus Christ" (Moses 6:57). So one name for Jesus Christ is *Son of Man*. It is important to understand this name for Christ, as that title will be used in some of the testimonies by Jesus Christ.

Just after the miracle of feeding the five thousand, some approached Him with the question, "What shall we do, that we might work the works of God? Jesus answered and said unto them, This is the work of God, that ye believe on him whom he hath sent." He was telling them to accept Him as the promised Savior. They then asked the question, "What sign shewest thou then, that we may see, and believe thee? what dost thou work? Our fathers did eat manna in the desert." Their tradition was that the Messiah would again bring manna from heaven, not just one meal, even though it be a miraculous meal. Jesus then gave a testimony that none could misunderstand: "My Father giveth you the true bread from heaven. For the bread of God is he which cometh down from heaven, and giveth life unto the world. . . . I am the bread of life: he that cometh to me shall never hunger; and . . . never thirst" (John 6:28–35). Jesus further confirmed His testimony, saying, "This is the will of him who hath sent me, that ye receive the Son; . . . and he who receiveth the testimony, and doeth the will of him who sent me, I will raise up in the resurrection of the just" (Joseph Smith Translation, John 6:44 [in John 6:44, footnote *a*]). Only a Savior could be the Living Bread with the power to raise men in the Resurrection of the just.

To His disciples, Jesus taught, "If any man will come after me, let him deny himself, and take up his cross, and follow me. For whosoever will save his life shall lose it: and whosoever will lose his life for my sake shall find it. For what is a man profited, if he shall gain the whole world, and lose his own soul? or what shall a man give in exchange for his soul? For the Son of man shall come in the glory of his Father with his angels; and then he shall reward every man according to his works" (Matthew 16:24–27; see also Mark 8:34–35; Luke 9:23–24). Only the Savior will have the power to judge.

During the Transfiguration experience, the Apostles heard the voice of Elohim, our Eternal Father, declare, "This is my beloved Son, in whom I am well pleased; hear ye him" (Matthew 17:5; see also Mark 9:7; Luke 9:35).

At another time, "while they abode in Galilee, Jesus said unto them, The Son of man shall be betrayed into the hands of men: And they shall kill him, and the third day he shall be raised again" (Matthew 17:22–23). Near the end of His ministry, Jesus gave that same testimony (see Matthew 20:17–19; Mark 10:32–34; Luke 18:31–34).

While in the temple during the Feast of Tabernacles, Jesus proclaimed, "Ye both know me, and ye know whence I am; and I am not come of myself, but he that sent me is true, whom ye know not. But I know him; for I am from him, and he hath sent me" (John 7:28–29). His bold claim that He was God's Son sent from the Father's presence incensed the Jewish leaders, and they again attempted to kill him for blasphemy. The record simply states that they could not, for His hour had not yet come.

On each day of the Feast of Tabernacles, one of the sons of Aaron would draw "living water" out of the pool of Siloam and carry it to the temple. Joyous blasts heralded its arrival at the temple. The ceremonial performances were designed to depict an outpouring of divine grace upon all men of all nations using water as the symbol of life. In this setting, Jesus testified, "If any man thirst, let him come unto me, and drink. He that believeth on me . . . out of his belly shall flow rivers of living water" (John 7:37–38).

The prophecies spoke plainly—and the Jewish leaders and teachers taught—that the Messiah would bring light to Israel and to all nations. During each night of the Feast of Tabernacles, the candelabra of the temple—seventy-five feet in height—was lighted to symbolize the sending forth of light to the city and the world. In this setting, Jesus testified, "I am the light of the world: he that followeth me shall not walk in darkness, but shall have the light of life" (John 8:12–13). Jesus Christ is the source of physical light in this world because He created that light. But Jesus Christ is also the exclusive source of spiritual light. Those who follow Jesus Christ will never walk in spiritual darkness.

Jesus powerfully testified, "If ye believe not that I am he [the Son of God], ye shall die in your sins" (John 8:24). Only the Savior can cleanse a person from sin. The first requirement to receive such grace from the Savior is to follow Him and to do things His way. If someone follows any other way, they will die in their sins.

In an intense exchange, His critics claimed spiritual privilege because of their direct genealogy to Abraham. Yet Jesus told them that although they were literal descendants, they did not exercise faith like Abraham and did works that Abraham would never do. Abraham worshipped Jehovah, yet they sought to slay the Jehovah that Abraham revered. Jesus declared, "If God were your Father, ye would love me; for I proceeded forth and came from God" (John 8:42).

Then Jesus gave them this challenge: "Which of you convinceth me of sin?" (John 8:46). No doubt the Jews were aware that the promised Messiah would be sinless and thus capable of effecting an infinite Atonement. In effect, Jesus was saying, "I am sinless, and only the Messiah can be sinless." His Apostles later testified that Jesus was indeed sinless (see Hebrews 4:15; 1 John 3:5). In our day, Jesus proclaimed Himself to be with no sin (see Doctrine and Covenants 45:4).

Jesus referenced a vision seen by Abraham: "The day cometh, that the Son of Man shall live. . . . Abram looked forth and saw the days of the Son of Man, and was glad, and his soul found rest, and he believed in the Lord" (Joseph Smith Translation, Genesis 15:11–12 [in Genesis 15:6, footnote *a*]). Declaring Himself to be the Savior as seen by Abraham, Jesus said, "Your father Abraham rejoiced to see my day; and he saw it, and was glad" (John 8:56). When His critics scoffed, Jesus gave a concluding testimony: "Verily, verily, I say unto you, Before Abraham was, I am" (John 8:58). Since the title *I AM* is another name for Jehovah, it could be better stated, "Before Abraham was I, Jehovah." There was no ambiguity in His testimony. There could be no greater claim to godhood—to being the Son of God, the promised Messiah—than those words.

At another time, Jesus testified, "I must work the works of him that sent me, while I am with you; the time cometh when I shall have finished my work, then I go unto the Father. As long as I am in the world, I am the light of the world" (Joseph Smith Translation, John 9:4–5 [in John 9:4, footnote *c*]).

The restoring of sight to a man born blind, who had been a beggar for years, is a remarkable story. The Pharisees tried to have the formerly blind man give credit to God, but the man was fearless in his testimony that Jesus was the healer. When the man was dismissed, Jesus approached him and asked, "Dost thou believe on the Son of God? He answered and said, Who is he, Lord, that I might believe on him? And Jesus said unto him, Thou hast both seen him, and it is he that talketh with thee" (John 9:35–37). Another incontrovertible testimony.

Jesus later testified:

> I am the door of the sheep. All that ever came before me who testified not of me are thieves and robbers. . . . I am the door: by me if any man enter in, he shall be saved. . . . I am come that they might have life, and that they might have it more abundantly. I am the good shepherd: the good shepherd giveth his life for the sheep. . . . As the Father knoweth me, even so know I the Father: and I lay down my life for the sheep. . . . Therefore doth my Father love me, because I lay down my life, that I might take it again. I have power to lay it down, and I have power to take it again. (Joseph Smith Translation, John 10:7–11, 15–18 [in John 10:8, footnote *a*])

Only the Savior would have power over life and death, which makes Him the Good Shepherd, the only door by which all humankind can be saved.

On another occasion, when Jesus walked in the temple, certain Jews approached him and said, "How long dost thou make us to doubt? If thou be the Christ, tell us plainly" (John 10:24). What? He had done so for nearly three years and had just testified that He had power over life and death. And Jesus provided another testimony: "I told you, and ye believed not; the works that I do in my Father's name, they bear witness of me. . . . I give unto [my sheep] eternal life; and they shall never perish. . . . I and my Father are one" (John 10:25–30). The testimony was clearly understood by them. Rather than believe, they took up stones with the intent of killing Him for blasphemy.

"Then certain of them came to him, saying, Good Master, we have Moses and the prophets, and whosoever shall live by them, shall he not have life? And Jesus answered, saying, Ye know not Moses, neither the prophets; for if ye had known them, ye would have believed on me; for to this intent they were written. For I am sent that ye might have life" (Joseph Smith Translation, Luke 14:35–37 [in Luke 14:34, footnote *a*]). Someone in the crowd asked Jesus why they needed Him since they had Moses and his law, which promised salvation. Christ's answer: All that Moses did and the law intended to do was to prepare a people who would accept the Messiah when He would come. He was that Messiah.

Later He gave similar testimony: "The law and the prophets testify of me; yea, and all the prophets who have written, even until John, have foretold of these days" (Joseph Smith Translation, Luke 16:17 [in Luke 16:16, footnote *a*]).

To Martha, Jesus testified, "I am the resurrection, and the life; he that believeth in me, though he were dead, yet shall he live: And whosoever liveth and believeth in me shall never die" (John 11:25–26).

Raising Lazarus from the dead was meant to be a witness to all that Jesus was the Son of God (see John 11:19–44).

When Jesus cleansed the temple the second time during the last week of His mortal life, He declared the Lord's temple to be His: "My house shall be called the house of prayer; but ye have made it a den of thieves" (Matthew 21:13; see also Mark 11:17; Luke 19:46). The temple has always been considered the house of the Lord. Jesus just proclaimed Himself to be the Lord.

While at the Jerusalem temple, the Jewish leaders had spent hours trying to show that Jesus was a fraud, but they had been humiliated and defeated. Jesus then became the interrogator. "What think ye of Christ? They say unto him, The Son of David. He saith unto them, How then doth David in spirit call him Lord, saying, The Lord said unto my Lord, Sit thou on my right hand, till I make thine enemies thy footstool? If David then call him Lord, how is he his son?" (Matthew 22:41–45; see also Mark 12:35–33; Luke 20:41–44)? How could Christ be called David's son and still be David's Lord? There is only one answer: Christ would be David's son by human birth but David's Lord as Jehovah before His birth. Implicit in Jesus's answer was His testimony that He was David's son and David's Lord.

Jesus said with power and authority, "Yet a little while is the light with you. Walk while ye have the light. . . . He that believeth on me, believeth not on me, but on him that sent me. . . . I am come a light into the world, that whosoever believeth on me should not abide in darkness. . . . I have not spoken of myself; but the Father which sent me" (John 12:35, 44, 46, 49).

"Ye call me Master and Lord: and ye say well; for so I am" (John 13:13).

"I am the way, the truth, and the life: no man cometh unto the Father, but by me" (John 14:6). Salvation comes through Christ, and Jesus of Nazareth is that Christ.

"I am the true vine, and my Father is the husbandman. . . . As the branch cannot bear fruit of itself, except it abide in the vine; no more can ye, except ye abide in me. I am the vine, ye are the branches; He that abideth in me, and I in him, the same bringeth forth much fruit; for without me ye can do nothing. If a man abide not in me, he is cast forth as a branch, and is withered" (John 15:1–6).

"I came forth from the Father, and am come into the world; again, I leave the world, and go to the Father" (John 16:28).

"This is life eternal, that they might know thee the only true God, and Jesus Christ, whom thou hast sent" (John 17:3). It is life eternal to know that Jesus of Nazareth is the Christ, the Only Begotten Son of God. So declared Jesus boldly.

During His trial before Caiaphas, the high priest asked, "Art thou the Christ, the Son of the Blessed? And Jesus said, I am: and ye shall see the Son of man sitting on the right hand of power, and coming in the clouds of heaven" (Mark 14:61–62; see also Matthew 26:63–64). In that moment, there was no ambiguity, no room for doubt. Any person who had decency in their heart and life, hearing such a testimony from Jehovah Himself, would have fallen to their knees in humble, worshipful adoration. Jesus gave the same answer when He met with the Sanhedrin (see Luke 22:66–71).

In answer to Pilate's question, "Art thou a king?" Jesus answered, "To this end was I born, and for this cause came I into the world, that I should bear witness unto the truth" (John 18:37). Christ's kingdom was not a political one but a spiritual one. During the Millennium, Christ will be the political king of all the earth.

After His Resurrection, He ministered among the people and gave counsel to His Apostles for forty days. Then, as He was about to ascend to heaven, He declared, "All power is given unto me in heaven and in earth" (Matthew 28:18). Indeed, the Son of God, having wrought the Atonement, was given all power.

Jewish Leaders Knew That Jesus Was the Promised Messiah

Jesus gave the parable of the wicked husbandman, which provided a powerful witness that He was the Son of God and that His antagonists knew it! Here is the parable in full:

> There was a certain householder, which planted a vineyard, and hedged it round about, and digged a winepress in it, and built a tower, and let it out to husbandmen, and went into a far country:
>
> And when the time of the fruit drew near, he sent his servants to the husbandmen, that they might receive the fruits of it.
>
> And the husbandmen took his servants, and beat one, and killed another, and stoned another.
>
> Again, he sent other servants more than the first: and they did unto them likewise.
>
> But last of all he sent unto them his son, saying, They will reverence my son.
>
> But when the husbandmen saw the son, they said among themselves, This is the heir; come, let us kill him, and let us seize on his inheritance.
>
> And they caught him, and cast him out of the vineyard, and slew him.
>
> When the lord therefore of the vineyard cometh, what will he do unto those husbandmen?

> They say unto him, He will miserably destroy those wicked men, and will let out his vineyard unto other husbandmen, which shall render him the fruits in their seasons.
>
> Jesus saith unto them, Did ye never read in the scriptures, The stone which the builders rejected, the same is become the head of the corner: this is the Lord's doing, and it is marvellous in our eyes?
>
> Therefore say I unto you, The kingdom of God shall be taken from you, and given to a nation bringing forth the fruits thereof.
>
> And whosoever shall fall on this stone shall be broken: but on whomsoever it shall fall, it will grind him to powder.
>
> And when the chief priests and Pharisees had heard his parables, they perceived that he spake of them.
>
> But when they sought to lay hands on him, they feared the multitude, because they learned that the multitude took him for a prophet.
>
> And now his disciples came to him, and Jesus said unto them, Marvel ye at the words of the parable which I spake unto them?
>
> Verily, I say unto you, I am the stone, and those wicked ones reject me.
>
> I am the head of the corner. These Jews shall fall upon me, and shall be broken.
>
> And the kingdom of God shall be taken from them, and shall be given to a nation bringing forth the fruits thereof; (meaning the Gentiles.)
>
> Wherefore, on whomsoever this stone shall fall, it shall grind him to powder.
>
> And when the Lord therefore of the vineyard cometh, he will destroy those miserable, wicked men, and will let again his vineyard unto other husbandmen, even in the last days, who shall render him the fruits in their seasons.
>
> And then understood they the parable which he spake unto them, that the Gentiles should be destroyed also, when the Lord should descend out of heaven to reign in his vineyard, which is the earth and the inhabitants thereof. (Joseph Smith Translation, Matthew 21:33–56 [in Matthew 21:45, footnote *a*])

All who listened understood the history of the Israelites. Over the years, many prophets (servants) had been rejected or slain as they cried repentance to the people. Then the Lord taught that when the time came for the Son to be sent, the husbandmen of the time would know that it was the Son! Those chief priests, elders, Pharisees, Rabbinists, scribes, and rulers knew the Heir, yet they chose to willfully cast Him out and slay Him to preserve their kingdom.

Later, Jesus again condemned the Jewish leaders for willfully rejecting Him when they knew He was the promised Messiah: "Ye bear testimony against your fathers, when ye, yourselves, are partakers of the same wickedness. Behold your fathers did it through ignorance, but ye do not" (Joseph Smith Translation, Matthew 23:33–35 [in Matthew 23:36, footnote *a*]).

Book of Mormon and Latter-day Witnesses

Those are the witnesses during the mortal ministry of Jesus Christ. But there are more witnesses as recorded in the Book of Mormon and the words of modern-day prophets. The greatest witness that Jesus is the Christ is His Resurrection. Many have testified that they saw the resurrected Jesus. Those witnesses will be covered in a later chapter of this book.

Any attorney armed with these testimonies given by Jesus of Nazareth, combined with the host of other witnesses, would convince any judge and jury that Jesus, born of Mary, is the Son of God.

There are many today who consider themselves more "enlightened" by their higher education or social status who attempt to rationalize away the divinity of Jesus Christ. Their arguments reveal how unenlightened they are. "O the vainness, and the frailties, and the foolishness of men! When they are learned they think they are wise, and they hearken not unto the counsel of God, for they set it aside, supposing they know of themselves, wherefore, their wisdom is foolishness and it profiteth them not. And they shall perish. But to be learned is good if they hearken unto the counsels of God" (2 Nephi 9:28–29). To the cynics, I ask: Where are your witnesses that Jesus is *not* the Christ? Where are your witnesses that Jesus did not rise from the grave a resurrected, glorified being? When one humbly accepts the testimonies found in the Bible and the Book of Mormon, and the testimonies of modern-day prophets, then there can be no argument regarding Jesus Christ. He is the majestic Messiah!

The Majesty of Christ's Miracles

Miracles were but one manifestation that Jesus was no mere mortal. The number of miracles He performed caused no small stir in the country and added greatly to His fame. Our Lord ministered in all parts of the land of Palestine. Though not all accepted Him, thousands had their hearts changed as they heard His testimony, repented of their sins, and followed Him. One could argue that those quiet, unseen miracles are among the greatest miracles.

The Lord told Joseph Smith, "Faith cometh not by signs, but signs follow those that believe. Yea, signs come by faith, not by the will of men, nor as they please, but by the will of God" (Doctrine and Covenants 63:9–10). The prophet Moroni wrote, "Ye receive no witness until after the trial of your faith" (Ether 12:6). Moroni continued, "For if there be no faith among the children of men God can do no miracle among them; wherefore, he showed not himself until after their faith. And neither at any time hath any wrought miracles until after their faith; wherefore they first believed in the Son of God" (Ether 12:12, 18).

We must remember that the miracles performed by Jesus Christ were primarily to build the faith and testimonies of those who already had faith. If one's testimony begins by witnessing a miracle, it will have little lasting power unless one continues in faith and obedience. At times, His miracles were to declare His divinity.

We have little conception of the number of physical miracles performed by our Lord. Multitudes thronged his way each day, bringing their diseased and deformed, their deaf, blind, and dumb. No attempt was made by the Gospel writers to record every miracle. Their intent was to preserve select examples of His purposes and powers. These are the physical miracles preserved by the Gospel writers. They are listed in chronological order, as best as can be determined. Each miracle is a witness that Jesus is the Christ!

Jesus Turned Water into Wine

The first recorded miracle was at a marriage feast in Cana. Mary seemed to be in charge of the wedding festivities. Scholars generally feel that some member of Mary's family was being married. Perhaps Jesus Himself had a personal obligation to look out for the well-being of the guests. We read the following from John 2:1–11:

> And the third day there was a marriage in Cana of Galilee; and the mother of Jesus was there:
>
> And both Jesus was called, and his disciples, to the marriage.
>
> And when they wanted wine, the mother of Jesus saith unto him, They have no wine.
>
> Jesus saith unto her, Woman, what have I to do with thee? mine hour is not yet come.
>
> His mother saith unto the servants, Whatsoever he saith unto you, do it.
>
> And there were set there six waterpots of stone, after the manner of the purifying of the Jews, containing two or three firkins apiece.
>
> Jesus saith unto them, Fill the waterpots with water. And they filled them up to the brim.
>
> And he saith unto them, Draw out now, and bear unto the governor of the feast. And they bare it.
>
> When the ruler of the feast had tasted the water that was made wine, and knew not whence it was: (but the servants which drew the water knew;) the governor of the feast called the bridegroom,

> And saith unto him, Every man at the beginning doth set forth good wine; and when men have well drunk, then that which is worse: but thou hast kept the good wine until now.
>
> This beginning of miracles did Jesus in Cana of Galilee, and manifested forth his glory; and his disciples believed on him.

Prior to His birth, Jesus, as Jehovah, never did for man what man could do for himself. So there must have been no other option for Mary than to turn to Jesus for divine help.

Bible scholars have determined that a firkin is equivalent to nine gallons. Each waterpot contained two to three firkins of water. In all, there were about 100–160 gallons. We can well imagine the sense of reverential awe that came into the hearts of those who were aware of what Jesus had done. Just a short time before, Jesus had refused to turn stones into bread to feed His own famished soul. Now He provided sweet wine for others that they might add to their pleasure as they rejoiced with a bride and groom in their happiness. The faith of His disciples was strengthened in Him.

Elder Bruce R. McConkie quotes Farrar thusly: "The miracles of Christ were miracles addressed not to a cold and skeptic curiosity, but to a loving and humble faith. Their primary object was the alleviation of human suffering, or the illustration of sacred truths, or, as in this instance, the increase of innocent joy. An obscure village, an ordinary wedding, a humble home, a few faithful peasant guests—such a scene, and no splendid amphitheater or stately audience, beheld one of Christ's greatest miracles of power."[17]

Jesus Healed Many on the Passover Day

A short time later, John tells us, "Now when he was in Jerusalem at the passover, in the feast day, many believed in his name, when they saw the miracles which he did" (John 2:23). This is the first Passover during Christ's official ministry. No doubt, He attended every Passover since at least the age of twelve, when He was found teaching in the temple. But this time, He makes Himself known. During the Passover, Jesus apparently performed many miracles, none of which

17. Bruce R. McConkie, *The Mortal Messiah* (Deseret Book, 1981), 1:451.

are named or described. John simply testified that many believed on His name because of all the miracles.

Jesus Healed the Nobleman's Son

Again, we read:

> So Jesus came again into Cana of Galilee, where he made the water wine. And there was a certain nobleman, whose son was sick at Capernaum.
>
> When he heard that Jesus was come out of Judæa into Galilee, he went unto him, and besought him that he would come down, and heal his son: for he was at the point of death.
>
> Then said Jesus unto him, Except ye see signs and wonders, ye will not believe.
>
> The nobleman saith unto him, Sir, come down ere my child die.
>
> Jesus saith unto him, Go thy way; thy son liveth. And the man believed the word that Jesus had spoken unto him, and he went his way.
>
> And as he was now going down, his servants met him, and told him, saying, Thy son liveth.
>
> Then inquired he of them the hour when he began to amend. And they said unto him, Yesterday at the seventh hour the fever left him.
>
> So the father knew that it was at the same hour, in the which Jesus said unto him, Thy son liveth: and himself believed, and his whole house. (John 4:46–53)

While in Cana, a nobleman approached him. The nobleman was likely a civil or military officer in Herod's court. The nobleman entreated Jesus to come to Capernaum and heal his dying son. He likely thought that the Savior's physical presence was required for such healing to occur. Christ gave a gentle rebuke to the nobleman: "Except ye see signs and wonders, ye will not believe" (verse 48). Christ paid little heed to those who confessed belief simply because of His miracles. He wanted people to develop a deep faith that comes from the Spirit. Christ had no intention of going to Capernaum to perform a great miracle or sign. So Christ tested the faith of the nobleman by saying, "Go thy way; thy son liveth."

In response, the nobleman did show great faith. He did not question the Lord. He did not second-guess. Whereas he had rushed to Jesus to ask for His intervention in healing his son, he now leisurely returned to his home, knowing there was nothing to be anxious about. His servants met him and imparted the good news that his son had been healed. The nobleman was not surprised at all to learn that such healing occurred at the same hour that Christ pronounced the words "Go thy way; thy son liveth."

This can be referred to as a dual healing: One healed the body of the son, and the other cured unbelief and planted faith in the heart of the father. This story bears witness that Christ is not limited by geographical location. He speaks and disease flees; healing occurs. As the God and Creator, He governs all things.

Jesus Cast Out an Unclean Spirit

"And in the synagogue there was a man, which had a spirit of an unclean devil, and cried out with a loud voice, Saying, Let us alone; what have we to do with thee, thou Jesus of Nazareth? art thou come to destroy us? I know thee who thou art; the Holy One of God. And Jesus rebuked him, saying, Hold thy peace, and come out of him. And when the devil had thrown him in the midst, he came out of him, and hurt him not" (Luke 4:33–35; see also Mark 1:23–26).

In the premortal world, Lucifer and his followers were cast out of heaven for rebellion. Their fate? Never to experience mortality nor to receive a body, a most treasured possession. "The demons that take possession of men, overruling their agency and compelling them to obey Satanic bidding, are the unembodied angels of the devil, whose triumph it is to afflict mortals, and if possible, to impel them to sin."[18] Under certain circumstances, the full extent of which we don't fully understand, the devils may enter into another's body. We do know that a person's wickedness leaves them more vulnerable to having their body possessed by an evil spirit. We do know that a person is playing with fire, so to speak, by delving into the dark side even just out of curiosity. Any activity that takes one to the edge of darkness and induces fear makes a person more vulnerable to such demonic possession. The

18. James E. Talmage, *Jesus the Christ* (1916), 183.

safest course to follow is to have "virtue garnish thy thoughts unceasingly" (Doctrine and Covenants 121:45).

The spirits who followed Lucifer know that Jesus was foreordained in the premortal world to be the Savior of all humankind. They know that He created the earth and that all things are subject to Him. These evil spirits know they were cast out of heaven through the power of Jesus Christ. They have no veil over their memories, so they know the Master of the universe when they see Him.

It's instructive to note Christ's response. He silenced the demon. He wanted no such testimony. A testimony from one of Lucifer's minions has no converting power. Only a testimony given by the Holy Ghost is acceptable to the Lord. Who cares what the devils say? An evil tree will not bring forth good fruit.

Christ then commanded the evil spirit to depart from the man's body. The demon had to obey even though it was against his will. With one final burst of hatred, the demon tore the man, threw him in agony in their midst, cried out with a defiant voice, and departed from the man. This story also teaches us that knowledge regarding Jesus of Nazareth is not enough; we must exercise faith in the Lord in order to be saved.

Jesus Healed Peter's Mother-in-law

"Simon's wife's mother lay sick of a fever, and anon they tell him of her. And he came and took her by the hand, and lifted her up; and immediately the fever left her" (Mark 1:30–31; see also Luke 4:38–39; Matthew 8:14–15). It is no surprise that Jesus would bless the family of a believer.

Jesus Healed Many Others from Diseases and Devils

"And he healed many that were sick of divers diseases, and cast out many devils" (Mark 1:34; see also Luke 4:40–41; Matthew 8:16; Matthew 4:23–24). Such healings were done because Jesus had compassion.

Jesus Healed a Leper

"And there came a leper to him, beseeching him, and kneeling down to him, and saying unto him, If thou wilt, thou canst make me clean. And Jesus, moved with compassion, put forth his hand, and touched him, and saith unto him, I will; be thou clean. And as soon as he had spoken, immediately the leprosy departed from him, and he was cleansed" (Mark 1:40–42; see also Matthew 8:1–3; Luke 5:12–13).

Never having been exposed to leprosy, I probably can't imagine the horrors of the disease. "As the disease spreads, nails loosen and drop off, the gums are absorbed, and the teeth decay and fall out; the breath is a stench, the nose decays; fingers, hands, feet may be lost, or the eyes eaten out. [One] feels that he is being eaten as by a fiend, who consumes him slowly in a long remorseless meal that will not end until he be destroyed. Leprosy in biblical times, in addition to its desolating physical effects, was looked upon as the symbol of sin and uncleanness, signifying that as this evil disease ate away and destroyed the physical body, so sin eats away and corrupts the spiritual side of man. It had been chosen as such a symbol because it was considered to be the worst of all diseases, one that could not be cured except by divine intervention."[19]

Luke tells us that this man was "full of leprosy," indicating that the disease was in its last stages; the man's body was likely severely ravished. The man approached Jesus with great faith. In his mind, there was no question whether Jesus could heal him, only whether He would do so.

The Levitical law stated that if someone touched a leper, then they would also be unclean. Ignoring the letter of the law, the Lord reached out and touched the man, and according to all three accounts, the Lord instantly rewarded the man's faith by saying, "I will; be thou clean." The hand of Jesus was not polluted by touching the leper, but the leper's whole body was cleansed by the touch of that holy hand. The healing was instant.

---

19. Bruce R. McConkie, *The Mortal Messiah,* 2:44–45.

It was believed by the religious leaders that only divine power could heal a leper. Jesus had just healed a leper—a miracle that would be a witness of His divinity. So it's curious that Jesus added a new dimension, not so far seen. He asked the cured leper to keep the miracle secret. But the great miracle was too much for the cleansed leper to keep to himself. He was near death, which would have made the healing a welcome relief. Now he had physical vigor and beauty again! The healed leper was living proof of the majesty of Jesus Christ!

Jesus Healed the Man with Palsy

> And again he entered into Capernaum after some days; and it was noised that he was in the house.
>
> And straightway many were gathered together, insomuch that there was no room to receive them, no, not so much as about the door: and he preached the word unto them.
>
> And they come unto him, bringing one sick of the palsy, which was borne of four.
>
> And when they could not come nigh unto him for the press, they uncovered the roof where he was: and when they had broken it up, they let down the bed wherein the sick of the palsy lay.
>
> When Jesus saw their faith, he said unto the sick of the palsy, Son, thy sins be forgiven thee.
>
> But there were certain of the scribes sitting there, and reasoning in their hearts,
>
> Why doth this man thus speak blasphemies? who can forgive sins but God only?
>
> And immediately when Jesus perceived in his spirit that they so reasoned within themselves, he said unto them, Why reason ye these things in your hearts?
>
> Whether is it easier to say to the sick of the palsy, Thy sins be forgiven thee; or to say, Arise, and take up thy bed, and walk?
>
> But that ye may know that the Son of man hath power on earth to forgive sins, (he saith to the sick of the palsy,)
>
> I say unto thee, Arise, and take up thy bed, and go thy way into thine house.
>
> And immediately he arose, took up the bed, and went forth before them all; insomuch that they were all amazed, and glorified

> God, saying, We never saw it on this fashion. (Mark 2:1–12; see also Matthew 9:1–8; Luke 5:17–26)

As Jesus was teaching the gospel to the assembled multitudes in His home city, Capernaum, four men approached the house. They were carrying a man with palsy on his bed. Because of the crowded multitude, they were unable to pass through, so they ascended to the roof. They made an opening in the thatch-type roof and then lowered the palsied man on his bed to the room where Jesus was teaching.

The man was paralyzed, helpless, and mute. His eyes made the entreaty that his voice could not. Jesus knew the desire of his heart, and He knew what to do. He first pronounced him spiritually clean: "Thy sins be forgiven thee."

The Pharisees and lawyers present were aghast. Only God can forgive sins, they reasoned; in this, they were right. If they had eyes to see and ears to hear, they would have accepted Jesus as their Christ and King. But their hearts were hardened, and they couldn't see through their prejudices and hatred.

Jesus declared His divinity to the believer and unbeliever. In essence, He said to them, "I am who I have proclaimed to be: the Son of God, the promised Messiah. You are right that only God can forgive sins—and I am God. I have the power to heal people of their sins and of their physical deformities. As evidence of my testimony, I so do now."

Again, the healing was instant. None could deny the miracle. He who claimed to forgive sins had proved His divine power by turning the living death of palsy into joyous life of physical health—and spiritual cleanness. Such is the majesty of Jesus Christ!

Jesus Healed a Lame Man at Bethesda Pool

"Now there is at Jerusalem by the sheep market a pool, which is called in the Hebrew tongue Bethesda, having five porches. And a certain man was there, which had an infirmity thirty and eight years. When Jesus saw him lie, and knew that he had been now a long time in that case, he saith unto him, Wilt thou be made whole? Jesus saith unto him, Rise, take up thy bed, and walk. And immediately the man was made whole, and took up his bed, and walked" (John 5:1–12).

This was the second Passover feast during Christ's ministry. This lame man did not cry out for help. Jesus saw the sufferer, knew that he had been lame for thirty-eight years, knew the spiritual stature of the man, and simply asked whether he would like to be made whole. With no administration of any kind, He commanded the impotent man to be made whole, which happened instantly!

Jesus Healed a Man's Withered Hand

"And he entered again into the synagogue; and there was a man there which had a withered hand. And they watched him, whether he would heal him on the sabbath day; that they might accuse him. And he saith unto the man which had the withered hand, Stand forth. And he saith unto them, Is it lawful to do good on the sabbath days, or to do evil? to save life, or to kill? But they held their peace. And when he had looked round about on them with anger, being grieved for the hardness of their hearts, he saith unto the man, Stretch forth thine hand. And he stretched it out: and his hand was restored whole as the other" (Mark 3:1–5; see also Matthew 12:9–13; Luke 6:6–10).

On another Sabbath day, Jesus entered the synagogue to teach. A man with a withered right hand was present. Whether he was there to learn from the Master or was placed there as an unwitting dupe is not clear, but the Pharisees used him as bait. Giving no heed to their apostate views of the Sabbath, Jesus healed the withered hand, which should have raised shouts of praise and thanksgiving that God dealt so compassionately among them.

Jesus Healed the Sick

"Great multitudes followed him, and he healed them all" (Matthew 12:15; Mark 3:7–10).

Jesus Healed the Sick on the Mount

Prior to giving His great Sermon on the Mount, we read, "And they that were vexed with unclean spirits: and they were healed. And the whole multitude sought to touch him: for there went virtue out of him, and healed them all" (Luke 6:18–19).

Jesus Healed the Centurion's Servant

> Now when he had ended all his sayings in the audience of the people, he entered into Capernaum.
>
> And a certain centurion's servant, who was dear unto him, was sick, and ready to die.
>
> And when he heard of Jesus, he sent unto him the elders of the Jews, beseeching him that he would come and heal his servant.
>
> And when they came to Jesus, they besought him instantly, saying, That he was worthy for whom he should do this:
>
> For he loveth our nation, and he hath built us a synagogue.
>
> Then Jesus went with them. And when he was now not far from the house, the centurion sent friends to him, saying unto him, Lord, trouble not thyself: for I am not worthy that thou shouldest enter under my roof:
>
> Wherefore neither thought I myself worthy to come unto thee: but say in a word, and my servant shall be healed.
>
> For I also am a man set under authority, having under me soldiers, and I say unto one, Go, and he goeth; and to another, Come, and he cometh; and to my servant, Do this, and he doeth it.
>
> When Jesus heard these things, he marvelled at him, and turned him about, and said unto the people that followed him, I say unto you, I have not found so great faith, no, not in Israel.
>
> And they that were sent, returning to the house, found the servant whole that had been sick. (Luke 7:1–10; see also Matthew 8:5–13)

Jesus was now in His home city, Capernaum. A Roman garrison was stationed there. One of its officers, a centurion, had a servant near death. This centurion was no ordinary Gentile upon whom the curse of disbelief rested. He may have been a convert to the gospel; at least he was a friend to the Jews. Hearing that Jesus was in their city, he besought the elders of the Jews to intercede on his behalf. He himself felt unworthy to be in Jesus's presence. Jesus and the group following Him began the journey to the centurion's house to heal the servant. The centurion sent friends to tell Jesus that He need not come to the house in order for his servant to be healed. As a centurion, he commanded his soldiers and it was done. He expressed faith that so long as Jesus said the word, the desired healing would be done. It was profound in logic and perfect in faith. Those in the group marveled at such faith. Christ blessed such faith with an instant healing.

Jesus Raised a Widow's Son from the Dead

> And it came to pass the day after, that he went into a city called Nain; and many of his disciples went with him, and much people.
>
> Now when he came nigh to the gate of the city, behold, there was a dead man carried out, the only son of his mother, and she was a widow: and much people of the city was with her.
>
> And when the Lord saw her, he had compassion on her, and said unto her, Weep not.
>
> And he came and touched the bier: and they that bare him stood still. And he said, Young man, I say unto thee, Arise.
>
> And he that was dead sat up, and began to speak. And he delivered him to his mother. (Luke 7:11–15)

The day after the healing of the centurion's servant, a young man lay dead. The funeral was over, and he was being transported to the designated place for burial. Jesus and His fellow travelers encountered the sorrowing group as they approached the city of Nain. It is doubtful that such a meeting, however, was just happenstance. His words were straightforward and simple. There was no struggle, no stretching of "himself upon the child three times," no pleading with the Lord, as when Elijah raised the son of the widow of Zarephath from death (see 1 Kings 17). Jesus, with a power that comes from knowing who He really was, simply said, "Arise," and the dead youth sat up. The Lord tenderly "delivered him to his mother." It had been just a short time ago when He healed the leper, an act that all recognized could only be done with divine authority. Only recognized great prophets, with authority from Jehovah, had ever raised people from the dead. He who claimed to be Jehovah now—with great simplicity, as it were—raised a youth from the dead!

Jesus Healed Many

"And in that same hour he cured many of their infirmities and plagues, and of evil spirits; and unto many that were blind he gave sight" (Luke 7:21).

Jesus Healed Women of Infirmities and Devils

"And certain women, which had been healed of evil spirits and infirmities, Mary called Magdalene, out of whom went seven devils" (Luke 8:2). Mary Magdalene became one of the closest friends and devoted disciples Christ had among women. Her devotion was unwavering. While other women tarried afar off in the time of His mortal agony, she stood close by the cross along with Jesus's mother. She was among the first at the sepulchre on the Resurrection morning and was the first mortal to look upon the resurrected Lord.

Jesus Healed a Possessed, Blind, and Dumb Man

"Then was brought unto him one possessed with a devil, blind, and dumb: and he healed him, insomuch that the blind and dumb both spake and saw" (Matthew 12:22).

Jesus Calmed the Raging Sea

> And when they had sent away the multitude, they took him even as he was in the ship. And there were also with him other little ships.
>
> And there arose a great storm of wind, and the waves beat into the ship, so that it was now full.
>
> And he was in the hinder part of the ship, asleep on a pillow: and they awake him, and say unto him, Master, carest thou not that we perish?
>
> And he arose, and rebuked the wind, and said unto the sea, Peace, be still. And the wind ceased, and there was a great calm.
>
> And he said unto them, Why are ye so fearful? how is it that ye have no faith? (Mark 4:36–40; see also Matthew 8:23–26; Luke 8:22–25)?

This was a ferocious storm. All authors record that they were fearful for their lives. In the midst of this ravaging storm, Jesus slept! His body needed rest just like ours do. He was at peace, and at that moment, His wearied body needed rest. Following the sequence that Mark and Luke follow, Christ arose, immediately rebuked the wind and the sea, and then asked the question, "Why are ye fearful?" "Where is your faith?" or "How is it that ye have no faith?"

Three observations: First, the storm didn't blow itself out; there was an immediate calm. To experienced fishermen who were likely used to storms on the sea, having it become instantly calm at Jesus's word would have been most amazing. To see mighty and pounding waves become still as glass, not over a period of thirty minutes or so but instantly, must have stunned those men. That's what caused them to wonder.

Second, it is also a wonderful illustration of how the elements quickly obey their Creator. Because the elements obey so quickly—so unlike most men—Mormon wrote that man was less than the dust of the earth (see Helaman 12).

Third, His disciples had faith; for that precise reason, they awoke Jesus. They had an expectation that He could and would save them. They may not have known what exactly He would do to affect the rescue, but they had faith in Him. Their lack of faith was in themselves. They didn't have faith that they could exercise the priesthood given to them and, in the name of their Master, cause the elements to obey. They didn't have the vision that they could speak in the name of Christ and have their words possess the same power and authority as though Christ Himself spoke. If they had that kind of faith, they could have stilled the storm without arousing their weary Lord.

Finally, some see great symbolism in this story. They liken the Church (or our own personal lives) to a ship sailing through the waves of the world, being tossed about by the forces of evil. Yet the ship never sinks; its faithful passengers never drown so long as Christ sails the ship. He may seem asleep, but in times of great peril, He will hearken to His servants and rescue the Church (or us) with the words "Peace, be still."

Jesus Cast Out Legions of Devils

> And when he was come out of the ship, immediately there met him out of the tombs a man with an unclean spirit,
>
> Who had his dwelling among the tombs; and no man could bind him, no, not with chains:
>
> Because that he had been often bound with fetters and chains, and the chains had been plucked asunder by him, and the fetters broken in pieces: neither could any man tame him.

> And always, night and day, he was in the mountains, and in the tombs, crying, and cutting himself with stones.
>
> But when he saw Jesus afar off, he ran and worshipped him,
>
> And cried with a loud voice, and said, What have I to do with thee, Jesus, thou Son of the most high God? I adjure thee by God, that thou torment me not.
>
> For he said unto him, Come out of the man, thou unclean spirit.
>
> And he asked him, What is thy name? And he answered, saying, My name is Legion: for we are many.
>
> And he besought him much that he would not send them away out of the country.
>
> Now there was there nigh unto the mountains a great herd of swine feeding.
>
> And all the devils besought him, saying, Send us into the swine, that we may enter into them.
>
> And forthwith Jesus gave them leave. And the unclean spirits went out, and entered into the swine: and the herd ran violently down a steep place into the sea, (they were about two thousand;) and were choked in the sea. (Mark 5:2–13; see also Matthew 8:28–33; Luke 8:27–34)

When Satan and his angels were cast out of heaven for rebellion, their great curse was to be denied bodies. It is apparent from this experience that they would rather possess the bodies of beasts rather than having no tabernacle at all. When the devils knew they had no choice but to leave the man's body, they asked Jesus not to torment them by, according to Mark, having them cast out of the country, or, according to Luke, by casting them into the deep. The "deep" means the eternal abyss of eternal torment that shall be their eventual inheritance. Speaking to this, Elder Bruce R. McConkie writes, "Apparently they were assigned to tempt those in that area and feared the wrath of Lucifer if they failed to bend to his will. We do know that all things are governed by law, and that Satan is precluded from taking possession of the bodies of the prophets and other righteous people. There must be circumstances of depression and sin and physical weakness that, within the restrictions of divine control, permit evil spirits to enter human bodies."[20]

Jesus Healed Jairus's Daughter

"And, behold, there cometh one of the rulers of the synagogue, Jairus by name; and when he saw him, he fell at his feet, And besought him greatly, saying, My little daughter lieth at the point of death: I pray thee, come and lay thy hands on her, that she may be healed; and she shall live. And Jesus went with him" (Mark 5:22–24).

While on the way to Jairus's home, they were delayed by another woman who sought healing. After the delay, the following occurred:

> There came from the ruler of the synagogue's house certain which said, Thy daughter is dead: why troublest thou the Master any further?
>
> As soon as Jesus heard the word that was spoken, he saith unto the ruler of the synagogue, Be not afraid, only believe.
>
> And he suffered no man to follow him, save Peter, and James, and John the brother of James.
>
> And he cometh to the house of the ruler of the synagogue, and seeth the tumult, and them that wept and wailed greatly.
>
> And when he was come in, he saith unto them, Why make ye this ado, and weep? the damsel is not dead, but sleepeth.
>
> And they laughed him to scorn. But when he had put them all out, he taketh the father and the mother of the damsel, and them that were with him, and entereth in where the damsel was lying.
>
> And he took the damsel by the hand, and said unto her, Talitha cumi; which is, being interpreted, Damsel, I say unto thee, arise.
>
> And straightway the damsel arose, and walked; for she was of the age of twelve years. (Mark 5:35–42; see also Matthew 9:18–26); Luke 8:41–56)

Jesus returned to His home in Capernaum. One of the first to meet Jesus was Jairus, a ruler of the synagogue. We know that Jesus preached often in Capernaum, so Jesus and Jairus likely knew each other. Though a leading clergyman, it is obvious that Jairus had faith in Christ. He approached Jesus with the proper reverence due Him.

20. Bruce R. McConkie, *The Mortal Messiah,* 2:281–82.

Jesus had performed miracles in divers ways, with or without oil, with or without the laying on of hands, always as the occasion required. Jairus requested that Jesus come and lay hands on his dying daughter—the most official and proper method—and heal her. No doubt, Jairus had witnessed such administrations of the sick. Jesus agreed to go to Jairus's house to heal his daughter.

On their way, they were delayed because of another woman who sought a miracle. Immediately after speaking words of comfort and blessing to the woman, a messenger came to report that Jairus's daughter was dead. I find it interesting that the record never indicated any impatience on the part of Jairus, even while Jesus was ministering to the woman. Nevertheless, Jesus encouraged Jairus to continue to show faith, and they proceeded to his house. A large crowd was at the house, many of them paid mourners and musicians, as was the custom of the day. Jesus told them that she was not dead, to which they laughed and scorned Him, for they all knew she was dead. Jesus commanded all the unbelievers to leave, for He was going to perform this great miracle only in the presence of believers. Interestingly, the believers were Peter, James, John, and Jairus and his wife. Jairus and his wife no doubt had great faith in their friend. Again, faith preceded the miracle.

The majesty of Jesus Christ was evidenced again!

Jesus Healed a Woman with an Issue of Blood

This is the event that caused Jesus to be delayed while on His way to the home of Jairus.

> And a certain woman, which had an issue of blood twelve years,
>
> And had suffered many things of many physicians, and had spent all that she had, and was nothing bettered, but rather grew worse,
>
> When she had heard of Jesus, came in the press behind, and touched his garment.
>
> For she said, If I may touch but his clothes, I shall be whole.
>
> And straightway the fountain of her blood was dried up; and she felt in her body that she was healed of that plague.

> And Jesus, immediately knowing in himself that virtue had gone out of him, turned him about in the press, and said, Who touched my clothes?
>
> And his disciples said unto him, Thou seest the multitude thronging thee, and sayest thou, Who touched me?
>
> And he looked round about to see her that had done this thing.
>
> But the woman fearing and trembling, knowing what was done in her, came and fell down before him, and told him all the truth.
>
> And he said unto her, Daughter, thy faith hath made thee whole; go in peace, and be whole of thy plague. (Mark 5:25–34; see also Matthew 9:20–22; Luke 8:43–48)

A woman who had given everything she had to doctors to heal her of some sort of blood disease—all to no avail—inconspicuously approached Jesus from behind and touched the hem of His garment. She had complete faith that by so doing, she would be healed from her disease, but she didn't deem herself worthy of His direct, divine attention. She actually felt the disease leave her, and she was whole. Such healing and wholeness occurred because she had the faith to be healed by Christ.

Jesus stopped and asked the question, "Who touched me?" He knew who had touched Him, but this question was an opportunity for the woman to give an accounting, to return and report, so to speak. Peter and others found it incredulous that Jesus would even ask that question given the thronging multitudes that were pressing Him. In response to His question, no one initially volunteered. Luke tells us that when the woman "found that she could not be hid"—no one knew it was her, only she and Jesus, and she knew that Jesus knew—she came forth with great humility and gave a reporting—a confession—of what she did and the healing that resulted from her touch. Such is the majesty of Jesus!

Jesus Healed Two Blind Men

"And when Jesus departed thence, two blind men followed him, crying, and saying, Thou Son of David, have mercy on us. And when he was come into the house, the blind men came to him: and Jesus saith unto them, Believe ye that I am able to do this? They said unto him, Yea, Lord. Then touched he their eyes, saying, According to your faith be it unto you. And their eyes were opened" (Matthew 9:27–30).

Jesus Cast Out a Devil from a Dumb Man

"As they went out, behold, they brought to him a dumb man possessed with a devil. And when the devil was cast out, the dumb spake" (Matthew 9:32–33).

Jesus Healed the Sick

"And he could there do no mighty work, save that he laid his hands upon a few sick folk, and healed them" (Mark 6:5). This occurred in Nazareth where the people generally rejected Him because, in their estimation, He was just the carpenter's son. Because of their unbelief, Jesus could not perform great miracles in Nazareth, but He did heal a few who exhibited true faith.

Jesus Healed Sickness and Disease

"And Jesus went about all the cities and villages, teaching in their synagogues, and preaching the gospel of the kingdom, and healing every sickness and every disease among the people" (Matthew 9:35). When Jesus left Nazareth (probably for the last time), He again taught the gospel throughout Galilee. For those who exercised faith, He healed every sickness and disease.

Jesus Healed the Sick

"And Jesus went forth, and saw a great multitude, and was moved with compassion toward them, and he healed their sick" (Matthew 14:14; Luke 9:11). This setting was before He fed the five thousand.

Jesus Fed the 5,000

> And when the day began to wear away, then came the twelve, and said unto him, Send the multitude away, that they may go into the towns and country round about, and lodge, and get victuals: for we are here in a desert place.

> But he said unto them, Give ye them to eat. And they said, We have no more but five loaves and two fishes; except we should go and buy meat for all this people.
>
> For they were about five thousand men. And he said to his disciples, Make them sit down by fifties in a company.
>
> And they did so, and made them all sit down.
>
> Then he took the five loaves and the two fishes, and looking up to heaven, he blessed them, and brake, and gave to the disciples to set before the multitude.
>
> And they did eat, and were all filled: and there was taken up of fragments that remained to them twelve baskets. (Luke 9:11–17; see also Matthew 14:14–22; Mark 6:33–45; John 6:3–15)

Besides the baptism of Jesus, this is the only event, prior to His last week, recorded by all four Gospel authors. It underscores how significant of an effect this miracle had on the Apostles as well as on the entire multitude. It was springtime, two years since Jesus began His public ministry. Jesus and His disciples had wanted to get away to some solitary place to properly grieve and mourn the death of John the Baptist. A great multitude learned of His whereabouts and came to listen and to be blessed. As the evening was nearing, the Apostles asked that Jesus send the multitude away so that they could have the necessary time to procure food for their needs. John tells us Jesus knew beforehand what He was going to do and earlier had asked Philip how they were going to feed the multitude. Jesus was setting the stage to perform the miracle. He had all 5,000 men along with the women and children sit down in groups. Using the five barley loaves of bread and two fish that a young lad had, He multiplied the food so that all ate and were satisfied.

By feeding the 5,000, Jesus did two things: (1) He set the stage that would enable Him to teach that there was an eternal bread, a spiritual food, a hidden manna, which all must eat to gain eternal life; and (2) He fanned the flames of messianic expectancy into a raging fire—here at last was their promised King who would free them and feed them as Moses had fed their fathers.

"There was a tradition, taught by the Rabbis and firmly entrenched in the public mind, that when the Messiah came, he would feed them with bread from heaven. The miracle of manna had become a subject of the proudest remembrances and the fondest legends of the nation. It had even become a fixed belief that the Messiah would signalize His advent by a repetition of this stupendous miracle. Thus, when Jesus multiplied the five barley loaves and the two small fishes, it was as though the traditional sign had been given."[21]

Jesus Walked on the Sea of Galilee

Once the multitude of 5,000 had been fed, the Lord retreated to a mountain to talk with His Father. The Apostles reluctantly left the Savior—indeed, they were constrained to leave—and boarded a ship. We then read the following:

> And when even was come, the ship was in the midst of the sea, and he alone on the land.
>
> And he saw them toiling in rowing; for the wind was contrary unto them: and about the fourth watch of the night he cometh unto them, walking upon the sea, and would have passed by them.
>
> But when they saw him walking upon the sea, they supposed it had been a spirit, and cried out:
>
> For they all saw him, and were troubled. And immediately he talked with them, and saith unto them, Be of good cheer: it is I; be not afraid.
>
> And he went up unto them into the ship; and the wind ceased. (Mark 6:47–51; see also Matthew 14:24–33; John 6:16–21)

Mark said it was the fourth watch, meaning that it was between 3 and 6 a.m., so they had been at sea for hours. It was in the dark of night, made darker still because of the furious storm. The going was very tough; the Apostles' lives were in peril. John wrote they were about four to five miles out to sea. Yet Mark wrote that Jesus "saw them toiling." Obviously, Jesus didn't see them with His natural eyes, but He saw them by the power of the Spirit. I wonder how many of us are able to use our spiritual sensitivities to see others who are toiling in despair, discouragement, or other spiritual dangers?

In the dark of night, Christ walked across the storm-tossed, wild sea as though it was solid ground. He then calmed the storm. He could have done the easy thing by calming the winds and staying the

---

21. Bruce R. McConkie, *The Mortal Messiah,* 2:367–68.

storm while on the mount. But what lesson would have been learned if He had done that? Whose faith would have been strengthened if He had done that? Jesus chose the harder path—He walked those four or five miles to show His Apostles that He was truly the Son of God, with power over the elements. Additionally, His example also taught them that He was willing to face danger, to do difficult things, to be inconvenienced in order to rescue them from the storm. We too can have faith that the Lord will rescue us during the storms we face in life. Such majesty!

As Jehovah, Christ created the waters and the earth. By the voice of Enoch, He moved mountains and changed the course of rivers. By the voice of Noah, He sent forth the waters to submerge and baptize the earth. By the voice of Moses, He caused the Red Sea to be divided, to have the waters stand as walls on both the left hand and the right hand, allowing the Israelites to pass through on dry ground. As we understand that the Creator has dominion over His creations, it should not surprise us that He can walk on water.

Jesus Again Healed the Sick and Diseased

"And when they were come out of the ship, straightway they knew him, And ran through that whole region round about, and began to carry about in beds those that were sick, where they heard he was. And whithersoever he entered, into villages, or cities, or country, they laid the sick in the streets, and besought him that they might touch if it were but the border of his garment: and as many as touched him were made whole" (Mark 6:54–56; see also Matthew 14:35–36).

Perhaps these people had heard of the woman who had been cleansed from her blood disease of twelve years just by touching the hem of His garment. Because of their faith, they were all healed by the majestic Savior!

Jesus Cast Out a Devil from a Gentile's Daughter

"Behold, a woman of Canaan came out of the same coasts, and cried unto him, saying, Have mercy on me, O Lord, thou Son of David; my daughter is grievously vexed with a devil. Then Jesus answered and said unto her, O woman, great is thy faith: be it unto thee even as thou wilt. And her daughter was made whole from that very hour" (Matthew 15:21–28; see also Mark 7:24–30).

Jesus Healed a Man Who Was Deaf and Dumb

"And they bring unto him one that was deaf, and had an impediment in his speech; and they beseech him to put his hand upon him. And he took him aside from the multitude, and put his fingers into his ears, and he spit, and touched his tongue; And looking up to heaven, he sighed, and saith unto him, Ephphatha, that is, Be opened. And straightway his ears were opened, and the string of his tongue was loosed, and he spake plain" (Mark 7:32–37).

In this instance, Jesus did not follow standard procedure. First, He removed the man from the multitude; this was to be a private healing. Second, as the man could not hear, Jesus put His own fingers in the deaf man's ears and placed His own saliva on the deaf man's tongue in lieu of a verbal exhortation. Those procedures were likely done to increase the man's faith. Why did Jesus sigh? (See verse 34.) Was He just tired but too full of compassion not to tend to the needy? Perhaps it was a sigh of compassion and tenderness.

Jesus Healed the Lame, Blind, Dumb, and Maimed

"And great multitudes came unto him, having with them those that were lame, blind, dumb, maimed, and many others, and cast them down at Jesus' feet; and he healed them: Insomuch that the multitude wondered, when they saw the dumb to speak, the maimed to be whole, the lame to walk, and the blind to see: and they glorified the God of Israel" (Matthew 15:30–31).

Jesus Fed the Four Thousand

> Then Jesus called his disciples unto him, and said, I have compassion on the multitude, because they continue with me now three days, and have nothing to eat: and I will not send them away fasting, lest they faint in the way.
>
> And his disciples say unto him, Whence should we have so much bread in the wilderness, as to fill so great a multitude?

> And Jesus saith unto them, How many loaves have ye? And they said, Seven, and a few little fishes.
>
> And he commanded the multitude to sit down on the ground.
>
> And he took the seven loaves and the fishes, and gave thanks, and brake them, and gave to his disciples, and the disciples to the multitude.
>
> And they did all eat, and were filled: and they took up of the broken meat that was left seven baskets full.
>
> And they that did eat were four thousand men, beside women and children. (Matthew 15:32–38; see also Mark 8:1–9)

This setting is in Decapolis, a place with many Gentiles, so the symbolism did not stoke a messianic fever.

Jesus Healed a Blind Man

"And he cometh to Bethsaida; and they bring a blind man unto him, and besought him to touch him. And he took the blind man by the hand, and led him out of the town; and when he had spit on his eyes, and put his hands upon him, he asked him if he saw ought. And he looked up, and said, I see men as trees, walking. After that he put his hands again upon his eyes, and made him look up: and he was restored, and saw every man clearly" (Mark 8:22–25).

We know that Jesus had the power to heal in an instant; every miracle and healing heretofore had been done that way. Here, however, the Lord decides to heal the man in stages. Why? It was probably designed to increase faith in the man's heart. Similarly, putting saliva on the man's eyes, as well as every other detail associated with this miracle, was done for the same purpose. But a miracle performed in stages, or over a prolonged period of time, is no less a miracle than one performed in a split second.

It's also interesting to note that Jesus took the man by the hand and led him out of town before the miracle was performed. Usually, He would heal people on the spot. Perhaps those who brought him had no faith and had hoped to see some "circus act." Perhaps the conditions of the city were so sinful that the Lord wouldn't perform a sacred service in such an environment.

Jesus Healed a Demonic Boy

> And they brought him unto him: and when he saw him, straightway the spirit tare him; and he fell on the ground, and wallowed foaming.
>
> And he asked his father, How long is it ago since this came unto him? And he said, Of a child.
>
> And ofttimes it hath cast him into the fire, and into the waters, to destroy him: but if thou canst do any thing, have compassion on us, and help us.
>
> Jesus said unto him, If thou canst believe, all things are possible to him that believeth.
>
> And straightway the father of the child cried out, and said with tears, Lord, I believe; help thou mine unbelief.
>
> When Jesus saw that the people came running together, he rebuked the foul spirit, saying unto him, Thou dumb and deaf spirit, I charge thee, come out of him, and enter no more into him.
>
> And the spirit cried, and rent him sore, and came out of him: and he was as one dead; insomuch that many said, He is dead.
>
> But Jesus took him by the hand, and lifted him up; and he arose. (Mark 9:20–27; see also Matthew 17:14–21; Luke 9:37–43)

When Jesus and His three chief Apostles descended from the Mount of Transfiguration, they found the other Apostles surrounded by a great multitude in the midst of an unseemly contention. The Twelve had gone forth on missions, preaching, healing, and performing miracles. Yet they had failed to cast out a particular devil. Their failure was a source of great satisfaction to the scribes, and they were now ridiculing the Apostles because of their failure. Mark tells us that Jesus's appearance "greatly surprised" the people. Why it was a surprise we do not know.

In this particular case, casting out the devil required a faith that comes only by fasting and prayer. This suggests that just as there are greater degrees of righteousness, so there are greater degrees of evil and wickedness among the devils. It takes greater faith to cast out the more evil devils.

In Mark 9:24, the man expresses what many of us feel: "I believe; help thou mine unbelief." We believe Jesus has all power to bless and help the suffering Saints, but we need assurance that His divine help will be forthcoming in our own personal lives. He blesses others, but will He bless me?

Jesus Healed a Dumb Man and Cast Out an Evil Spirit

"And he was casting a devil out of a man, and he was dumb. And it came to pass, when the devil was gone out, the dumb spake" (Joseph Smith Translation, Luke 11:14 [in Luke 11:14, footnote *a*]).

Jesus Healed a Man Born Blind

"And as Jesus passed by, he saw a man which was blind from his birth. And his disciples asked him, saying, Master, who did sin, this man, or his parents, that he was born blind? Jesus answered, Neither hath this man sinned, nor his parents: but that the works of God should be made manifest in him . . . he spat on the ground, and made clay of the spittle, and he anointed the eyes of the blind man with the clay, And said unto him, Go, wash in the pool of Siloam, (which is by interpretation, Sent.) He went his way therefore, and washed, and came seeing" (John 9:1–7).

Jesus had healed the blind numerous times without anointing clay on their eyes. People had been healed by faith through the laying on of hands. So why did Jesus go through this ritual? He deliberately did so because it was against the Pharisaical definition of what constituted the breaking of the Sabbath. Making clay and applying a healing remedy to a sick person was prohibited by their apostate law. Applying spit to someone's eyes constituted Sabbath-breaking. So Jesus put the people in a position to choose between Him as the One who had been sent from God versus the elders and their false traditions.

Jesus Healed a Bound Woman

"And he was teaching in one of the synagogues on the sabbath. And, behold, there was a woman which had a spirit of infirmity eighteen years, and was bowed together, and could in no wise lift up herself. And when Jesus saw her, he called her to him, and said unto her, Woman, thou art loosed from thine infirmity. And he laid his hands on her: and immediately she was made straight, and glorified God" (Luke 13:10–13).

Acting upon His own initiative, without supplication from her or anyone else, Jesus healed her because He desired to bless humankind! The woman was healed instantly and began to glorify God.

Jesus Healed a Man with Dropsy

"And it came to pass, as he went into the house of one of the chief Pharisees to eat bread on the sabbath day, that they watched him. And, behold, there was a certain man before him which had the dropsy. And Jesus answering spake unto the lawyers and Pharisees, saying, Is it lawful to heal on the sabbath day? And they held their peace. And he took him, and healed him, and let him go" (Luke 14:1–4). Dropsy is now known as edema, which is an increase of fluid in organs.

Jesus Raised Lazarus from the Dead

> Now a certain man was sick, named Lazarus, of Bethany, the town of Mary and her sister Martha.
>
> (It was that Mary which anointed the Lord with ointment, and wiped his feet with her hair, whose brother Lazarus was sick.)
>
> Therefore his sisters sent unto him, saying, Lord, behold, he whom thou lovest is sick.
>
> When Jesus heard that, he said, This sickness is not unto death, but for the glory of God, that the Son of God might be glorified thereby.
>
> Now Jesus loved Martha, and her sister, and Lazarus.
>
> When he had heard therefore that he was sick, he abode two days still in the same place where he was.
>
> Then after that saith he to his disciples, Let us go into Judæa again.
>
> His disciples say unto him, Master, the Jews of late sought to stone thee; and goest thou thither again?
>
> Jesus answered, Are there not twelve hours in the day? If any man walk in the day, he stumbleth not, because he seeth the light of this world.
>
> But if a man walk in the night, he stumbleth, because there is no light in him.

These things said he: and after that he saith unto them, Our friend Lazarus sleepeth; but I go, that I may awake him out of sleep.

Then said his disciples, Lord, if he sleep, he shall do well.

Howbeit Jesus spake of his death: but they thought that he had spoken of taking of rest in sleep.

Then said Jesus unto them plainly, Lazarus is dead.

And I am glad for your sakes that I was not there, to the intent ye may believe; nevertheless let us go unto him.

Then said Thomas, which is called Didymus, unto his fellow-disciples, Let us also go, that we may die with him.

Then when Jesus came, he found that he had lain in the grave four days already.

Now Bethany was nigh unto Jerusalem, about fifteen furlongs off:

And many of the Jews came to Martha and Mary, to comfort them concerning their brother.

Then Martha, as soon as she heard that Jesus was coming, went and met him: but Mary sat still in the house.

Then said Martha unto Jesus, Lord, if thou hadst been here, my brother had not died.

But I know, that even now, whatsoever thou wilt ask of God, God will give it thee.

Jesus saith unto her, Thy brother shall rise again.

Martha saith unto him, I know that he shall rise again in the resurrection at the last day.

Jesus said unto her, I am the resurrection, and the life: he that believeth in me, though he were dead, yet shall he live:

And whosoever liveth and believeth in me shall never die. Believest thou this?

She saith unto him, Yea, Lord: I believe that thou art the Christ, the Son of God, which should come into the world.

And when she had so said, she went her way, and called Mary her sister secretly, saying, The Master is come, and calleth for thee.

As soon as she heard that, she arose quickly, and came unto him.

Now Jesus was not yet come into the town, but was in that place where Martha met him.

> The Jews then which were with her in the house, and comforted her, when they saw Mary, that she rose up hastily and went out, followed her, saying, She goeth unto the grave to weep there.
>
> Then when Mary was come where Jesus was, and saw him, she fell down at his feet, saying unto him, Lord, if thou hadst been here, my brother had not died.
>
> When Jesus therefore saw her weeping, and the Jews also weeping which came with her, he groaned in the spirit, and was troubled,
>
> And said, Where have ye laid him? They said unto him, Lord, come and see.
>
> Jesus wept.
>
> Then said the Jews, Behold how he loved him!
>
> And some of them said, Could not this man, which opened the eyes of the blind, have caused that even this man should not have died?
>
> Jesus therefore again groaning in himself cometh to the grave. It was a cave, and a stone lay upon it.
>
> Jesus said, Take ye away the stone. Martha, the sister of him that was dead, saith unto him, Lord, by this time he stinketh: for he hath been dead four days.
>
> Jesus saith unto her, Said I not unto thee, that, if thou wouldest believe, thou shouldest see the glory of God?
>
> Then they took away the stone from the place where the dead was laid. And Jesus lifted up his eyes, and said, Father, I thank thee that thou hast heard me.
>
> And I knew that thou hearest me always: but because of the people which stand by I said it, that they may believe that thou hast sent me.
>
> And when he thus had spoken, he cried with a loud voice, Lazarus, come forth.
>
> And he that was dead came forth, bound hand and foot with graveclothes: and his face was bound about with a napkin. Jesus saith unto them, Loose him, and let him go. (John 11:1–44)

By the time messengers reported on Lazarus's condition, he was already dead, a fact that Jesus knew by divine inspiration. Jesus tarried for two more days, and it probably took one day to travel to Bethany for a total of four days since the death of Lazarus. According to Jewish tradition, the spirit no longer remained in the body after four days, and the corpse was considered as the dust of the earth. Decay and decomposition were in full swing; the finality of death was a reality. The body was eaten by worms, every vital organ was in the process of rotting away.

Jesus wanted all the Jewish nation to recognize that only by the power of God—only the promised Messiah—could perform such a miracle. He wanted all possible rationalizations and explanations to be eliminated, and that's why he waited for Lazarus to be dead for four days. Because of the majesty of Jesus, a ghastly, horrible figure did not emerge from the grave. A vigorous Lazarus came forth.

Jesus Healed Ten Lepers

> And it came to pass, as he went to Jerusalem, that he passed through the midst of Samaria and Galilee.
>
> And as he entered into a certain village, there met him ten men that were lepers, which stood afar off:
>
> And they lifted up their voices, and said, Jesus, Master, have mercy on us.
>
> And when he saw them, he said unto them, Go shew yourselves unto the priests. And it came to pass, that, as they went, they were cleansed.
>
> And one of them, when he saw that he was healed, turned back, and with a loud voice glorified God,
>
> And fell down on his face at his feet, giving him thanks: and he was a Samaritan.
>
> And Jesus answering said, Were there not ten cleansed? but where are the nine?
>
> There are not found that returned to give glory to God, save this stranger.
>
> And he said unto him, Arise, go thy way: thy faith hath made thee whole. (Luke 17:11–19)

It is likely that these ten lepers had gathered at a spot that gave them a high probability of seeing the Master. They cried out in faith to be healed. Interestingly, Jesus did not heal them on the spot. Rather, He instructed them to go to the priests in order to be pronounced clean, a requirement of the Mosaic law. It required their deepest faith to commence the journey, for they were not yet healed. Somewhere along the way, they became clean, probably degree by degree, of that dreadful disease.

Sadly, only one of the ten lepers returned to give thanks to his healer. The others probably rushed home to their loved ones to rejoice in their newfound health. To the one who returned, the Savior said, "Thy faith hath made thee whole." Since all of them had been healed physically, this can only mean that the one received added spiritual blessings that were withheld from the nine.

Well might we remember, "And in nothing doth man offend God, or against none is his wrath kindled, save those who confess not his hand in all things" (Doctrine and Covenants 59:21). McConkie wrote:

> Are we more grateful for our blessings than were the healed lepers who hastened on their ways, heedless of the beneficent goodness of the One whose words had made them new creatures? Well might we remember that he, who in his life healed men physically, is the one who, in his death, made it possible for all men to be healed spiritually. Well might we rejoice because he who cleansed the lepers, when he dwelt on earth, is the one who, through his atoning sacrifice, enables all men to cast off their leprous bodies of corruption, exchanging them for those glorious bodies which are refreshed and renewed in immortality.[22]

Jesus Healed Barimeus from Blindness

> And they came to Jericho: and as he went out of Jericho with his disciples and a great number of people, blind Bartimæus, the son of Timæus, sat by the highway side begging.
>
> And when he heard that it was Jesus of Nazareth, he began to cry out, and say, Jesus, thou Son of David, have mercy on me.
>
> And many charged him that he should hold his peace: but he cried the more a great deal, Thou Son of David, have mercy on me.
>
> And Jesus stood still, and commanded him to be called. And they call the blind man, saying unto him, Be of good comfort, rise; he calleth thee.
>
> And he, casting away his garment, rose, and came to Jesus.

---

22. Bruce R. McConkie, *The Mortal Messiah*, 3:284–86.

> And Jesus answered and said unto him, What wilt thou that I should do unto thee? The blind man said unto him, Lord, that I might receive my sight.
>
> And Jesus said unto him, Go thy way; thy faith hath made thee whole. And immediately he received his sight, and followed Jesus in the way. (Mark 10:46–52; see also Matthew 20:29–34; Luke 18:35–43)

There are some contradictions regarding the details of this story. The above is Mark's account. Matthew tells us that the healing occurred as they departed Jericho and that two men were healed from their blindness. Mark agrees with Matthew in the timing of the miracle but only speaks of Bartimaeus. Luke tells us that it occurred as they were approaching Jericho and only speaks of one blind man. Matthew writes that Jesus touched the eyes, which is not mentioned by the other witnesses. Mark tells us that the disciples helped Bartimaeus approach the Lord only after being called by Jesus. But the essence of the story is the same. A blind beggar, Bartimaeus, showed his faith by repeatedly calling Jesus "Son of David," a messianic title. Such faith qualified him for the blessing of being healed.

Jesus Healed All the Blind and Lame in the Temple

"And the blind and the lame came to him in the temple; and he healed them" (Matthew 21:14). This was just after His second cleansing of the temple.

Jesus Healed the Ear of Malchus

"Then Simon Peter having a sword drew it, and smote the high priest's servant, and cut off his right ear. The servant's name was Malchus. Then said Jesus unto Peter, Put up thy sword into the sheath: the cup which my Father hath given me, shall I not drink it?" (John 18:10–11) "Suffer ye thus far. And he touched his ear, and healed him" (Luke 22:51; see also Mark 14:47). Unconcerned about Himself, having no ill feelings toward those who were about to arrest him, Jesus told Peter to sheath the sword and then tenderly restored Malchus's ear to full health.

JESUS ATONED FOR THE SINS OF THE WORLD

See Matthew 26:36–46; Mark 14:32–42; Luke 22:40–46. Commentary to be found in a subsequent chapter.

JESUS ROSE FROM THE DEAD

The Resurrection of Jesus as evidenced by His numerous appearances is the greatest miracle He performed (see Matthew 28; Mark 16; Luke 24; John 20–21). Commentary is to be found in a subsequent chapter.

The prophet Moroni asked, "Have miracles ceased because Christ hath ascended into heaven?" He provides his own answer: "Nay; for it is by faith that miracles are wrought. . . . If [miracles] have ceased wo be unto the children of men, for it is because of unbelief, and all is vain" (Moroni 7:27, 37).

Jesus continues His miracles today among thousands and millions of His faithful disciples. I mention but one miracle that happened in our family. My wife delivered all our children by C-section. After one delivery, she experienced a sharp, hot pain in her abdomen, and she had a fever. An X-ray revealed that she had an infected cyst. The doctor wanted to do an immediate surgery, but my wife declined and asked that it be done the next day. At home, with complete faith that the Lord could heal her, she asked for a priesthood blessing. The next morning, she had no pain at all. An X-ray revealed that the cyst had disappeared, and she was mending nicely from the C-section. Flabbergasted, the doctor had no explanation for the healing. That was a miracle!

Elder Ronald A. Rasband taught, "The Lord performs miracles to remind us of His power, His love for us, His reach from the heavens to our mortal experience, and His desire to teach of that which is of most worth."[23] Christ's many miracles, both small and great, provide another witness that He is the Son of God!

---

23. Ronald A. Rasband, "Behold! I Am a God of Miracles," *Liahona*, May 2021, 111.

The Majesty of Christ's Mortal Ministry

How can a God be born into mortality? How can He take upon Himself flesh and blood? A child—any child—must have progenitors; he must have parents, both a father and a mother. An angel will tell the Virgin Mary that she shall be the mother. Elohim, our Heavenly Father, the God of all Gods, shall be the father. It is just that simple, and it lies at the foundation of true religion; without it, Christ becomes just another man.

And so, a God was born. A new star appeared overhead. The angels sang praises, the shepherds came to worship their King. Later, wise men would visit Him, bringing gifts. But for the most part, though Israel talked about the coming of a Messiah and Savior, because of general apostasy, they did not know of His birth, and they did not accept their Savior when He ministered among them.

We read in John 21:25, "And there are also many other things which Jesus did, the which, if they should be written every one, I suppose that even the world itself could not contain the books that should be written." Perhaps John used hyperbole, but it's true that the testimonies of Matthew, Mark, Luke, and John do not come close in giving us a full and complete account of the life and ministry of our

Savior. We have enough to come to know that Jesus of Nazareth is the Son of God.

It is easy to get caught up with all the wondrous miracles that Jesus performed. But most of His time was spent teaching and ministering. How can we describe His life and ministry? There has been a plethora of books written on this subject, so I will just mention a few events that illuminate His majesty and help us know that He is the Promised Messiah, foreordained before the foundations of this world. Some events will help us understand what we need to do to be faithful disciples, which will enable us to return to our Heavenly Father's presence.

The Baptism of Jesus Christ

We start with His baptism under the hands of John the Baptist:

> Then cometh Jesus from Galilee to Jordan unto John, to be baptized of him.
>
> But John forbad him, saying, I have need to be baptized of thee, and comest thou to me?
>
> And Jesus, answering, said unto him, Suffer me to be baptized of thee, for thus it becometh us to fulfill all righteousness. Then he suffered him.
>
> And John went down into the water and baptized him.
>
> And Jesus when he was baptized, went up straightway out of the water; and John saw, and lo, the heavens were opened unto him, and he saw the Spirit of God descending like a dove and lighting upon Jesus.
>
> And lo, he heard a voice from heaven, saying, This is my beloved Son, in whom I am well pleased. Hear ye him. (Joseph Smith Translation, Matthew 3:13–17 [in Matthew 3:15, footnote *a*]; see also Mark 1:9–11; Luke 3:21–22; John 1:28–34)

The baptism of Jesus Christ should testify to every honest in heart that the Godhead is composed of three separate beings. Jesus Christ, the Son, was baptized. God the Father spoke from heaven, proclaiming that He was pleased with His Son. The Holy Ghost descended in the bodily spirit form that He is, and His descent was like unto a dove.

Speaking of the sign of the dove, the Prophet Joseph Smith taught, "The sign of the dove was instituted before the creation of the world, a witness for the Holy Ghost, and the devil cannot come in the sign of a dove. The Holy Ghost is a personage and is in the form of a personage. It does not confine itself to the form of a dove, but in the sign of the dove. The Holy Ghost cannot be transformed into a dove; but the sign of a dove was given to John to signify the truth of the deed, as the dove is an emblem or token of truth and innocence."[24]

Why was the Savior baptized? He had no sin to be remitted. He lived a perfect, sinless life. There is no better explanation than found in the Book of Mormon, specifically 2 Nephi 31. Nephi tells us five reasons why Jesus Christ was baptized: (1) to signify his humility before the Father, (2) as a covenant of obedience, (3) to receive the gift of the Holy Ghost, (4) to gain an inheritance in the celestial kingdom, and (5) as an example to all men. Christ is our exemplar; He has shown all of us that baptism by one who has been called by God and armed with priesthood power (as was the Baptist) is necessary on our path to God.

Jesus Was Tempted

Most of us are familiar with the three temptations Jesus resisted from Satan prior to His ministry (see Matthew 4). The first temptation was to inappropriately use His powers to satisfy the needs of the flesh (i.e., to satiate His hunger). The second temptation was to inappropriately use His powers for the glory of men. The third temptation was to inappropriately use His powers for the riches and power of this world. All men and women are likewise tempted to some degree for the needs of the flesh, to attain the glory of men, and to obtain power and riches. The overarching temptation was to prove who He was; "if thou be the Son of God" was the message from the tempter.

Jesus was well acquainted with temptation during His mortal life. Some have speculated whether Jesus could even be tempted, or if all temptations were easily shrugged off because of His nature. We must remember that Jesus inherited mortal qualities from His mother, Mary. As a mortal, He could and was tempted just like any of us. Paul writes, "Though he were a Son, yet learned he obedience by the things which he suffered" (Hebrews 5:8). We also read that Jesus was

24. *Teachings of the Prophet Joseph Smith*, sel. Joseph Fielding Smith (1976), 276.

"in all points tempted like as we are, yet without sin" (Hebrews 4:15). Peter also testified regarding Jesus, "Who did no sin, neither was guile found in his mouth" (1 Peter 2:22). That would be the Savior's test in life, to be sinless. When we sin, we can turn to the Savior to be rescued. The Savior would have no such relief valve. He had to be sinless.

Lucifer knew that Jesus was chosen in premortality to save and redeem man. He knew Jesus could only fulfill that mission if He committed no sin. I am convinced that Jesus was subjected to constant temptations throughout His life. It was much, much more than the three temptations in the wilderness. During Christ's mortality, Lucifer had his one and only chance to get revenge, to beat Jesus by having Him sin, and to get all our souls in the process.

In the King James Version of the Bible, we then read, "Then the devil leaveth him, and, behold, angels came and ministered unto him" (Matthew 4:11). The Prophet Joseph made a significant change to that verse that gives us an insight into the character of Jesus: "And now Jesus knew that John was cast into prison, and he sent angels, and, behold, they came and ministered unto him [John]." Angels did not come to Jesus after those temptations to minister to *Him*, although that would have been understandable. Unconcerned about His physical, mental, and spiritual needs, Jesus sent angels to minister to the Baptist. Forgetting self and ministering to others was a character hallmark throughout His ministry and highlights His majesty!

Christ's Apostles

The calling of the Twelve Apostles was crucial to Christ's ministry (see Matthew 10:1–4; Mark 3:13–19; Luke 6:12–16). It was so important to the Savior that He secluded Himself all night to pray before selecting the Apostles. He wanted to find those who He had called in the premortal world—those whom Nephi saw in vision six hundred years earlier. Christ built His Church upon the foundation of Apostles and prophets, with Jesus Christ being the chief cornerstone (see Ephesians 2:20). "And he gave some apostles and some prophets" (Ephesians 4:11). Why? "For the perfecting of the saints, for the work of the ministry, for the edifying of the body of Christ. Till we all come in the unity of the faith, and of the knowledge of the Son of God. That we henceforth be no more children, tossed to and fro, and carried about with every wind of doctrine, by the sleight of men, and cunning craftiness, whereby they lie in wait to deceive" (Ephesians 4:12–14).

The Lord's Apostles were expected to learn as much as they could from their Master, for it was their commission to guide the Church after Christ ascended to heaven. They were to preach the gospel in all nations (see Matthew 28:19).

The Lord gave Peter (and the rest of the Apostles) priesthood power, including the "keys of the kingdom of heaven; and whatsoever thou shalt bind on earth shall be bound in heaven; and whatsoever thou shalt loose on earth shall be loosed in heaven" (Matthew 16:19). The Apostles as a quorum receive revelation from Jesus Christ to administer the affairs of the kingdom.

The Apostles, as ambassadors of the Lord, speak truth and provide steady direction and guidance as they receive revelation from Jesus Himself. Without them, the members of the Church, like all other people, wander into strange paths. Both Peter and Paul prophesied of the impending apostasy that would cover the whole earth until the Lord would again restore His Church. Apostate ways were already creeping into the Church shortly after Christ's Ascension, which was the focus of some of Paul's writings as he tried to correct such heresies. The Apostles were scattered about in various quarters of the earth, so they couldn't reconstitute the quorum when deaths occurred. With their deaths, the priesthood was taken from the earth and the flock of sheep was left alone to be devoured by ravening wolves; eventually, the Apostasy became complete and worldwide. In our dispensation, the Lord reestablished His Church with the same apostolic authority.

Just six days later (per Matthew and Mark) or eight days later (per Luke), Jesus took Peter, James, and John on a mount. There, Moses and Elijah appeared and gave additional priesthood keys to the three Apostles who were the First Presidency in the meridian of times. Both Moses and Elijah, instead of tasting death, had been translated—taken into heaven with physical bodies—so they could return in order to confer keys upon Peter, James, and John. President Joseph Fielding Smith wrote:

> They had a mission to perform, and it had to be performed before the crucifixion of the Son of God, and it could not be done in the spirit. They had to have tangible bodies. Christ is the first fruits of the resurrection; therefore, if any former prophets had a work to perform preparatory to the mission of the Son of God, or to the dispensation of the meridian of times, it was essential that they be preserved to fulfill that mission in the flesh. For that reason, Moses disappeared from among the people and was taken up into the mountain, and the people thought he was buried by the Lord. The Lord preserved him, so that he could come at the proper time and restore his keys on the heads of Peter, James, and John, who stood at the head of the dispensation of the meridian of time. He reserved Elijah from death that he might also come and bestow his keys upon the heads of Peter, James, and John and prepare them for their ministry.[25]

About 1,800 years later, both Moses and Elijah, now as resurrected beings, also appeared to the Prophet Joseph and Oliver Cowdery to confer upon them the same keys they had given to Peter, James, and John (see Doctrine and Covenants 110).

JESUS NEVER FOCUSED ON HIMSELF

Because of His mother, Jesus had the same mortal needs as we all do. He needed food, drink, rest, and shelter. He was subject to the full range of emotions as any mortal. On one particular day, Jesus and His Apostles were tired and wanted to get away to some solitary place to get some rest and to properly grieve and mourn the recent death of John the Baptist. So they got on a boat on the Sea of Galilee and sailed for a distant shore. Their departure was noted by some who spread the word, and a great multitude awaited them when they reached shore. As He always did, Jesus majestically forgot His own physical needs. Instead, He turned His attention to the people. Matthew and Mark wrote that Jesus had "great compassion" for the people. Jesus spent many hours with them. Mark wrote that "he began to teach them many things." Matthew wrote that "he healed their sick."

---

25. *Doctrines of Salvation*, comp. Bruce R. McConkie (1955), 2:110–11.

There is no written record, no evidence whatsoever, that Jesus did things His way, or in accordance with His timetable. He spent much time in prayer and meditation to determine His Father's will. Once the Father's will was determined, Jesus went about doing it. No matter how difficult the task, Jesus simply did it. The Savior testified, "My meat is to do the will of him that sent me, and to finish his work" (John 4:34). He also said, "I came down from heaven, not to do mine own will, but the will of him that sent me" (John 6:38). "I can of mine own self do nothing; because I seek not mine own will, but the will of the Father which hath sent me" (John 5:30). "I do nothing of myself; but as my Father hath taught me, I speak these things" (John 8:28).

Abinadi witnessed that the "will of the Son [would be] swallowed up in the will of the Father" (Mosiah 15:7). The only time we have record wherein Jesus asked for some relief was during the Gethsemane experience, but His spiritual submissiveness always triumphed, and He placed His desires secondary to the Father's desires: "Nevertheless not my will, but thine, be done" (Luke 22:42).

The Sacrament

During the Last Supper, Jesus introduced the ordinance of the sacrament (see Matthew 26:26–29; Mark 14:22–24; Luke 22:19–20). It is surprising that so little was preserved regarding the introduction of this gospel ordinance. We don't have one word about it from John. The other gospel writers gave us little. The full significance of what occurred that night must be gleaned from latter-day revelation. Christ also instituted the sacrament to the Nephites when He visited them after His Ascension, and we can glean more from that account as found in 3 Nephi 18:1–14 and 20:1–9. Gratefully, we are given more details from the revelations given to the Prophet Joseph. They can be found in Doctrine and Covenants 20:75–79 and 27:1–14.

From the latter-day revelation, we more fully understand that:

1. Jesus gave His life to ransom humankind from both physical and spiritual death;
2. the broken bread of the sacrament symbolizes His broken flesh as He died for us, and we are to eat the bread in remembrance of His great suffering and sacrifice for us;

3. the water of the sacrament symbolizes the blood He spilt in Gethsemane and on Calvary, and we are to drink in remembrance of His great sacrifice;
4. the sacrament is a holy ordinance that must be administered by those having priesthood authority;
5. it is administered to those who have been baptized, as it is the ordinance whereby faithful Saints can renew the covenants made at baptism;
6. those who partake promise to always remember the Son in all their walks of life;
7. those who partake promise to keep the commandments of God;
8. those who partake also promise to take upon them the name of the Son, meaning that they will set themselves apart from the world and live in such a way as to honor His name and, by so doing, direct others toward Him;
9. partaking of the sacrament unworthily will condemn the partaker; and
10. if one is true to the sacramental covenants, then the Lord will bless the partaker with His Spirit.

What does it mean to partake of the sacrament unworthily? All mortals sin; none of us are perfect. But one must approach the sacrament with a humble heart, with a contrite spirit, and with a determination to repent, to do better tomorrow, and be the best disciple of Christ they can be. If a person partakes of the sacrament without a repentant attitude and without a resolve to do better, then they partake of it unworthily.

THE TEACHINGS OF JESUS

The teachings of Jesus were majestic! Following His teachings will lift one up from the telestial to the celestial. However, it is not within the scope of this book to cover all his majestic teachings. His teachings do change people. Following His teachings would make this world a much better place, and it would ultimately shackle Satan. However, His gospel message had been preached from the days of Adam, and it will be preached to the end of the earth. Although Jesus spoke with authority and with great power, His mission was not specifically to preach His gospel.

Jesus performed many miracles. Violent nature obeyed His word and became calm. The blind were made to see, the deaf were made to hear, the lame were made to walk, the maim were healed, and even some who were dead were brought back to life. But miracles have been done by His authorized servants throughout all history and will continue till the end of time. Christ's mission was not to perform miracles.

While others could preach the Savior's gospel and even perform a ministry of miracles, only He could accomplish His foreordained mission: to redeem humankind. His mission was to "bring to pass the immortality and eternal life of man" (Moses 1:39). No other could do it. His mission centered on Gethsemane, the cross, the tomb, and His resurrection.

The Majesty of Christ's Atonement

Christ came to earth to perform the Atonement; no one else could do it. The plan of salvation works only because of the Atonement. Much has been said and written about the Atonement of Jesus Christ. Hence, my intent is not to write a complete treatise regarding the Atonement, but some things need to be written and pondered regarding His Gethsemane and Calvary experience to fully appreciate the majesty of Jesus Christ. Before His formal ministry even began, Jesus gained a knowledge of His mission. He knew He had come to bear the burden of the sins of us all. He knew He would suffer humiliations and insults from His enemies. He knew He would be lifted up on the cross. He knew He would rise from the grave.

His greatest test would be to face the terrible pains that would come as He suffered the pains and sufferings of all humankind. The Lord knew this. When Jesus traveled to Jerusalem during His last week, the gravity of it all must have weighed heavily on His heart and mind. Mark recorded that "Jesus went before them; and they were amazed; and as they followed, they were afraid" (Mark 10:32). There must have been a mighty struggle between Christ's spirit and the natural anguish of His flesh, which shrank from that great sacrifice. Such struggle was felt by the Apostles. Though they didn't fully understand the cause of the struggle, they were afraid because of the powers of darkness that were at work in that struggle.

Following the Last Supper, Jesus took His Apostles—except Judas—to the Garden of Gethsemane. Sorrow and grief always accompany pain. Such sorrow began as the group entered the garden. Matthew and Mark record that even before separating Himself from the group, Jesus exclaimed that He felt very sorrowful.

Leaving eight of the Apostles at some point, he took Peter, James, and John deeper into the garden. Then the terrible work of the Atonement began in earnest. Mark used the word "sore amazed" to describe the experience (Mark 14:33). One respected New Testament scholar says that the Greek word for "sore amazed" is best rendered as "terrified surprise." What could possibly cause the Savior to feel terrified and surprised? For all the Savior knew, there was one thing He did not know. Because He had lived a sinless life, He did not know the physical, spiritual, mental, or emotional feelings of sin—until Gethsemane. Now, as He experienced the effects of sin, it surprised and terrified Him. Elder Neal A. Maxwell once said, "Jesus knew cognitively what He must do, but not experientially. He had never personally known the exquisite and exacting process of an atonement before. Thus, when the agony came in its fullness, it was so much, much worse than even He with his unique intellect had ever imagined!"[26]

Jesus Experienced All Our Temptations

In Gethsemane, Jesus felt and experienced "temptations of every kind" (Alma 7:11). Jesus experienced every temptation that anyone has had to face. Why? "In that he himself hath suffered being tempted, he is able to succour them that are tempted" (Hebrews 2:18). "He will take upon him their infirmities, that his bowels may be filled with mercy, according to the flesh, that he may know according to the flesh how to succor his people according to their infirmities" (Alma 7:12).

Jesus knows exactly what you and I are going through because He has already experienced it! He is perfectly equipped to support and comfort each one of us in our moments of grief and sorrow. Jesus knows by experience what it feels like to be hungry, thirsty, tired,

---

26. Neal A. Maxwell, "Willing to Submit," *Ensign*, May 1985, 72–73.

snubbed, ridiculed, excluded, abused, and addicted. He knows how you feel when you sin. In short, He chose to endure all the experiences of mortality so that He could be in a position to succor us. The word *succor* means to run to help and support in times of hardship or distress. He became perfectly equipped to support and comfort each one of us in our moments of grief and sorrow because of our sins.

Elder Neal A. Maxwell taught, "Have you ever thought that there was no way that Jesus could know the suffering which we undergo as a result of our stupidity and sin (because he was sinless) except he bear those sins of ours in what I call the awful arithmetic of the Atonement? Jesus now knows, according to the flesh, how to succor us and how to help us as a result of that suffering, which knowledge could have come in no other way."[27]

Wrong is the individual who contends that Jesus cannot really empathize with the one who yields to temptation since He never once yielded. Such reasoning is fallacious. The insightful C. S. Lewis wrote, "A silly idea is current that good people do not know what temptation means. Only those who try to resist temptation know how strong it is. A man who gives in to temptation after five minutes simply does not know what it would have been like an hour later. That is why bad people know very little about badness. They have lived a sheltered life by always giving in. We never find out the strength of the evil impulse inside us until we try to fight it."[28] Someone who resists temptation really understands the power of temptation. The fact that Jesus perfectly resisted all temptation gives Him the power to understand our temptations and help deliver us from evil.

Jesus Suffered for All Our Sins and All Our Pains

In some way incomprehensible to us, Jesus took upon Himself the sins of the world. He suffered for the most wicked actions of the vilest sinners as well as the unwitting transgressions of the meek. He suffered for those He knew would repent, and also for those He knew would not repent or accept His offering. The spiritual and physical

---

27. *Third Annual Church Educational System Religious Educators' Symposium on the Old Testament* (The Church of Jesus Christ of Latter-day Saints, 1979), 17.

28. *The Inspirational Writing of C. S. Lewis* (Inspirational Press, 1987), 337–38.

feelings brought about by sin, as well as the full effects of all sins and violent acts ever committed, were literally placed upon the Savior and suffered by Him. He acted in our place to take the consequences and sorrows of wicked behavior, which each of us deserves, so that we could be free from the devastating effects of sin. He did this all the while withstanding the merciless fury and attacks against Him launched by Satan.

In His tremendous suffering in the Garden of Gethsemane, and again experienced on the cross, "Jesus Christ did not just assume the punishment for our sins—he took the guilt as well. The sin, the experience itself with all of its negative consequences and ramifications, and not just the penalty for sin, became His. If Jesus had assumed only the punishment for our sins but not the sins themselves, then when the penalty was paid, we would merely be 'guilty but forgiven,' instead of being sanctified through the Atonement, being perfect in Christ, and being innocent and worthy of the kingdom of God and the presence of the Father."[29]

But Christ's suffering was more than for the sins of the world. Alma taught, "He shall go forth, suffering pains and afflictions and temptations of every kind; and this that the word might be fulfilled which saith he will take upon him the pains and the sicknesses of his people. . . . He will take upon him their infirmities" (Alma 7:11–12). Jacob confirmed that truth: "He suffereth the pains of all men, yea, the pains of every living creature, both men, women, and children, who belong to the family of Adam" (2 Nephi 9:21). He suffered for our pains, sicknesses, and infirmities. Think of your sicknesses and multiply that by billions. Think of your physical, emotional, and mental pains and multiply that by billions. Think of your infirmities and addictions, bodily and otherwise, and multiply that by billions. Elder Neal A. Maxwell called such suffering "enormity multiplied by infinity."[30]

He willingly suffered it all. Why? So He could empathize with our sicknesses, pains, and afflictions and properly give us comfort. He

---

29. Stephen E. Robinson, *Believing Christ the Parable of the Bicycle and Other Good News* (Deseret Book, 1992), 117.

30. Maxwell, "Willing To Submit," 73.

understands all addictions, all depression, all loneliness, and all else that afflicts humankind. No one can say to Him, "You don't understand." He understands completely, for in Gethsemane, He experienced everything you may go through. "Thus, when we are tempted to think that our sins have put us beyond the understanding or reach of our Savior, we are simply mistaken, and we grossly underestimate the scope of the Atonement. However low we may fall, our Redeemer has already been there."[31] Though sinless, our Savior knows the pain and suffering that comes from sin.

How could He take that burden by Himself? A mere mortal couldn't, as death would bring welcome relief before such a burden could be fully realized. Only a God could do it. Yet His suffering was so great that He bled from every pore. Some critics have scoffed at the notion that Jesus actually sweat blood. But latter-day revelation has confirmed that such a thing happened (see Doctrine and Covenants 19:16–19). Our finite minds simply do not understand the depth of His suffering and pain.

Elder James E. Talmage wrote:

> Christ's agony in the garden is unfathomable by the finite mind, both as to intensity and cause. It was not physical pain, nor mental anguish alone, that caused Him to suffer such torture as to produce an extrusion of blood from every pore; but a spiritual agony such as only God was capable of experiencing. No other man, however great his powers of physical or mental endurance, could have suffered so; for his human organism would have succumbed, and would have produced unconsciousness and welcome oblivion. In some manner, actual and terribly real though to man incomprehensible, the Savior took upon Himself the burden of the sins of humankind from Adam to the end of the world.[32]

Some have thought that Jesus used His godlike attributes to soften the blows He experienced in Gethsemane. Such is not the case. Paul taught, "For verily he [the Savior] took not on him the nature of angels; but he took on him the seed of Abraham. Wherefore in all things it behoved him to be made like unto his brethren" (Hebrews 2:16–17).

---

31. Robinson, *Believing Christ*, 120–21.

32. Talmage, *Jesus the Christ* (1916), 613.

In other words, Jesus refused to use His divine powers to soften the blows. By choice, Jesus did not call down legions of angels to deliver Him in the Garden of Gethsemane, although He indeed possessed the power to do so. He suffered like a mortal (the seed of Abraham) and used His divine powers to prevent succumbing to death so that He could drain the whole cup.

Sometime during this excruciating night when the burdens seemed to be crushing Him, Jesus pleaded with His Father if the cup could be removed. But His plea was always given in a spirit of meekness: "Nevertheless not as I will, but as thou wilt" (Matthew 26:39). Matthew gives an interesting perspective. He tells us that the plea was made, and then He visited His Apostles and found them sleeping. He returned to continue the work of the Atonement and prayed, "Father, if this cup may not pass away from me, except I drink it, thy will be done" (Matthew 26:42). In other words, Christ first prayed for relief. Sometime between that prayer and His return from visiting the three Apostles, He received the answer from the Father that He must drink the full cup. His second prayer is one of resignation; He would drink the full cup because it was His Father's will (see Matthew 26:36–46; Mark 14:32–42; Luke 22:40–46).

Andrew C. Skinner gives this wonderful insight, "Rather than diminishing the Savior's accomplishment in Gethsemane by mentioning his personal preference to avoid suffering, we actually magnify it. . . . He demonstrated the human impulse to look for ways out of the horrors and agonies that constituted Gethsemane. The Savior's human nature wrestled with his divine nature. Yet, he was perfectly obedient. Most impressively, his obedience was informed obedience, not blind submission." He continues, "Will there not come a time—or many times—in our life when we will wrestle with conflicting impulses? Will there not come a time when each one of us will consciously have to choose to be obedient, to subjugate our desires and preferences to the will of God, to yield our agency to Deity?"[33]

To help His suffering Son, the Father did send an angel, strengthening Him (see Luke 22:43). Most likely, a priesthood blessing was

33. Andrew C. Skinner, *The Savior's Final Week: Gethsemane* (Deseret Book, 2014), 62–63.

given. What an honor for that angel! Some have speculated that the angel was Adam, which would seem reasonable. In truth, we don't know the identity of the angel.

JESUS SUFFERED ALONE

Undoubtedly, the greatest terrifying surprise to our Savior was the withdrawal of the Father and the Spirit. Just as He cried out while on the cross, "My God, my God, why hast thou forsaken me?" (Matthew 27:46), it is most likely that the Father withdrew from the Son in Gethsemane. Though humankind had consistently rejected Him, Jesus could always count on the support and comforting love of His Father. During His ministry, Jesus enjoyed the fulness of the Spirit (see Joseph Smith Translation, John 3:34). Is it possible that Heavenly Father had really forsaken Him? Could God have abandoned Him in this most sacred and terrible hour? The answer is yes. Even the choicest Son of God had to understand being forsaken. Perhaps that was the culmination of descending below all things.

I do not doubt that it was a gut-wrenching experience for the Father to see His Only Begotten Son suffer so exquisitely. It would have been a natural fatherly reaction to rescue His Son. However, the Father needed His Son to drink the full cup, to complete the Atonement, because He also loved you and me. Failure to complete the Atonement would have had catastrophic consequences for us. I appreciate the thought expressed by Elder Melvin J. Ballard:

> He (Father in Heaven) loved His Son, and He could have saved Him. He might have rescued Him from the insult of the crowds. He might have rescued Him when the crown of thorns was placed upon His head. He saw Him drag the cross through the streets of Jerusalem and faint under its load. He saw the Son finally upon the cross upon Calvary. . . .
>
> In that hour I think I see our dear Father behind the veil looking upon these dying struggles until even He could not endure it any longer; and like the mother who bids farewell to her dying child and has to be taken out of the room so as not to look upon the last struggles, so He bowed His head and hid in some part of His universe. His great heart almost breaking for the love that He had for His Son. Oh, in that moment when He might have saved

> His Son, I thank Him and praise Him that He did not fail us, for He had not only the love of His Son in mind, but He also had love for us. I rejoice that He did not interfere, and that His love for us made it possible for Him to endure to look upon the sufferings of His Son and give Him finally to us, our Savior and Redeemer. Without Him, without His sacrifice, we would have remained, and we would never have come glorified into His presence.[34]

I too am grateful to the Father for not intervening. We need to remember that when we go through our Gethsemanes, God will respond appropriately—as He always does. His response may not provide immediate relief, however. Because of some greater divine design, our Father in Heaven doesn't rescue us when and how we like. We simply need to put our trust in the Lord.

Jesus Was Buffeted by Satan

Two conditions resulted from the withdrawal of the Father's power and influence. First, He was engulfed by spiritual death and hell. Second, He became completely vulnerable to the powers of Satan. We know that Satan attempted to destroy Joseph Smith when he walked into that grove of trees to pray. It is reasonable to assume that Satan threw everything he had at Jesus in Gethsemane. Unspeakable horror was at work that night in Gethsemane when eternity hung in the balance. "In that hour of anguish Christ met and overcame all the horrors of Satan, the prince of this world could inflict. The frightful struggle incident to the temptations immediately following the Lord's baptism was surpassed and overshadowed by this supreme contest with the power of the devil."[35]

In one sense, Gethsemane entailed great risk. The Savior's experience in the garden was not without danger. Not only did Christ suffer greatly for the pains and sins of all humankind, but He was fighting against everything Satan threw at Him. Jesus could have failed in that garden. So in one sense, He might have failed and the whole plan of salvation would have been frustrated.

---

34. Melvin Joseph Ballard, *Melvin J. Ballard: Crusader for Righteousness* (Bookcraft, 1966), 135–37.

35. Talmage, *Jesus the Christ* (1916), 613.

In another sense, there was no risk at all, for our Father in Heaven absolutely knew that Christ would not fail. The majesty of Jesus Christ lies in the fact that He experienced the same temptations and enticements of a natural man, yet he instantly rejected them. "He suffered temptations but gave no heed unto them" (Doctrine and Covenants 20:22). He condescended below all things—He suffered everything Satan could throw at Him—yet He was victorious!

His Blood, Sweat, and Tears

Perhaps because the Father withdrew His support and Spirit, Jesus took a couple of breaks from the terrific struggle to seek strength from his chief Apostles. Perhaps He went to His Apostles to ensure that all was well with them—that they had not been overcome by Satan in this vicious battle with the darkness. Whatever the reason, He found them sleeping. Christ was truly alone in this struggle. Lest we judge these Apostles too harshly, I find Luke's words instructive: "And when he rose up from prayer, and was come to his disciples, he found them sleeping for sorrow" (Luke 22:45). These Apostles dearly loved their Lord. They were seeing Him go through unspeakable pain. They were witnesses to Him bleeding from every pore. Somewhere in that process, it became too unbearable for them. They sought relief by simply closing their eyes and sleeping. Those Apostles told the Lord, "The spirit truly is ready, but the flesh is weak" (Mark 14:38).

Elder Orson F. Whitney had a remarkable vision regarding Gethsemane. He writes:

> I seemed to be in the Garden of Gethsemane, a witness of the Savior's agony. I saw Him as plainly as ever I have seen anyone. Standing behind a tree in the foreground, I beheld Jesus, with Peter, James, and John, as they came through a little wicket gate at my right. Leaving the three Apostles there, after telling them to kneel and pray, the Son of God passed over to the other side, where He also knelt and prayed.
>
> As He prayed the tears streamed down His face, which was toward me. I was so moved at the sight that I also wept, out of pure

> sympathy. My whole heart went out to Him; I loved Him with all my soul, and longed to be with Him as I longed for nothing else.[36]

The Gospel authors mention blood and sweat but do not mention tears. Elder Whitney saw the tears of sorrow and suffering. Jesus prayed for relief—each prayer being more intense—but relief did not come. There would be no relief until justice had been fully satisfied.

Jesus Christ overcame sin. He had the power to do so because He was the Son of God and lived a sinless life. He was willing to take the punishment for sin for each of us because of His infinite love for each of us!

Though terribly difficult to endure, Jesus finished the Gethsemane experience for no more reason than that it was His Father's will. In the premortal world, He proclaimed, "Father, thy will be done" (Moses 4:2). That same attitude remained with Him throughout His life. "I must be about my Father's business" (Luke 2:49). "The Son can do nothing of himself, but what he seeth the Father do" (John 5:19). Such lowliness of heart, such spiritual submissiveness, is simply majestic!

Part of the probationary test of this life is to learn to do the will of the Father and His Son. What I want should never take precedence over what They want. We must learn to subject our will to Theirs.

Elder Maxwell taught, "Jesus' character necessarily underwrote His remarkable atonement. Without Jesus' sublime character there could have been no sublime atonement!"[37] His majestic character was manifest during His final hours during the judicial trials and ultimately His Crucifixion.

His Arrest and Trials

With the Gethsemane experience complete, Jesus and His Apostles exited the garden only to be met by Judas, who was leading a band of Pharisees, chief priests, some temple guards, and some Roman soldiers who had come to arrest Jesus. The temple guards and the Roman soldiers, no doubt, were a hardened group who had made many prior

---

36. Orson F. Whitney, *Through Memories Halls* (Press of Zion's Printing and Publishing Company, 1930), 82.

37. Neal A. Maxwell, *O How Great the Plan of God*, Address to CES Religious educators, February 3, 1995, Temple Square Assembly Hall.

arrests. To ensure that Jesus—and not some impostor—was arrested, Judas had conspired previously with the chief priests and Pharisees that he would identify Jesus with a kiss. The Greek text implies that Judas not only kissed but covered Him with kisses, kissing Him repeatedly and loudly.[38] As it was the custom to greet friends and guests with a kiss, Judas wanted to ensure the sign was clear and certain.

Even with the sign given, the armed group stood still. Why? I like to think that Jesus had a majestic appearance that left them in awe and unsure of how to proceed. As the literal Son of God, He had just prayed mightily to his Father in Gethsemane and had been strengthened by an angel. At any rate, the armed group stood in awe of the Lord. Knowing the purpose of their appearance and to help them do what needed to be done, Jesus stepped forward and without hesitation asked, "Whom seek ye?" They answered, "Jesus of Nazareth," to which Jesus replied, "I am he." John tells us that the group "went backward, and fell to the ground" (John 18:6). This hardened group was shocked at His words and His demeanor, and they were overcome by His magnificence! Jesus simply could not be arrested without His own consent.

After the same exchange was repeated, the officials gathered the courage to approach Him because of His willing attitude to be arrested. Luke tells us that someone asked whether they should smite with the sword. Not waiting for an answer, Peter quickly smote off the ear of Malchus, the servant of the high priest. It is likely that Peter's intent was to strike the head or neck but got the ear when Malchus made a defensive move to thwart the strike. Peter was going to defend His Master. Remarkably, unconcerned about Himself, and having no ill feelings toward those who were about to arrest Him, Jesus told Peter to sheath the sword and then tenderly restored Malchus's ear to full health. The Savior's majestic character was on full display.

Despite the magnificence of Jesus, regardless of His tender touch that restored a severed ear, the hearts of the Pharisees and chief priests were hardened. Surely prodded by them, the temple guards and Roman soldiers at last came and arrested Jesus, but they honored His request that His Apostles and disciples be allowed to go free. Their

---

38. Bruce R. McConkie, *The Mortal Messiah* (Deseret Book, 1981), 4:130.

agreeableness might have been temporary or with a time condition (such as "you've got two minutes") as the Apostles fled. Jesus chided the Pharisees and chief priests for coming in the middle of the night with swords and staves to arrest Him when they had ample opportunity to do so while He taught daily in the temple. They had no answer for the Man of Righteousness, as they were involved in a dastardly deed and they knew it. Jesus could have called the legions of heaven to come and rescue Him, but He didn't. He went willingly; for this cause came He into the world.

Jesus went through a series of illegal trials that night. Elder James E. Talmage details the various illegalities.[39] There is one fact that becomes crystal clear as one reads the various accounts of the trials: Those who judged Jesus were murderous thugs. During the unholy proceedings of the first trial in front of Annas, one person profaned the situation even more with an infamous blow to Jesus's face. It was to be the first of many that night. As evidence that He had truly overcome the world, Jesus didn't lash out at the man for such a blow as most men would have, but His reply was with genuine gentleness: "If I have spoken evil, bear witness of the evil; but if well, why smitest thou me?" (John 18:23).

During the second trial in front of Caiaphas, Jesus remained silent as one false witness after another spewed lies. He could have easily silenced the false witnesses. But His role at this time was not to live but to die at the hands of these evil men. His majestic silence agitated and infuriated those evil men. With unbelievable contempt and fury, Caiaphas yelled at Jesus—knowing that He was the promised Messiah—"I adjure thee by the living God, that thou tell us whether thou be the Christ, the Son of God" (Matthew 26:63). Elder Bruce R. McConkie wrote it well: "How intense was the hatred of that hour! How many unseen demons must have laughed in the background as the legal high priest in Israel, speaking in Jehovah's name, adjured Jehovah himself to proclaim His own divine sonship! No doubt the prince of devils himself was there; what is more natural than to expect

39. Talmage, *Jesus the Christ* (1916), 645–48.

the master of all evil come face to face with Him that is the embodiment of all that is good."[40]

To such a direct question, Jesus gave a direct answer: "I am." In that answer there was no ambiguity, no room for doubt. As He had done many times before, Jesus boldly declared Himself to be the Son of God, their promised Messiah, the Savior of the world. Rather than being humbled by such a direct testimony, they elected to cry "blasphemy." Under Jewish law, the crime of blasphemy was met with capital punishment. The Sanhedrin did not have the power to impose capital punishment. But they all shouted that Jesus was worthy of death. Their Jehovah was worthy of death because He testified that He was Jehovah. Then they belittled and mistreated their Jehovah with derision, mocking, cursing, slapping, and showers of spittle. The Savior bore this horrible abuse with quiet dignity and majesty.

After being formally condemned in front of a full quorum of the Sanhedrin, Jesus was taken to Pilate to obtain his permission to kill Jesus. When asked by Pilate, Jesus confirmed that He was born to be the King of the Jews but not at this time. He had no soldiers who would rescue Him. His kingdom was a spiritual one, one not of this world. Pilate had the authority to release Jesus, and when he told the Jews that he found nothing worthy of capital punishment, he was stunned by their animosity. The chief priests then accused Jesus of many other crimes, to which Jesus maintained majestic silence. His silent yet majestic suffering caused Pilate to marvel. Jesus is our exemplar in all things; silence is often the best response to private trials.

Jesus had only silence during the trial in front of Herod. Herod had beheaded John the Baptist. Can you imagine the Savior's contempt for him? Rather than condemning Herod as the Lord Jehovah, Jesus remained silent. As they ridiculed and mocked Him, as they sarcastically dressed Him in an elegant robe, He maintained majestic silence.

Jesus was taken back to Pilate for a second trial, where Pilate declared that Jesus was innocent of their accusations. Having come to that conclusion, there was only one honorable thing to do: release Jesus. But the Jewish leaders wanted nothing less than His blood.

---

40. McConkie, *The Mortal Messiah*, 4:154.

Despite Pilate's attempts to appease them, their cries of "Crucify him!" became vociferous. Pilate again approached Jesus and must have been struck with awe by His majestic silence. The Lord's plan did not call for Jesus to be released. It was the time for His death. Indeed, as the Son of God, Jesus could have called down the armies of heaven to rescue Him, but that was not the will of the Father. Having been weakened by past decisions, and lacking a resolute character, Pilate released Jesus into the hands of the Jews to be crucified.

The whole process, from arrest to crucifixion, moved at an alarmingly rapid pace. After the Last Supper, it is estimated that Jesus spent about four hours in Gethsemane. His arrest had to be late Thursday evening. All the Jewish trials occurred that night. The Roman trials began at 6 a.m., and Jesus was nailed to the cross at around 9 a.m. From arrest to crucifixion was less than twelve hours.

The Cross

Gethsemane was not the end of the bitter cup. On the cross, Jesus again had to endure physical and mental suffering to make the final payment for our sins as well as our sorrows, sicknesses, and afflictions. "In some way, incomprehensible to us, Gethsemane, the cross, and the empty tomb join into one grand and eternal drama, in the course of which Jesus abolishes death, and out of which comes immortality for all and eternal life for the righteous."[41]

During my lifetime, it has been my perception that throughout the Church, there has been more and more emphasis on Gethsemane (and that is good) but with a correspondingly less emphasis on the cross. Both need to share the same podium for the roles they played in the Atonement. The ancient prophet Enoch saw in vision "the Son of Man lifted up on the cross" (Moses 7:55). Nephi writes, "I, Nephi, saw that he was lifted up upon the cross and slain for the sins of the world" (1 Nephi 11:33).

When the camp of Israel was wandering in the Sinai desert, the Lord sent a plague of poisonous serpents with the intent that they would humble themselves and repent. Moses was instructed to make a brass serpent and set it on a pole. Those who looked at the serpent

---

41. McConkie, *The Mortal Messiah*, 4:224.

would be healed. The Book of Mormon prophets understood the symbolism of the brass serpent. "Did [Moses] not bear record that the Son of God should come? And as he lifted up the brazen serpent in the wilderness, even so shall he be lifted up who should come. And as many as should look upon that serpent should live, even so as many as should look upon the Son of God with faith, having a contrite spirit, might live" (Helaman 8:14–15).

For the meridian Saints, the cross was a powerful symbol of Christ's suffering and atoning sacrifice. Paul wrote, "For the preaching of the cross is to them that perish foolishness; but unto us which are saved it is the power of God" (1 Corinthians 1:18). To the Galatian Saints, Paul wrote, "God forbid that I should glory, save in the cross of our Lord Jesus Christ" (Galatians 6:14). To the Ephesian Saints, Paul taught that man was reconciled to God by the cross (see Ephesians 2:16). Again, in Hebrews we read, "Looking unto Jesus the author and finisher of our faith; who for the joy that was set before him endured the cross, despising the shame, and is set down at the right hand of the throne of God" (Hebrews 12:2).

A powerful witness of the symbolism of the cross was made by the resurrected Jesus when He appeared to the Nephites: "My Father sent me that I might be lifted up upon the cross . . . that I might draw all men unto me" (3 Nephi 27:14). Jesus also emphasized His Gethsemane experience: "I have drunk out of that bitter cup which the Father hath given me, and have glorified the Father in taking upon me the sins of the world" (3 Nephi 11:11). Thus, both the cross and Gethsemane are inseparable in defining the work of Christ's Atonement.

The Savior used the imagery of the cross to teach fundamental doctrines. "Then said Jesus unto his disciples, if any man will come after me, let him deny himself, and take up his cross, and follow me. And now for a man to take up his cross, is to deny himself all ungodliness, and every worldly lust, and keep my commandments" (Joseph Smith Translation, Matthew 16:25–26 [in Matthew 16:24, footnote *a*]). Taking up your cross means to eschew the world, to put off the natural man, to stop doing things your own way, but rather to follow the Lord, no matter how inconvenient, no matter if it causes you to stretch yourself beyond your comfort zone.

I love how Jacob used the imagery of the cross: "We would to God that we could persuade all men not to rebel against God, to provoke him to anger, but that all men would believe in Christ, and view his death, and suffer his cross and bear the shame of the world" (Jacob 1:8). The world will mock and ridicule those who are doing their best to follow Christ. Jacob urges those followers of Christ to bear the shame of the world as Jesus bore the shame of the cross.

Christ's Last Words Show His Character

Shortly after Jesus was nailed to the cross, Satan made a last attempt to destroy Him and thwart the plan of God: "If thou be the Son of God, come down from the cross" (Matthew 27:40). "Let Christ the King of Israel descend now from the cross, that we may see and believe" (Mark 15:32). It was a repeat of Satan's temptation to the Savior while in the wilderness prior to His formal ministry. He was taunted to prove Himself—to show His great power as the Christ. Jesus was in a weakened state. His body and spirit writhed in unimaginable pain and agony. His powers to fight were at their lowest. Jesus was most vulnerable to temptation. It had to be an insidious, alluring temptation. Magnificently, Jesus gave no heed to it.

Much has been written about the final words uttered by Jesus while on the cross. What He said is a good encapsulation of who He was. "It might well be stated as a rule of human nature that when a man reaches his greatest extremity, a moment of extreme danger, pain, emotion, or critical need or death, the true nature of his soul becomes evident. Is he basically thoughtful or selfish, courageous or cowardly, self-absorbed or concerned with others?"[42]

The first words by Jesus are known widely: "Father, forgive them; for they know not what they do" (Luke 23:34). Suffice it to say that those words were not directed toward Annas, Caiaphas, or the other Jewish leaders who had sought to kill him for a long time. They knew they were killing the Son of God, and they will one day face the awful consequences for it. Nor were those words directed at Pilate, whose cowardice allowed the Crucifixion to happen. They were directed at

42. *The Life and Teachings of Jesus and His Apostles* (The Church of Jesus Christ of Latter-day Saints, 1979), 185.

the soldiers who were simply following orders. The Savior did not forgive them of their sins, but rather, He simply did not lay this singular act of nailing Him to the cross at their door. Remarkably, as unfathomable pain tortured His body, Christ was thinking of others.

Elder Jeffrey R. Holland wrote:

> How could he forgive his tormenters at that moment? Surely, he doesn't need to think of others every minute all the time, and especially not with this pack of jackals who are laughing and spitting, stripping him of his clothing and his rights and his dignity. Who cares whether or not they know what they are doing! This is cruel and barbaric and insulting injustice to the purest and only perfect life ever lived. This is yet one more amazing evidence that he really was perfect. . . .
>
> Surely the reason Christ said, "Father, forgive them," was because even in the weakened and terribly trying hour he faced, he knew that this was the message he had come through all eternity to deliver. All of the meaning and all of the majesty of all those dispensations—indeed, the entire plan of salvation—would have been lost had he forgotten that not *in spite* of injustice and brutality and unkindness and disobedience but precisely *because* of them had he come to extend forgiveness to the family of man. Anyone can be pleasant and patient and forgiving on a good day. A Christian has to be pleasant and patient and forgiving on all days.[43]

Jesus was crucified between two thieves. One of the thieves joined the others in mocking and ridiculing Him. The other thief rebuked the first thief with these words: "Dost not thou fear God, seeing thou art in the same condemnation? . . . We receive the due reward of our deeds: but this man hath done nothing amiss" (Luke 23:40–41). How did he know that Jesus was sinless? Had he heard Jesus teach? Had he witnessed His miracles? Did he have a testimony of Jesus but just hadn't overcome the natural man?

Despite intense suffering, Jesus did not look inward with pity. He looked outward to the thief and gave him as much comfort as He could in the moment: "To day shalt thou be with me in paradise"

---

43. Jeffrey R. and Patricia T. Holland, *On Earth as It Is in Heaven* (Deseret Book, 1989), 200–201, 209.

(Luke 23:43; see also Joseph Smith Translation, Matthew 27:44). Apostate Christianity is confused with that statement simply because it lacks an understanding of the spirit world, or because it has rejected modern-day revelation that teaches of the spirit world. *Paradise* is not heaven. Latter-day revelation has taught us that paradise is a place where we continue to prepare for a celestial heaven. Joseph Smith taught that the Savior said, "This day thou shalt be with me in the world of spirits."[44] So the thief was not promised eternal glory, only a place—in a world of spirits—where he could be taught the gospel by legal administrators. Jesus did not forgive the thief; He did not lend credence to death-bed repentance.

Then Jesus expressed concern for His mother, Mary. "When Jesus therefore saw his mother, and the disciple standing by, whom he loved, he saith unto his mother, Woman, behold thy son! Then saith he to the disciple, Behold thy mother! And from that hour that disciple took her unto his own home" (John 19:26–27). We can confidently assume that Joseph had died or Jesus would not have been concerned for His mother's welfare. It's also probable that the Savior's half brothers had not yet accepted Jesus as the Son of God and were not part of the household of faith. Jesus wanted His mother to be nurtured in the gospel faith by one of His faithful Apostles.

The Savior thought of others to the very end of His life. He asked for mercy for those who unwittingly sinned by nailing the Son of God to the cross. He gave some comfort to the mercy-seeking thief. He demonstrated concern and love for His mother. His words demonstrated His character.

When Jesus had paid the full price, when He had drunk the full bitter cup, He then said, "Father, it is finished, thy will is done" (Joseph Smith Translation, Matthew 27:50 [in Matthew 27:50, footnote *a*]). "Into thy hands I commend my spirit" (Luke 23:46). The Creator of this world and worlds without number voluntarily gave up His spirit. He did so only when He had completed His mission as foreordained in the premortal heavens—only when He had done His Father's will. It is believed that He died from a literal broken heart—a

44. *Teachings of the Prophet Joseph Smith*, sel. Joseph Fielding Smith (1976), 309.

manifestation of His great love for us and of His sadness that so many rejected Him.

The Nephite prophet Jacob taught that Jesus would "come among the Jews, among those who are the more wicked part of the world; and they shall crucify him . . . and there is none other nation on earth that would crucify their God" (2 Nephi 10:3). Jesus was born in the meridian of time among the Jews precisely because it was His mission to die so that He could bring to pass the Resurrection for all humankind and eternal life for the obedient.

Though terribly difficult to endure, Christ did emerge from the garden and the cross as the victor over sin and hell. His garments were red with His blood as proof of that victory. Though the earth groaned in sorrow over the death of its Creator, surely all in heaven sighed a collective sigh of relief—and then shouted in wondrous joy—that Christ won the battle over Satan.

Christ's Mission Was the Atonement

The mission of Jesus Christ was to overcome physical death and sin (spiritual death). Gethsemane, the cross, the Garden Tomb, and His Resurrection constituted His mission. No one has suffered as much as Christ when He took upon Himself the sins as well as the pains, sicknesses, and infirmities of all humankind. Such suffering occurred both in Gethsemane and on the cross. Only a God could so suffer. Only when He knew the Father had accepted His sacrifice did He voluntarily allow His spirit to depart His body.

The Atonement of Jesus Christ began in Gethsemane. It ended with the empty tomb and His Resurrection. Jesus Christ, as the Only Begotten Son of God and the only sinless person to live on the earth, was the only one capable of making an Atonement for humankind. Elder Bruce R. McConkie taught, "Nothing in the entire plan of salvation compares in any way in importance with that most transcendent of all events, the atoning sacrifice of our Lord. It is the most important single thing that has ever occurred in the entire history of created things; it is the rock foundation upon which the gospel and all other things rest."[45]

---

45. McConkie, *Mormon Doctrine*, 2nd ed. (1966), 60.

"Salvation comes because of the atonement. Without it the whole plan of salvation would be frustrated and the whole purpose of creating and populating of the earth would come to naught. With it the eternal purposes of the Father will roll forth, the purpose of creation be preserved, the plan of salvation made efficacious, and men will be assured of a hope of the highest exaltation."[46]

The Savior's Atonement was infinite—it covers all people. Elder Patrick Kearon taught, "If you are prone to worry that you will never measure up, or that the loving reach of Christ's infinite Atonement mercifully covers everyone else but not you, then you misunderstand. *Infinite* means infinite. *Infinite* covers you and those you love."[47]

I don't understand how Jesus Christ could vicariously pay for all our sins, but He did so at the price of His much suffering in Gethsemane and death on the cross. I stand all amazed at His magnificent love that He would be willing to pay that price. With Him having paid that price, Paul could write, "Ye are bought with a price: therefore glorify God in your body, and in your spirit" (1 Corinthians 6:20). In Doctrine and Covenants 45:3–5, we read, "Listen to him who is the advocate with the Father, who is pleading your cause before him—Saying: Father, behold the sufferings and death of him who did no sin, in whom thou wast well pleased; behold the blood of thy Son which was shed, the blood of him whom thou gavest that thyself might be glorified; Wherefore, Father, spare these my brethren that believe on my name, that they may come unto me and have everlasting life." It gives Christ the right to claim those who enter into His gospel covenant.

We will never fully comprehend while in mortality *how* He accomplished what He did, but we must never fail to understand *why* He did what He did. All that He did was prompted by His unselfish, infinite love for us. He did for us what we could not do for ourselves. He paid a great price to do so. He taught, "Greater love hath no man than this, that a man lay down his life for his friends" (John 15:13). I marvel at his majestic love!

46. Joseph Fielding Smith, *Doctrines of Salvation*, comp. Bruce R. McConkie (1955), 1:121–38.

47. Patrick Kearon, "God's Intent Is to Bring You Home," *Liahona*, May 2024, 88.

The Majesty of Christ While in the Grave

As noted in the first chapter, we lived as spirit children of our Heavenly Father in a premortal sphere. A spirit is a personage that lives forever, as God is its Creator. A spirit simply never dies. Mortal birth and life represent the union of a spirit with a physical body. Mortal death represents a separation of the spirit from the physical body. When death occurs, the physical body returns to the dust of the earth while the spirit goes to another sphere, a sphere called the *spirit world*. In our premortal world, one could say we lived in a world of spirits but along with those who had resurrected bodies, such as our Father in Heaven. We wanted a body like our Father in Heaven, and that is one primary reason we were eager for our mortality: to gain a physical body. In the spirit world, we will not live with anyone who has a resurrected body; we will not return to our Father in Heaven. It is a world in which we wait for the Resurrection—a time to continue to progress and learn. It is an extension of mortality.

The Book of Mormon prophet Alma, who lived before Christ, taught, "Now, concerning the state of the soul [i.e., spirit] between death and the resurrection—Behold, it has been made known unto me by an angel, that the spirits of all men, as soon as they are departed from this mortal body, yea, the spirits of all men, whether they be good or evil, are taken home to that God who gave them life" (Alma 40:11). Then to clarify what he meant, Alma continued, "The spirits of those who are righteous are received into a state of happiness, which is called paradise, a state of rest, a state of peace, where they shall rest from all their troubles and from all care, and sorrow. . . . The spirits of the wicked, yea, who are evil . . . these shall be cast out into outer darkness; there shall be weeping, and wailing, and gnashing of teeth, and this because of their own iniquity. . . . This is the state of the souls of the wicked . . . as well as the righteous in paradise, until the time of their resurrection" (Alma 40:12–14).

Some have misunderstood Alma's words "taken home to that God who gave them life." It is clear from Alma's clarification that our spirits do not go directly into the presence of God when we die. But they do go to a sphere of spirits that is under God's direction and control. Mortals cannot dwell in the presence of God, but they can be visited by God. But even to be visited by God for a short period of time requires a transfiguration of the mortal body. We read, "For no man has seen God at any time in the flesh, except quickened by the Spirit of God. Neither can any natural man abide the presence of God, neither after the carnal mind. Ye are not able to abide the presence of God now, neither the ministering of angels; wherefore, continue in patience until ye are perfected" (Doctrine and Covenants 67:11–13). One does not become "perfected" until after the Resurrection. So the same principle applies to non-resurrected spirits. Just as God can visit mortals, so He can visit the spirit world.

Note that Alma taught that the righteous will enjoy rest from their troubles, worldly cares, and sorrows; they will enjoy peace. They are in paradise. This mortal probationary period is complete for those who have made covenants with the Lord and kept those covenants in faithfulness. They have proven themselves to the Lord. Although they are no longer troubled by worldly cares, they are anxiously engaged in doing the work of the Lord.

But such is not the case for the unrighteous. Alma tells us that they will be in darkness, meaning they will have little to no hope. They are in what we call *spirit prison*. For the unrighteous, the spirit world is an extension of one's mortal probationary period, which implies that Satan and his minions are still at work in spirit prison. The majesty of Jesus Christ is manifest again as we learn that He has not forgotten them.

While Christ's body lay in the tomb, His spirit went to the spirit world—to paradise in the spirit world. That understanding gives new light to His words to one of the thieves while on the cross: "To day shalt thou be with me in paradise" (Luke 23:43). The thief was not promised eternal glory but paradise in the spirit world, a good place where he could learn and progress.

Jesus Appeared to the Saints in the Spirit World

In a marvelous vision given to the Prophet Joseph F. Smith in 1919, we read:

> As I pondered over these things which are written, the eyes of my understanding were opened, and the Spirit of the Lord rested upon me, and I saw the hosts of the dead, both small and great.
>
> And there were gathered together in one place an innumerable company of the spirits of the just, who had been faithful in the testimony of Jesus while they lived in mortality;
>
> And who had offered sacrifice in the similitude of the great sacrifice of the Son of God, and had suffered tribulation in their Redeemer's name.
>
> All these had departed the mortal life, firm in the hope of a glorious resurrection, through the grace of God the Father and his Only Begotten Son, Jesus Christ.
>
> I beheld that they were filled with joy and gladness, and were rejoicing together because the day of their deliverance was at hand.
>
> They were assembled awaiting the advent of the Son of God into the spirit world, to declare their redemption from the bands of death.
>
> Their sleeping dust was to be restored unto its perfect frame, bone to his bone, and the sinews and the flesh upon them, the spirit and the body to be united never again to be divided, that they might receive a fulness of joy.
>
> While this vast multitude waited and conversed, rejoicing in the hour of their deliverance from the chains of death, the Son of God appeared, declaring liberty to the captives who had been faithful;

And there he preached to them the everlasting gospel, the doctrine of the resurrection and the redemption of mankind from the fall, and from individual sins on conditions of repentance.

But unto the wicked he did not go, and among the ungodly and the unrepentant who had defiled themselves while in the flesh, his voice was not raised;

Neither did the rebellious who rejected the testimonies and the warnings of the ancient prophets behold his presence, nor look upon his face.

Where these were, darkness reigned, but among the righteous there was peace;

And the saints rejoiced in their redemption, and bowed the knee and acknowledged the Son of God as their Redeemer and Deliverer from death and the chains of hell.

Their countenances shone, and the radiance from the presence of the Lord rested upon them, and they sang praises unto his holy name.

I marveled, for I understood that the Savior spent about three years in his ministry among the Jews and those of the house of Israel, endeavoring to teach them the everlasting gospel and call them unto repentance;

And yet, notwithstanding his mighty works, and miracles, and proclamation of the truth, in great power and authority, there were but few who hearkened to his voice, and rejoiced in his presence, and received salvation at his hands.

But his ministry among those who were dead was limited to the brief time intervening between the crucifixion and his resurrection;

And I wondered at the words of Peter—wherein he said that the Son of God preached unto the spirits in prison, who sometime were disobedient, when once the long-suffering of God waited in the days of Noah—and how it was possible for him to preach to those spirits and perform the necessary labor among them in so short a time.

And as I wondered, my eyes were opened, and my understanding quickened, and I perceived that the Lord went not in person among the wicked and the disobedient who had rejected the truth, to teach them;

But behold, from among the righteous, he organized his forces and appointed messengers, clothed with power and authority, and

> commissioned them to go forth and carry the light of the gospel to them that were in darkness, even to all the spirits of men; and thus was the gospel preached to the dead.
>
> And the chosen messengers went forth to declare the acceptable day of the Lord and proclaim liberty to the captives who were bound, even unto all who would repent of their sins and receive the gospel.
>
> Thus was the gospel preached to those who had died in their sins, without a knowledge of the truth, or in transgression, having rejected the prophets.
>
> These were taught faith in God, repentance from sin, vicarious baptism for the remission of sins, the gift of the Holy Ghost by the laying on of hands,
>
> And all other principles of the gospel that were necessary for them to know in order to qualify themselves that they might be judged according to men in the flesh, but live according to God in the spirit.
>
> And so it was made known among the dead, both small and great, the unrighteous as well as the faithful, that redemption had been wrought through the sacrifice of the Son of God upon the cross.
>
> Thus was it made known that our Redeemer spent his time during his sojourn in the world of spirits, instructing and preparing the faithful spirits of the prophets who had testified of him in the flesh;
>
> That they might carry the message of redemption unto all the dead, unto whom he could not go personally, because of their rebellion and transgression, that they through the ministration of his servants might also hear his words. (Doctrine and Covenants 138:11–37)

Jesus Christ organized the priesthood and gave them authority to preach the gospel to those who are in spirit prison. Before Christ's visit to the spirit world, those in paradise and those in spirit prison did not intermingle. Christ gave the righteous the authority and commission to go to the spirit prison and preach the gospel so they could receive hope in Christ and repent. There are many in paradise, such as the thief next to Jesus on the cross, who also will hear the gospel message.

The Church of Jesus Christ is organized in the spirit world, and missionary work is carried out under the direction of the priesthood. That missionary work will continue until all have heard the message. We are taught that "the faithful elders of this dispensation, when they depart from mortal life, continue their labors in the preaching of the gospel . . . among those who are in darkness and under the bondage of sin in the great world of the spirits of the dead" (Doctrine and Covenants 138:57).

Missionary Work in the Spirit World

"Life and work and activity all continue in the spirit world. Men have the same talents and intelligence there which they had in this life. They possess the same attitudes, inclinations, and feelings there which they had in this life. As far as eternal truths are concerned, they continue to walk in the same path they were following in this life."[48] That same teaching is found in the Book of Mormon: "That same spirit which doth possess your bodies at the time that ye go out of this life, that same spirit will have power to possess your body in that eternal world" (Alma 34:34).

The apostolic word and the scriptures teach that one leaves mortality and enters the spirit world with the same attitudes and feelings. But just as one's attitudes and feelings can change in this life, they can change in the spirit world. For those who made poor choices in mortality, the spirit world is a time to use agency to change, progress, and develop. Before the Lord proclaims that His work is finished, every living person who has lived or who will yet live will have an opportunity to hear the gospel message. Using their agency, they can accept or reject that message. Some will accept the gospel and change; others won't. Those who accept the gospel message can repent and receive the grace of Jesus Christ. Thus, the Lord, through ordained messengers, is calling all in the spirit world to come unto Him, just as He is doing so here. President Russell M. Nelson has often reminded us that the Lord is gathering Israel—His elect—on both sides of the veil. When a person in the spirit prison does repent, they will join the righteous in paradise. That is why the Prophet Joseph wrote, "Hades, paradise,

48. McConkie, *Mormon Doctrine*, 2nd ed. (1966), 762.

spirits in prison, are all one: it is a world of spirits. The righteous and the wicked all go to the same world of spirits until the resurrection."[49]

President Brigham Young taught that in the spirit world, one would have no thirst, no hunger, no need for sleep, and no weariness. One would have energy and vigor and would be full of life.[50] So I can well imagine that the missionary work is going forth with much more vigor than here on earth for no other reason than spirits do not get fatigued. They can do the Lord's work twenty-four hours a day.

A primary obstacle here in mortality that prevents people from accepting the gospel is the traditions of the fathers: "And that wicked one cometh and taketh away light and truth, through disobedience, from the children of men, and because of the tradition of their fathers" (Doctrine and Covenants 93:39). In the Book of Mormon, we read that the Lamanites would not believe gospel truths because of the traditions of their fathers (see Mosiah 1:5; Alma 9:16). Such traditions will likely have a lesser pull in the spirit world. The very fact that they are living after their mortal death will cause many to question the traditions. More vigor from the missionary force combined with less resistance to the gospel message leads me to believe that conversions in the spirit world far exceed what we experience here.

As a young missionary, I was riding a bus from one city to another. Seated next to me was a young man who was wearing a military uniform. He was fulfilling his mandatory one-year service in the military for his country. We had a pleasant conversation about Jesus Christ. The young man asked me if I could answer one pressing question that had bothered him. He asked me what would happen to the millions who had never even heard of Jesus Christ. When I told him of the majestic and merciful plan the Lord had to teach everyone about Jesus Christ and His gospel either in this life or in the next life, his heart was filled with joy. I never saw or heard from him again. But I did leave a Book of Mormon with him and bore my testimony.

---

49. *Teachings of the Prophet Joseph Smith*, sel. Joseph Fielding Smith (1976), 310.

50. *Journal of Discourses*, 17:142.

One's Purpose May Be Fulfilled in the Spirit World

The noble and great in premortality were foreordained to accomplish a mission when they left the Lord's presence. For many, that mission will not be completed in this mortal life. It will be completed in the spirit world. I have counseled those who come to me for a patriarchal blessing to keep an eternal perspective—to have faith in God's timing. I mention two examples that illustrate this principle.

I received a patriarchal blessing recommend from a bishop for a ninety-two-year-old sister. I pondered what the Lord might say to her when she was at the sunset of her mortal life. When I laid my hands upon her head, my eyes were opened, and the Lord's words came. Everything that was said to her revealed the Lord's will and desires for her when she passed through the veil. All of her mission was to be accomplished in the spirit world.

A young man in his teens received his patriarchal blessing. He was promised that the Lord would call him to fulfill a full-time mission, conditioned upon his faithfulness. A few years later, that mission call came. Just before he entered the missionary training center, he drowned. As people grieved, questions arose concerning his patriarchal blessing and the promise that he would serve a mission. I know in my heart that that young man did serve a mission. His field of labor, however, was in the spirit world. It is possible that some blessings will not occur in this life but will be realized sometime in eternity.

Redemption Work for the Dead

As with all other believing disciples, those in the spirit world must receive the saving gospel ordinances of baptism and those associated with the temple. Take special note from President Smith's vision that the missionaries will teach those in the spirit world all gospel principles of salvation, including vicarious baptism for the dead. Paul references this vicarious work in his epistle to the Corinthians: "Else what shall they do which are baptized for the dead, if the dead rise not at all? why are they then baptized for the dead?" (1 Corinthians 15:29).

The missionaries will also teach other vicarious ordinances belonging to the temple of the Lord. Performing gospel ordinances vicariously for the dead is one of the great works being done in temples throughout the world. All who will ever live on this earth will have those ordinances performed for them, either while living or by proxy when they are dead. But none will be forced to accept those ordinances. All will have agency to reject the gospel message and the proxy ordinances. The Lord recognized that in these words: "For what doth it profit a man if a gift is bestowed upon him, and he receive not the gift? Behold, he rejoices not in that which is given unto him, neither rejoices in him who is the giver of the gift" (Doctrine and Covenants 88:33).

Christ's work in the spirit world opened up the grand and glorious work that redeems the dead. Christ was able to vicariously take upon Himself the sins of all humankind and thus open the door of salvation to all of us. We can vicariously open the door of salvation by performing the gospel ordinances for the dead one name at a time. In this sense, each of us can be the saviors of men (see Doctrine and Covenants 103:9–10). "The dead who repent will be redeemed, through obedience to the ordinances of the house of God, And after they have paid the penalty of their transgressions, and are washed clean, shall receive a reward according to their works, for they are heirs of salvation" (Doctrine and Covenants 138:58–59).

The words the angel Moroni said to the young Prophet Joseph Smith are the foundational doctrines pertaining to this work for the dead: "Behold, I will reveal unto you the Priesthood, by the hand of Elijah the prophet, before the coming of the great and dreadful day of the Lord. And he shall plant in the hearts of the children the promises made to the fathers, and the hearts of the children shall turn to their fathers. If it were not so, the whole earth would be utterly wasted at his coming" (Doctrine and Covenants 2:1–3).

Elijah did come. He appeared to the Prophet Joseph and Oliver Cowdery in the Kirtland Temple on April 3, 1836. It was Passover Sunday for the Jews. President Joseph Fielding Smith noted, "I am informed, on the third day of April, 1836, that the Jews, in their homes at the Paschal feast, opened their doors for Elijah to enter. On that very day Elijah did enter—not in the home of the Jews to partake of the Passover with them—but he appeared in the house of the Lord, erected to his name and received by the Lord in Kirtland, and there bestowed his keys to bring to pass the very things for which these

Jews, assembled in their homes, were seeking."[51] Elijah restored the priesthood keys by which families can be sealed throughout eternity.

Who are the fathers and children as quoted by Moroni? The following quotation helps answer this question:

> The fathers are our dead ancestors who died without the privilege of receiving the gospel, but who received the promise that the time would come when that privilege would be granted them. The children are those now living who are preparing genealogical data and who are performing the vicarious ordinances in the temples. The turning of the hearts of the children to the fathers is placing or planting in the hearts of the children that feeling and desire which will inspire them to search out the records of the dead. Moreover, the planting of the desire and inspiration in their hearts is necessary. This they must have in order that they might go into the house of the Lord and perform the necessary labor for their fathers, who died without a knowledge of the gospel, or without the privilege of receiving the fulness of the gospel.[52]

What are the promises made to the fathers? We must go back to our premortal world to fully understand. In premortality, all of us were taught the plan of salvation. We knew what needed to be done in order to return to our Heavenly Father. We were also taught that because we would live in a fallen world, many would use their agency to follow paths that would not lead them back to their heavenly home. Those choices would have devastating effects on their posterity. Consequently, many knew they would live in the world without the saving doctrines and ordinances of the gospel of Jesus Christ. Anxious about their eternal happiness, they were promised by the Lord that His plan of salvation would have a path to save them. They were promised they would be taught the gospel in the spirit world and that the saving ordinances would be performed by proxy by the faithful Saints of the latter days:

> In our preexistent state, in the day of the great council, we made a certain agreement with the Almighty. The Lord proposed a plan, conceived by him. We accepted it. Since the plan is intended for all

51. *Doctrines of Salvation*, comp. Bruce R. McConkie (1955), 2:100–101.

52. Joseph Fielding Smith, *Doctrines of Salvation,* 2:127–28.

> men, we become parties to the salvation of every person under that plan. We agreed, right then and there, to be not only saviors for ourselves but measurably, saviors for the whole human family. We went into a partnership with the Lord. The working out of the plan became then not merely the Father's work, and the Savior's work, but also our work. The least of us, the humblest, is in partnership with the Almighty in achieving the purpose of the eternal plan of salvation.[53]

Why would the earth be cursed and utterly wasted were it not for the priesthood keys restored by Elijah? Because the grand, ultimate objective for the plan of salvation is for us to return to heaven as families and to continue the family unit throughout eternity. In premortality, we saw what God enjoyed, and we wanted the same. That could only be possible with the sealing keys of the priesthood. Without those keys, the family unit would not continue through eternity, so the whole purpose of the Lord's plan of salvation would have been utterly frustrated.[54]

They who accept the gospel in the spirit world are anxious for the saving ordinances to be done for them. I have always been fascinated with the testimony related by President Wilford Woodruff, who served as the first president of the St. George Temple, which was dedicated on April 6, 1877 (the first temple dedicated following the exodus of the Saints to the West). President Woodruff testified:

> Those men who laid the foundation of this American government and signed the Declaration of Independence were the best spirits the God in heaven could find on the face of the earth. They were choice spirits, not wicked men. General Washington and all the men that labored for the purpose were inspired of the Lord. . . . Every one of those men called upon me two consecutive nights and demanded at my hands that I should go forth and attend to the ordinances of the House of God for them. . . . Said they: "You have had the Endowment House for a number of years, and yet nothing has ever been done for us. We laid the foundation of the

53. *History of the Church,* 6:59–61.

54. Joseph Fielding Smith, *Doctrines of Salvation,* 2:121–22.

> government you now enjoy, and we never apostatized from it, but we remained true to it and were faithful to God."
>
> I straightway went into the baptismal font and called upon Brother McCallister to baptize me for the signers of the Declaration of Independence, and fifty other eminent men, making one hundred in all, including John Wesley, Columbus, and others. When Brother McCallister had baptized me for the one hundred names, I baptized him for twenty-one, including General Washington and his forefathers, and all the Presidents of the United States, except three. Sister Lucy Bigelow Young went forth into the font and was baptized for Martha Washington and her family, and seventy of the eminent women of the world. I told these brethren that it was their duty to go into the temple and labor until they had got endowments for all of them. They did it. Would those spirits have called upon me, as an Elder in Israel to perform that work if they had not been noble spirits before God? They would not.[55]

We learn the following from a marvelous revelation given to the Prophet Joseph on May 6, 1833: "For man is spirit. The elements are eternal, and spirit and element, inseparably connected, receive a fulness of joy; And when separated, man cannot receive a fulness of joy" (Doctrine and Covenants 93:33–34). We also know that the dead look upon the long absence of their spirits from their bodies as a bondage, and they anxiously await their resurrection so "that they might receive a fulness of joy" (Doctrine and Covenants 138:17). Resurrection with an immortal body that will live forever in a state of happiness is a grand objective of the Lord's plan of happiness.

Thus we see that time in the spirit world is temporary—a waiting period between the mortal state and the resurrected state. Although those in paradise will be free from the negative aspects of mortality, they will not be completely happy until they are resurrected. In the due time of the Lord, all will be called forth from the grave, "but every man in his own order" (1 Corinthians 15:23). When all are resurrected, the spirit world will have no inhabitants.

---

55. In Conference Report, Apr. 1898; Wilford Woodruff Journal, Aug. 21, 1877.

The Majesty of Christ's Resurrection

Elder Bruce R. McConkie taught the following:

> At the moment when Christ died, nothing could have seemed more abjectly weak, more pitifully hopeless, more absolutely doomed to scorn, and extinction and despair than the Church which He had founded. It numbered but a handful of followers, of whom the boldest had denied his Lord, and the most devoted had forsaken Him and fled. How was it that these dull and ignorant men triumphed over the deadly fascinations of sensual mythologies, conquered kings and their armies, and overcame the world? What was it that thus caused strength to be made perfect out of abject weakness? There is one, and only one possible answer—the resurrection from the dead. All this vast revolution was due to the power of Christ's resurrection.[56]

The spiritual power of Peter, Paul, and the other Apostles, the strength of their testimonies, and the resulting conversion power emanated from their perfect knowledge that Christ had overcome death. To the question "How shall we know that Jesus is the Son of God?" Paul gives this answer: He is "declared to be the Son of God with power . . . by the resurrection from the dead" (Romans 1:4).

56. Bruce R. McConkie, *The Mortal Messiah* (Deseret Book, 1981), 4:259.

The testimonies that proclaim that Jesus rose from the dead are the greatest witness that He is indeed the Son of God, the promised Messiah, the Savior and Redeemer of all humankind. It is evidence that He has powers over death and has the power to resurrect us all.

"On that first Easter day at the appointed moment, how and in what way it was done we know not, the spirit of Christ entered again into His body. That Spirit, now housed in its eternal home, now inseparably connected with its body, became the first immortal soul. Christ is risen; the victory is won; death is abolished. His resurrection was the creation of an immortal soul; a reuniting of body and spirit in immortality."[57] A resurrected being has a body of flesh and bones that occupies space.

On that first Easter Sunday, Mary Magdalene, Salome, and Mary, the mother of James and John (and perhaps other women, such as Martha and Mary) rose early to go to the tomb to further prepare the body of Jesus with spices and aloes. The work of Joseph of Arimathea and Nicodemus had been done in haste before the Sabbath commenced, and, might I add, their work simply didn't have a woman's touch. Little did they know that the spirit of Jesus Christ had returned from the spirit world and had entered again into His body. In connection with His Resurrection, two angels descended from heaven and rolled back the stone from the tomb's door, which the chief priests had placed there to prevent His body from being stolen and having a story fabricated about His resurrection. The angels' appearance greatly frightened the Roman guards who collapsed as though they were dead (see Matthew 28:4). The stone being rolled away from the door was an announcement to the world that Christ overcame death.

When they saw the empty tomb, the women were frightened. Then they saw two angels who announced the glorious news. Matthew wrote that the angels said to them, "Fear not ye: for I know that ye seek Jesus, which was crucified. He is not here: for he is risen, as he said. Come, see the place where the Lord lay. And go quickly, and tell his disciples that he is risen from the dead" (Matthew 28:5–7). Luke recorded the angels saying, "Why seek ye the living among the

---

57. Joseph Fielding Smith, *Doctrines of Salvation*, comp. Bruce R. McConkie (1955), 2:258.

dead? He is not here, but is risen: remember how he spake unto you when he was yet in Galilee, Saying, The Son of man must be delivered into the hands of sinful men, and be crucified, and the third day rise again" (Luke 24:5–7). The angels reminded them of Christ's teachings regarding His death and Resurrection.

Yet, a resurrection had never happened in history—the women didn't fully comprehend the momentous declaration of the angels. Though they saw angels and heard their testimony regarding the Resurrection of their Savior, they ran to Peter and John with great fear that someone had indeed stolen the body of Jesus.

Peter and John rushed to the tomb with that same fear because they didn't hear the women testify regarding the glorious news of the Resurrection; all they heard was that the body of Jesus was missing. John outran his friend, but out of respect and deference for the position that Peter held, he did not enter the tomb until Peter had done so. There they witnessed the burial clothes that had not been unwrapped but through which a resurrected body had passed! They neither saw nor heard the two angels. Upon seeing the burial clothes but no body, John straightway testified that he knew what had happened—his beloved Lord had resurrected. Then he apologized for his fellow Apostles, as they did not fully understand the scriptures, which stated that He must rise again (see Matthew 28:1–8; Mark 16:1–8; Luke 24:1–12; John 20:1–10).

Jesus First Appeared to Mary Magdalene

Mary Magdalene had returned to the tomb. When Peter and John returned to their homes, she remained in the general area. Jesus first appeared to Mary Magdalene in the garden of the tomb (see John 20:11–18, Matthew 28:2–4, Mark 16:9–11). Filled with grief for the loss of the one she adored and worshipped, and fearing that perhaps His body had been stolen as she witnessed an empty tomb, Jesus appeared to her. When He spoke her name, "Mary," the recognition came instantly. With soul-filled exuberance, she cried, "Oh, my Master!" She rushed toward Him.

What Jesus said next has been the source of some interpretative concern. The King James Bible quotes Jesus as saying, "Touch me not." However, the Joseph Smith Translation reads, "Hold me not"

(John 20:13–17). Various translations from the Greek give the meaning as "Do not hold me any longer," giving the inference that Mary was already holding Him. She was holding the body of a resurrected person, proving that a resurrected being is corporeal. For reasons of His own, the risen Lord singled out Mary Magdalene to be the first witness of His resurrection. She was the first mortal ever to see, hear, and touch a resurrected being.

Jesus Appeared to Other Women

Christ appeared to the other faithful, believing women who had come earlier in the morning with Mary Magdalene to prepare the body of Jesus (see Matthew 28:5–10; Mark 16:10; Luke 24:10–11). These women included (1) Mary the mother of Joseph; (2) Joanna, the wife of Chuza who was Herod's steward; and (3) Salome, the mother of James and John. It is likely that His mother was part of that group as well as Mary and Martha from Bethany. There could have been more. These were women who had shown exceeding faith in Jesus. The group likely were those who hovered in sorrow around the cross. Jesus met them with a cry of "All hail." The recognition was immediate. In awe and reverence, "they came and held him by the feet, and worshipped him" (Matthew 28:9). Words of peace and comfort were surely said; emotions and feelings were surely joyous and intense.

Jesus Appeared to Peter

Christ appeared to Peter. It was necessary that Jesus appear to His senior Apostle who would lead the Church. We do not know where or under what circumstances He came to Peter, or what words or counsel He gave. In the upper room, with Peter present, the witness is borne, "The Lord is risen indeed, and hath appeared to Simon" (Luke 24:34), and Paul says, "He was seen of Cephas, then of the twelve" (1 Corinthians 15:5).

Jesus Appeared to Two Disciples on the Road to Emmaus

Jesus appeared to two disciples on their way to Emmaus (see Luke 24:13–32). It was the afternoon of the day of His Resurrection. Two disciples not of the Twelve—one called Cleopas, the other undoubtedly Luke—were walking the eight miles from Jerusalem to Emmaus. They were thinking and pondering and speaking of only one thing—the Lord Jesus Christ, including His death and reports relative to His Resurrection. There was a sense of anxiety and perplexity and wonder in their words as they communed and reasoned together.

A stranger, Jesus Himself, drew nigh and walked with them. It suited His purpose not to be recognized, and so their eyes were covered with a veil. He asked, "What manner of communications are these that ye have one to another, as ye walk, and are sad?" (Luke 24:17). Cleopas was surprised. How could anyone who had been in Jerusalem that week not be aware of the tumult surrounding the trials and crucifixion of the most renowned person in all of Palestine? So Cleopas asked, "Art thou only a stranger in Jerusalem, and hast not known the things which are come to pass there in these days?" (verse 18).

Jesus asked, "What things?" They replied, "Concerning Jesus of Nazareth, which was a prophet mighty in deed and word before God and all the people: And how the chief priests and our rulers delivered him to be condemned to death, and have crucified him" (verses 19–20). Herein lay their sorrow; their friend had suffered and died. All His promises and teachings seemed uncertain now.

Jesus then quoted from Moses and other prophets and expounded from the scriptures "the things concerning himself" (verse 27). How wonderful it would be to know what He said. They may have walked for as long as two hours. Perhaps someday the conversations of the Emmaus walk will be revealed.

Nearing Emmaus, Jesus acted as though He would travel on. The two disciples invited Him to stay with them, and Jesus consented. As they sat to eat, "he took bread, and blessed it, and brake, and gave to them" (verse 30). It is as though He removed the veil from their eyes. He was doing what He had done before. "They knew him; and he vanished out of their sight" (verse 31).

Then the two disciples said, "Did not our heart burn within us, while he talked with us by the way, and while he opened to us the scriptures?" (verse 32). Cleopas and Luke now knew for themselves that Jesus was risen. Feeling that they must tell the others, they returned immediately to Jerusalem.

Jesus Appeared in the Upper Room

Later that evening, He appeared to His disciples in an upper room in Jerusalem (see Luke 24:33–47; John 20:19–23; Mark 16:13). Both men and women were gathered together in that upper room. Ten of the Apostles were present; Thomas was absent. The whole group was eating an evening meal and witnessing to each other what they had seen and heard. Surely, Peter recounted the appearance of the risen Lord to him.

Into this dinner meeting came Cleopas and Luke, returning from Emmaus. They heard the accounts of the others and shared their experience with the Lord. As they shared experiences, Jesus materialized in front of them. His first words were the familiar "Peace be unto you." Mark tells us that Jesus upbraided them for their unbelief and hardness of heart because they believed not the testimony of Mary Magdalene and the other women. The inference is that they didn't give much credence to their witness until they heard Peter's testimony that he had seen the Lord. Jesus then said, "Behold my hands and my feet, that it is I myself: handle me, and see; for a spirit hath not flesh and bones, as ye see me have" (verse 39). He stood there as a man with a body—not of flesh and blood, as mortals have, but of flesh and bones and spirit, as an immortal being. A resurrected body of flesh and bones is tangible; it can be felt. Though He had come through walls into the enclosed room, yet He is a tangible being. It is apparent that resurrected beings, though having flesh and bones, operate under higher laws that give them power to move through physical objects.

Then they felt the nail marks in his hands and wrists. While they were amazed at this experience, Jesus asked, "Have ye here any meat?" (verse 41). Their meal of broiled fish and honeycomb was handed to him and—marvel of all marvels—he ate! A resurrected body can eat food. The body, though immortal, is tangible and real. The favored faithful in that upper room had seen the risen Lord!

Jesus Appeared Again in the Upper Room

Christ appeared to the eleven Apostles, now including Thomas (see John 20:24–29). Once again, it was Sunday, the first weekly anniversary of Christ's Resurrection. The disciples had begun the practice of worshipping on Sunday rather than on the Jewish Sabbath. They were again in the upper room. During the week, the disciples had borne witness to Thomas, "We have seen the Lord" (John 20:25). Thomas had believed in the Resurrection but not in the literal materiality of His body. He said, "Except I shall see in his hands the print of the nails, and put my finger into the print of the nails, and thrust my hand into his side, I will not believe" (verse 25).

Thomas was now present with the others in the upper room. All of a sudden, as happened the week before, Jesus "stood in the midst" (verse 26). Then to Thomas came the command, "Reach hither thy finger, and behold my hands; and reach hither thy hand, and thrust it into my side; and be not faithless, but believing" (verse 27). Thomas complied. He now felt and handled as the others had done. He was now a living, personal witness of the materiality of the resurrected body of Jesus. Thomas worshipfully cried, "My Lord and my God" (verse 28).

Thomas, who once offered to go with Jesus to Bethany, there to die with Him, saw and believed. He has been called, somewhat unkindly, Doubting Thomas. Whatever they may have been, his doubts were of a passing and transitory nature. He became and remained a believer in the full sense.

Jesus Appeared to His Apostles at the Sea of Galilee

Jesus appeared to some of His disciples at the shores of the Sea of Galilee. After Jesus rose from the dead, the Apostles were commanded to go to Galilee and meet Jesus on a mountain according to a prior appointment. As they awaited the day, and needing to supply their families with this world's goods, Peter said, "I go a fishing" (John 21:3). Six of the eleven were with him. They all went forth into a ship and spent the whole night fishing in the Sea of Galilee. They caught nothing. In the morning, Jesus stood on the shore, but the disciples didn't know it was Him. He called out, "Children, have ye any meat?"

(verse 5). They answered no. Jesus then said, "Cast the net on the right side of the ship, and ye shall find" (verse 6). These experienced fishermen did so and immediately the net was so full that "they were not able to draw it for the multitude of fishes" (verse 6). John, who seems to have been more spiritually sensitive than the rest, said to Peter, "It is the Lord." The impetuous Peter jumped from the ship and swam to shore to meet his Master. The others changed into a small ship and dragged the net and the fish about a hundred yards to the shore (see John 21:2–13). Again, the resurrected Lord dined with them and taught the disciples much.

Jesus Appeared on a Galilean Mountain

Christ appeared to over five hundred in one setting, most likely on a Galilean mountain (see 1 Corinthians 15:6; Matthew 28:16–20; Mark 16:15–18). That may have been the greatest of all the appearances of the risen Lord to His disciples. Recounting the Lord's resurrected appearances, Paul writes, "He was seen of above five hundred brethren at once" (1 Corinthians 15:6). This was likely the appearance on the mountain. When Paul speaks of more than five hundred brethren being present on one occasion, we have every reason to believe there may have been five hundred or more women also present as well as many children.

In this setting, Jesus bore this testimony of Himself: "All power is given unto me in heaven and in earth" (Matthew 28:18). A resurrected body adds eternal blessing that cannot be gained in any other way. Even a God must be resurrected to inherit, possess, and receive all things. In this setting, the Lord gave the Apostles the charge to go into all the world and preach the gospel. He taught them all the doctrines of His gospel, particularly faith, repentance, baptism, the Holy Ghost, and the gifts of the Spirit.

Jesus Appeared to James, His Half Brother

Paul tells us "after that, he was seen of James" (1 Corinthians 15:7). This is understood to be the half brother of Jesus, Mary's and Joseph's son. James became one of the Twelve and a mighty pillar of strength and righteousness in due course. Elder Bruce R. McConkie quotes Farrar thusly:

> Respecting this appearance to James we know nothing further, unless there be any basis of true tradition in the story preserved to us in the Gospel of the Hebrews. We are there told that James, the first Bishop of Jerusalem, and the Lord's brother, had, after the Last Supper, taken a solemn vow that he would neither eat nor drink until he had seen Jesus risen from the dead. Early, therefore, after His resurrection, Jesus had a table with bread brought out, blessed the bread, and gave it to James, with the words: "Eat thy bread now, my brother, since the Son of Man has risen from the dead."[58]

The Day of Ascension

Many were with the Savior during the day of His Ascension (see Act 1:1–14; Mark 16:19–20; Luke 24:50–53). The Lord Jesus was about to return to the presence of the Father. The Apostles were assembled together. Jesus led them out toward Bethany. They arrived at the Mount of Olives. His mortal work was done; the Atonement had been completed. With uplifted hands, Christ blessed His Apostles, and He was then "taken up; and a cloud received him out of their sight. And while they looked steadfastly toward heaven as he went up, behold, two men stood by them in white apparel" (Acts 1:9–10). They proclaimed, "Ye men of Galilee, why stand ye gazing up into heaven? this same Jesus, which is taken up from you into heaven, shall so come in like manner as ye have seen him go into heaven" (verse 11).

A man having a body of flesh and bones—a being who walked, talked, and ate with his disciples—ascended bodily into heaven. As He went up, so is He now; and as He is now, so will He be when He comes again to reign on earth for a thousand years; and as He will be during the Millennium, so will He remain through all eternity: a glorified, perfected, exalted Man.

Jesus Appeared in the Americas

Perhaps the greatest witness of Christ's literal Resurrection occurred on the American continent. Following His Ascension, He appeared to well over 2,500 people at the Bountiful temple grounds in

---

58. McConkie, *The Mortal Messiah,* 4:305.

the Nephite nation (see 3 Nephi 11–27). We read from that remarkable account:

> The Lord spake unto them saying:
>
> Arise and come forth unto me, that ye may thrust your hands into my side, and also that ye may feel the prints of the nails in my hands and in my feet, that ye may know that I am the God of Israel, and the God of the whole earth, and have been slain for the sins of the world.
>
> And it came to pass that the multitude went forth, and thrust their hands into his side, and did feel the prints of the nails in his hands and in his feet; and this they did do, going forth *one by one* until they had all gone forth, and did see with their eyes and did feel with their hands, and did know of a surety and did bear record, that it was he, of whom it was written by the prophets, that should come. (3 Nephi 11:13–15; emphasis added)

Can there be any more powerful witness that Jesus Christ did indeed rise from the dead? All 2,500 of those people felt His wounds! If each one took ten seconds to feel and gaze at him in worshipful awe, it would have been a seven-hour experience for them.

Three hundred years after His appearance to the Nephites in Bountiful, He appeared to a young prophet named Mormon, who wrote, "I was visited of the Lord, and tasted and knew of the goodness of Jesus" (Mormon 1:15). The prophet Moroni also testified, "I have seen Jesus, and . . . he hath talked with me face to face" (Ether 12:39).

Jesus Appeared in Our Dispensation

In the spring of 1820, Christ appeared to Joseph Smith, which began the "restitution of all things" (Acts 3:21). Joseph testified, "I saw two Personages, whose brightness and glory defy all description, standing above me in the air. One of them spake unto me, calling me by name and said, pointing to the other—*This is My Beloved Son. Hear Him!*" (Joseph Smith—History 1:15–17).

Twelve years later, in 1832, He again appeared to Joseph Smith along with Sidney Rigdon. They gave this powerful testimony: "And now, after the many testimonies which have been given of him, this is the testimony, last of all, which we give of him: That he lives! For we saw him, even on the right hand of God; and we heard the voice bearing record that he is the Only Begotten of the Father" (Doctrine and Covenants 76:22–24).

On April 3, 1836, He again appeared to Joseph Smith along with Oliver Cowdery in the Kirtland Temple. They testified, "The veil was taken from our minds, and the eyes of our understanding were opened. We saw the Lord standing upon the breastwork of the pulpit. . . . His eyes were as a flame of fire; the hair of his head was white like the pure snow; his countenance shone above the brightness of the sun; and his voice was as the sound of the rushing of great waters, even the voice of Jehovah, saying: I am the first and the last; I am he who liveth, I am he who was slain; I am your advocate with the Father" (Doctrine and Covenants 110:1–4).

Undoubtedly, since we live in a dispensation of prophets and apostles, there have been other visits by the resurrected Lord that are not recorded in canonized scripture. Every prophet in this dispensation has given witness that Jesus of Nazareth is the very Christ. There have been over one hundred Apostles since the Restoration of the Lord's Church in 1830. Every one of those special witnesses has given testimony that Jesus of Nazareth is the Son of God, risen from the dead and who lives today. The Resurrection of Jesus Christ is proof positive that He has conquered death and is a witness of His divinity. The fact of the Resurrection is the most certain surety in all history. A host of witnesses—those in the biblical record, in the Book of Mormon, and by modern prophets—testify of the reality of the resurrected Lord Jesus Christ.

There have been millions more who can bear witness that Jesus is the Christ as they have felt and heard the whisperings of the Spirit. Some "have suffered the loss of all things, and do count them but dung" for Christ (Philippians 3:8). Saints in the meridian of times and Saints in this dispensation have faced perils of waters, perils of plains, and persecutions because of the testimony of Jesus Christ that beat in their hearts.

The majestic resurrection from the dead—above all else—proves that Jesus is the Christ, the Son of God, the promised Messiah.

THE MAJESTY OF CHRIST'S GRACE

"NO UNCLEAN THING CAN INHERIT THE KINGDOM OF HEAVEN" (Alma 11:37). Since all of us sin, none of us would return to heaven on our own merits. Gloriously, in Gethsemane, Jesus Christ suffered and atoned for our sins. But His Atonement for our sins doesn't come free. There is a price we must pay—a price determined by our Savior. We read that Christ cannot save us in our sins (see Alma 11:37). Furthermore, "He hath power given unto him from the Father to redeem them from their sins because of repentance" (Helaman 5:11). Christ will not save us *in* our sins—only *from* our sins.

Amulek taught, "Christ shall come among the children of men, to take upon him the transgressions of his people, and that he shall atone for the sins of the world. . . . There must be an atonement made, or else all mankind must unavoidably perish" (Alma 34:8–9). How exactly can the Savior take upon Himself our sins and redeem us? We must understand the law of justice and the law of mercy for proper appreciation of how Christ's Atonement works.

The law of justice demands consequences for actions. The gospel of Jesus Christ is founded upon law for the blessings and salvation of its people. When a law is obeyed, one receives blessings. "There is a law, irrevocably decreed in heaven before the foundations of this world, upon which all blessings are predicated; And when we obtain any blessing from God, it is by obedience to that law upon which it is predicated" (Doctrine and Covenants 130:20–21). When a law is broken by sin, the law of justice demands a penalty be paid. That penalty is banishment from the presence of God, for no unclean thing can dwell in His presence.

Jesus Christ came not to abolish the law but to fulfill it. But He introduced mercy to temper the enforcement of the law. The law of mercy recognizes the law of justice but introduces the possibility of a vicarious payment for the law that has been broken. It allows the sinner to escape punishment if they can find someone else who is both able and willing to take the punishment. We read, "Justice exerciseth all his demands, and also mercy claimeth all which is her own; and thus, none but the truly penitent are saved. What, do ye suppose that mercy can rob justice? I say unto you, Nay; not one whit" (Alma 42:24–25). We also read, "Mercy can satisfy the demands of justice, and encircles them in the arms of safety, while he that exercises no faith unto repentance is exposed to the whole law of the demands of justice" (Alma 34:16).

In 1977, Elder Boyd K. Packer gave a marvelous talk entitled "The Mediator." He gave an enlightening parable to help explain the workings of the laws of justice and mercy and how they relate to the Atonement of Jesus Christ:

> There once was a man who wanted something very much. It seemed more important than anything else in his life. In order for him to have his desire, he incurred a great debt.
>
> He had been warned about going into that much debt, and particularly about his creditor. But it seemed so important for him to do what he wanted to do and to have what he wanted right now. He was sure he could pay for it later.
>
> So he signed a contract. He would pay it off some time along the way. He didn't worry too much about it, for the due date seemed such a long time away. He had what he wanted now, and that was what seemed important.
>
> The creditor was always somewhere in the back of his mind, and he made token payments now and again, thinking somehow that the day of reckoning really would never come.

But as it always does, the day came, and the contract fell due. The debt had not been fully paid. His creditor appeared and demanded payment in full.

Only then did he realize that his creditor not only had the power to repossess all that he owned, but the power to cast him into prison as well.

"I cannot pay you, for I have not the power to do so," he confessed.

"Then," said the creditor, "we will exercise the contract, take your possessions, and you shall go to prison. You agreed to that. It was your choice. You signed the contract, and now it must be enforced."

"Can you not extend the time or forgive the debt?" the debtor begged. "Arrange some way for me to keep what I have and not go to prison. Surely you believe in mercy? Will you not show mercy?"

The creditor replied, "Mercy is always so one-sided. It would serve only you. If I show mercy to you, it will leave me unpaid. It is justice I demand. Do you believe in justice?"

"I believed in justice when I signed the contract," the debtor said. "It was on my side then, for I thought it would protect me. I did not need mercy then, nor think I should need it ever. Justice, I thought, would serve both of us equally as well."

"It is justice that demands that you pay the contract or suffer the penalty," the creditor replied. "That is the law. You have agreed to it and that is the way it must be. Mercy cannot rob justice."

There they were: One meting out justice, the other pleading for mercy. Neither could prevail except at the expense of the other.

"If you do not forgive the debt there will be no mercy," the debtor pleaded.

"If I do, there will be no justice," was the reply.

Both laws, it seemed, could not be served. They are two eternal ideals that appear to contradict one another. Is there no way for justice to be fully served, and mercy also?

There is a way! The law of justice can be fully satisfied and mercy can be fully extended—but it takes someone else. And so it happened this time.

The debtor had a friend. He came to help. He knew the debtor well. He knew him to be shortsighted. He thought him foolish to have gotten himself into such a predicament. Nevertheless, he wanted to help because he loved him. He stepped between them, faced the creditor, and made this offer.

"I will pay the debt if you will free the debtor from his contract so that he may keep his possessions and not go to prison."

As the creditor was pondering the offer, the mediator added, "You demanded justice. Though he cannot pay you, I will do so. You will have been justly dealt with and can ask no more. It would not be just."

And so the creditor agreed.

The mediator turned then to the debtor. "If I pay your debt, will you accept me as your creditor?"

"Oh yes, yes," cried the debtor. "You save me from prison and show mercy to me."

"Then," said the benefactor, "you will pay the debt to me and I will set the terms. It will not be easy, but it will be possible. I will provide a way. You need not go to prison."

And so it was that the creditor was paid in full. He had been justly dealt with. No contract had been broken. The debtor, in turn, had been extended mercy. Both laws stood fulfilled. Because there was a mediator, justice had claimed its full share, and mercy was fully satisfied.

Each of us lives on a kind of spiritual credit. One day the account will be closed, a settlement demanded. However casually we may view it now, when that day comes and the foreclosure is imminent, we will look around in restless agony for someone, anyone, to help us.

And, by eternal law, mercy cannot be extended save there be one who is both willing and able to assume our debt and pay the price and arrange the terms for our redemption.

Unless there is a mediator, unless we have a friend, the full weight of justice untempered, unsympathetic, must, positively must fall on us. The full recompense for every transgression, however minor or however deep, will be exacted from us to the uttermost farthing.

But know this: Truth, glorious truth, proclaims there is such a Mediator.

"For there is one God, and one mediator between God and men, the man Christ Jesus." (1 Tim. 2:5.)[59]

---

59. Boyd K. Packer, "The Mediator," *Ensign*, May 1977, 54–56.

When Jesus took upon Himself our sins, He satisfied the law of justice. Lehi said He "did answer the ends of the law" (2 Nephi 2:7). Thus, we read, "Having ascended into heaven, having the bowels of mercy; being filled with compassion towards the children of men; standing betwixt them and justice; having broken the bands of death, taken upon himself their iniquity and their transgressions, having redeemed them, and satisfied the demands of justice" (Mosiah 15:9). Because of the law of mercy, Jesus paid the price of our sins, conditioned on our repentance.

Christ's power gives us the opportunity to repent and be cleansed by His atoning sacrifice. We can then be justified to be in the Lord's presence. If repentance is not present, then the sinner must pay the price for sin. But even after paying the price for sin, the sinner cannot redeem oneself. All of us must look to the grace of Christ to be redeemed.

As we persist daily to put off the natural man—to cultivate the attributes of meekness, humility, patience, and charity, thereby incrementally developing a broken heart and a contrite spirit—we will still realize that, at the end of the day, we fall short. Our individual efforts, no matter how worthy and mighty, will not be enough. We need the grace of Christ. We read from the Bible Dictionary that grace connotes divine help given by the mercy and love of Jesus Christ. Then we read, "It is . . . through the grace of the Lord that individuals, through faith in the Atonement of Jesus Christ and repentance of their sins, receive strength and assistance to do good works that they otherwise would not be able to maintain if left to their own means. This grace is an enabling power . . . after they have expended their own best efforts. Divine grace is needed by every soul . . . because of man's weaknesses and shortcomings. However, grace cannot suffice without total effort on the part of the recipient." That is why Nephi wrote, "It is by grace that we are saved, after all we can do" (2 Nephi 25:23).

"After all we can do" is much more than just believing Christ is real. It is more than coasting through life pursuing only personal agendas. It is more than doing something worthwhile for others, or even heavenly things, one day a week. Those who yearn for salvation to be easy, with no obligation or commitment, are deceived.

Enabling Power

The principle of grace is this: God will enable us to do things in this life that are beyond our capacity if we give Him our best efforts. God will exalt us in the next life, which we have no power to accomplish by our own efforts, if we give our best efforts to do God's will in this life.

There are many examples found in the scriptures that illustrate the enabling power that comes from the grace of Jesus Christ. I mention just a few.

Lehi sent his sons back to Jerusalem to obtain the plates of brass from Laban. They failed in their first two attempts. They even had to run for their lives to escape Laban's wrath. Nephi's older brothers, having little faith, wanted to call it quits, for Laban "is a mighty man, and he can command fifty, yea, even he can slay fifty; then why not us?" (1 Nephi 3:31). Nephi was determined to do the Lord's will. Leaving his faithless brothers in a safe place, he ventured forth, "not knowing beforehand the things which I should do" (1 Nephi 4:6). We know how the story ends: By the power of God, he was able to obtain the plates. Nephi received enabling power to accomplish the impossible because he went outside of his comfort zone and exerted his best efforts to do the Lord's will.

Later, Nephi was commanded to construct a ship. He had no experience or knowledge of how to build a ship. His brothers, knowing Nephi had no such competence, called him a fool. Nephi stepped out of his comfort zone. Being enabled by God, he built the ship, and when it was completed, his brothers admitted that it was of fine workmanship (see 1 Nephi 17–18).

I share one personal experience because from it I learned so much about the enabling power that comes from Jesus Christ. I had just arrived in Finland to serve my full-time mission. My first companion was a zone leader. One duty of a zone leader is to work with and train other missionaries. My zone leader / companion was going to work with the district leader, and I was to work with the district leader's companion who had arrived in Finland with me. I was shocked when the zone leader gave us the assignment to teach a first discussion to a couple. About the only words and sentences we could speak were those things that we had memorized in the discussions. We had not yet developed the ear to understand what was being spoken. The zone leader counseled us to go with faith and that we would be all right.

Those with little faith would have resisted with "No way—that's outside of my comfort zone!" And that sentiment would have been understandable. But faith and receiving the enabling power from the Atonement requires stepping out of one's comfort zone. I went with a continual prayer in my heart that I would not fail God.

After an opening prayer, the discussion began. The test came when the investigators were asked how they felt about the principle they had just been taught. Their responses, and everything else they said during the discussion, were beyond my physical comprehension. But then I heard the still, small voice tell me what they were feeling. I would then be prompted to know what to say—but I didn't know how to say it in Finnish. I could adequately respond in English, just not in Finnish. Then the Spirit reminded me of scriptures I had learned during seminary or institute classes that would answer their questions. So I directed them to read those scriptures, which satisfied them. That is how the whole night went: They would ask questions that I didn't understand, the Spirit would tell me what needed to be said, and the scriptures would say what I couldn't say with my inadequate Finnish. It was an overpowering display of the Lord's enabling power, which led me through the darkness of inadequate speech and allowed me to teach true principles to those investigators. When we left, I was so elated and edified that I'm not sure my feet touched the ground. But I would not have experienced the enabling power of Jesus Christ had I not gone first with faith.

Many years later, I was called to be a stake patriarch. My first instinctive reaction was to say "I'm not capable of doing that calling." The Lord immediately reminded me of how He enabled me to teach that discussion in Finland. Today, every time I approach giving a patriarchal blessing, I do so not knowing beforehand the things that I should say. The Lord always gives me the enabling power to give a blessing that is pure revelation for that recipient.

My wife and I served two years in the mission office for the England London Mission. She served as the secretary for the mission president. She had never been a secretary and had no secretarial skills.

She had never taken typing classes. Soon she was given tasks that required Excel spreadsheets and Word documents. She literally did not know how to work with Excel or Word. Humbly, she approached the Lord and basically said, "I don't know how to do this, but I know You know." Although she got a little help from the APs, she was mostly taught by the Spirit in answer to her prayers. She was able to be a successful missionary in the mission office because of the enabling power of Jesus Christ.

Why We Will Suffer Like Christ Without Repentance

Having won the victory over death and hell, the Savior tells us the following:

> Repent, lest I smite you by the rod of my mouth, and by my wrath, and by my anger, and your sufferings be sore—how sore you know not, how exquisite you know not, yea, how hard to bear you know not.
>
> I, God, have suffered these things for all, that they might not suffer if they would repent;
>
> But if they would not repent they must suffer even as I.
>
> Which suffering caused myself, even God, the greatest of all, to tremble because of pain, and to bleed at every pore, and to suffer both body and spirit. (Doctrine and Covenants 19:15–18)

For years, I pondered over that passage. Why does a person have to suffer like Christ if they don't repent? Why does the suffering have to be so intense? Why couldn't it be less suffering, less hard to bear? Why will the Lord punish so severely?

I received my answer when a newly called Apostle visited our stake conference—Elder Russell M. Nelson, who had been a world-renowned heart surgeon. He spoke directly about those verses. He said that as a heart surgeon, in order to repair a heart, he had to inflict great pain. There was no way around it. He didn't like inflicting pain, but pain was a natural consequence for healing a heart. Over time, the pain disappeared, but the revitalized heart gave a newness of life.

In that same revelation, Jesus also teaches that our pain will end. Eternal or endless punishment doesn't mean that the suffering never ends; they are descriptive terms, not quantitative terms. *Eternal* or *Endless* are other names for God. Because of the love Jesus has for us, He does not want us to live through eternity suffering for our unrepentant sins. He does not want us to live throughout eternity with a desire to sin. In order to eliminate the suffering and give us a desire to do good, the natural man—which is an enemy to God, which encourages us to sin—must be rooted out of our systems.

President Nelson taught that Jesus Christ will remove the natural man and heal the soul for everyone—a process that will naturally cause great pain. There is no way around it. Christ took upon Himself that pain for us, conditioned on our repentance. With no repentance, exquisite pain will naturally occur when the natural man is removed and replaced with a disposition to do no evil. When the natural man is displaced, a person can live in happiness, within their sphere, throughout the eternities. God does not want to inflict pain upon any of His children. But removing the natural man is a painful "surgical" procedure. If we repent, our Savior has already suffered for that pain.

I am humbled and grateful to realize that Jesus can remove the natural man from all of us. Consequently, all of us can enjoy life in eternity to a much higher degree than we will ever experience here. What a wonderful, majestic expression of love for us! Such is the majesty of Jesus Christ!

The Majesty of Our Resurrection

"For as death hath passed upon all men, to fulfil the merciful plan of the great Creator, there must needs be a power of resurrection. . . . The grave must deliver up its captive bodies, and the bodies and the spirits of men will be restored one to the other; and it is by the power of the resurrection of the Holy One of Israel" (2 Nephi 9:6, 12). "It behooveth [Christ] and becometh expedient that he dieth, to bring to pass the resurrection of the dead" (Helaman 14:15).

The Book of Mormon prophet Jacob paints a frightening scenario if there were no Resurrection: "If the flesh should rise no more our spirits must become subject to that angel who fell from before the presence of the Eternal God, and became the devil, to rise no more. And our spirits must have become like unto him, and we become devils, angels to a devil, to be shut out from the presence of our God, and to remain with the father of lies, in misery, like unto himself" (2 Nephi 9:8–9). What a dreadful ending if there were no Resurrection! But knowing the reality of the Resurrection, Jacob rejoices and exclaims, "How great the importance to make these things known unto the inhabitants of the earth, that they may know that there is no flesh that can dwell in the presence of God, save it be through the merits, and mercy, and grace of the Holy Messiah, who layeth down his life according to the flesh, and taketh it again by the power of the Spirit, that he may bring to pass the resurrection of the dead, being the first that should rise" (2 Nephi 2:8). The Resurrection saves men from the devil.

Phrased a little differently, another prophet, Abinadi, taught that none of us would rise from the dead had not Jesus Christ been resurrected: "And if Christ had not risen from the dead, or have broken the bands of death . . . there could have been no resurrection" (Mosiah 16:7).

Paul eloquently taught:

> But now is Christ risen from the dead, and become the firstfruits of them that slept. . . .
>
> For as in Adam all die, even so in Christ shall all be made alive. . . .
>
> For this corruptible must put on incorruption, and this mortal must put on immortality.
>
> So when this corruptible shall have put on incorruption, and this mortal shall have put on immortality, then shall be brought to pass the saying that is written, Death is swallowed up in victory. O death, where is thy sting? O grave, where is thy victory? . . .
>
> But thanks be to God, which giveth us the victory through our Lord Jesus Christ. (1 Corinthians 15:20, 22, 53–57)

Other prophets provide additional witnesses that Christ would be the first to resurrect and that He would provide the power for all of us to rise from the dead: "The bands of death shall be broken, and the Son reigneth, and hath power over the dead; therefore, he bringeth to pass the resurrection of the dead" (Mosiah 15:20).

The teachings of Jesus and His Apostles of all ages are unmistakable—the Resurrection will be universal. It matters not whether one has been good or bad, intelligent or ignorant; nationality, race, or faith does not matter; all will be resurrected. There have been many throughout history who have searched for the fountain of youth. Paradoxically, the way to find the fountain of youth is to die! The fountain of youth will be given to all but only after we die—it is a gift from the majestic Jesus Christ.

Amulek taught:

> Now, there is a death which is called a temporal death; and the death of Christ shall loose the bands of this temporal death, that all shall be raised from this temporal death.
>
> The spirit and the body shall be reunited again in its perfect form; both limb and joint shall be restored to its proper frame. . . .
>
> Now, this restoration shall come to all, both old and young, both bond and free, both male and female, both the wicked and the righteous; and even there shall not so much as a hair of their heads be lost; but every thing shall be restored to its perfect frame. . . .
>
> I say unto you that this mortal body is raised to an immortal body . . . that they can die no more; their spirits uniting with their bodies, never to be divided. (Alma 11:42–45)

We will never die again! We will live forever! We will not be reincarnated into some other form!

Alma provided another witness regarding this complete restoration that is part of the Resurrection: "The soul shall be restored to the body, and the body to the soul; yea, and every limb and joint shall be restored to its body; yea, even a hair of the head shall not be lost; but all things shall be restored to their proper and perfect frame" (Alma 40:23).

Nature of a Resurrected Body

The nature of a resurrected body will be different than the mortal body. The mortal body consists of flesh, bones, and blood, the blood giving life to the body (see Genesis 9:3–6; Leviticus 17:11). But a resurrected body will consist of flesh, bones, and spirit, the spirit giving immortal life to the body.[60] Speaking of the physical death of the body and the subsequent resurrection of the body, Paul wrote, "So also is the resurrection of the dead. It is sown in corruption; it is raised in incorruption. . . . It is sown a natural body; it is raised a spiritual body. There is a natural body, and there is a spiritual body" (1 Corinthians 15:42, 44). Those who deny a literal resurrection use this scripture to justify their claims. They misunderstand the concept of a spiritual body. A spiritual body is a tangible body, such as Christ had

60. Joseph Fielding Smith, *Doctrines of Salvation*, comp. Bruce R. McConkie (1955), 2:284–86.

after His resurrection. In the premortal world, we had a spirit body. In the eternities, we will have a spiritual (meaning forever) physical body. The Resurrection is a purifying process for the body.

Final Judgment

Many scriptures inextricably link the Resurrection with the Final Judgment of God. During His earthly ministry, the Savior taught that by His power, all people would resurrect and then be judged. Ponder His testimony: "The dead shall hear the voice of the Son of God; and they that hear shall live. For as the Father hath life in himself; so hath he given to the Son to have life in himself; And shall come forth; they that have done good, unto the resurrection of life; and they that have done evil, unto the resurrection of damnation" (John 5:25–29).

The glorious news for all of us is the knowledge that our Savior, Jesus Christ, will be our judge. While ministering among men, Jesus even said, "The Father judgeth no man, but hath committed all judgment unto the Son" (John 5:22). Because of His experiences in Gethsemane and on the cross, Jesus completely understands each one of us. He will be our judge; He does not employ any servants for that role (see 2 Nephi 9:41).

The Book of Mormon prophet Jacob taught, "When all men shall have passed from this first death unto life, insomuch as they have become immortal, they must appear before the judgment-seat of the Holy One of Israel; and then cometh the judgment, and then must they be judged according to the holy judgment of God" (2 Nephi 9:15). Lehi taught, "All men come unto God; wherefore, they stand in the presence of him, to be judged of him according to the truth and holiness which is in him" (2 Nephi 2:10). And from John: "And I saw the dead, small and great, stand before God; and the books were opened . . . and the dead were judged out of those things which were written in the books, according to their works" (Revelation 20:12).

From Alma: "[Christ] shall rise again from the dead, which shall bring to pass the resurrection; that all men shall stand before him, to be judged at the last and judgment day, according to their works" (Alma 33:22). From Amulek: "All shall rise from the dead and stand before God, and be judged according to their works . . . whether they be good or whether they be evil" (Alma 11:41, 44).

At the judgment bar, "our words will condemn us, yea, all our works will condemn us; our thoughts will also condemn us" (Alma 12:14). In essence, our words, our works, and our thoughts determine who we have become. We will be judged based on who we have become.

Amulek taught, "We shall be brought to stand before God, knowing even as we know now, and have a bright recollection of all our guilt" (Alma 11:43). I find Amulek's words "a bright recollection of all our guilt" intriguing. Nephi also taught that same concept: "We shall have a perfect knowledge of all our guilt, and our uncleanness, and our nakedness; and the righteous shall have a perfect knowledge of their enjoyment, and their righteousness" (2 Nephi 9:14). As we go through mortality, we often forget things. That's just part of being human. However, as resurrected beings, when we meet God at the judgment bar, we will remember everything—including everything we experienced in premortality. The veil that God placed over our memories of the premortal world will be removed. It is likely that a good part of the anguish people will feel on Judgment Day will come as they realize who they were in the premortal world, the potential to which they were foreordained, and how they fell short of their foreordination.

I am grateful that the Lord's judgment is not comparative. He will not compare what I have done and have become according to a standard set by another. The parable of the talents (see Matthew 25:14–30) teaches that each of us will be judged in accordance to our capacity and talents. He who received five talents and doubled them to ten talents, and he who received two talents and doubled them to four talents, will receive the same mercy from Christ and will receive the same reward. I do not need to "measure up" to President Nelson or other incredibly righteous and gifted men and women all around me. I just need to do my best and measure up to myself based on my potential and capabilities, which the Father and the Son know perfectly.

Please note that this will be a *Final* Judgment. Nothing is found in the scriptures to indicate that progression can be made after this Final Judgment. All the prophets teach that now—meaning mortality and the spirit world—is the time to prepare to meet God; now is the time to change and progress. Because it is the Final Judgment, one cannot progress from a lower to a higher kingdom.

All Will See the Father and the Son at the Judgment Bar

The Father of our spirits will also be at the judgment bar to greet and love His children. Amulek writes that we will "be brought and be arraigned before the bar of Christ the Son, and God the Father" (Alma 11:44). This will be the fulfillment of the scripture that says, "The spirit shall return unto God who gave it" (Ecclesiastes 12:7). The prophet Samuel taught, "The resurrection of Christ redeemeth mankind, yea, even all mankind, and bringeth them back into the presence of the Lord" (Helaman 14:17). Every one of God's children will again feel of His love. If we learn nothing else from the parable of the prodigal son, we must learn that the Father's love is always present for His children, even if the prodigal children don't return. All of us will enjoy His presence for a time. Whether we can dwell with Him throughout the eternities will be determined by our judgment.

Alma writes, "And in this awful state [an unrepentant state] we shall not dare to look up to our God; and we would fain be glad if we could command the rocks and the mountains to fall upon us to hide us from his presence. But this cannot be; we must come forth and stand before him in his glory . . . and acknowledge . . . that all his judgments are just; that he is just in all his works, and that he is merciful unto the children of men" (Alma 12:14–15). We will fear because we will know that we fell short of God's expectations. However, our fears will dissipate as we feel the love of our Savior and of our Eternal Father. Whatever judgment we receive, it will likely be more rewarding than what we anticipate, and we will exclaim that His judgment is not only just but also merciful!

Judgment: The Celestial Kingdom

Jesus taught, "In my Father's house are many mansions" (John 14:2). That teaching from the Savior totally debunks the false understanding that there is just a heaven and a hell. Just as there are many degrees of righteousness and wickedness found among men, so there will be many mansions to accommodate the degrees of righteousness and wickedness.

In a series of panoramic visions received by the Prophet Joseph and witnessed also by Sidney Rigdon, the Lord revealed that there are three general kingdoms of glory: the celestial, the terrestrial, and the telestial. Those who are admitted into the celestial kingdom are those people who were valiant in their testimonies of Jesus Christ. They followed the doctrine of Christ and walked the covenant path. (The next chapter will explore these topics.) They will dwell with Heavenly Father and Christ throughout the eternities. They will receive all that the Father hath. They will be made perfect in all attributes through Jesus Christ (see Doctrine and Covenants 76:50–69). Everything found in the gospel of Jesus Christ, and everything that His Church does, is to help us attain the celestial kingdom.

There is one other observation that magnifies the majesty of Jesus Christ and His Atonement: "Little children are redeemed from the foundation of the world through mine Only Begotten; Wherefore, they cannot sin, for power is not given unto Satan to tempt little children, until they begin to become accountable before me" (Doctrine and Covenants 29:46–47). "All little children are alive in Christ, and also all they that are without the law. For the power of redemption cometh on all them that have no law; wherefore, he that is not condemned, or he that is under no condemnation, cannot repent; and unto such baptism availeth nothing" (Moroni 8:22). "Little children also have eternal life" (Mosiah 15:25). Little children who are not yet accountable for their actions, defined as age eight by the Lord (see Doctrine and Covenants 68:25–28), have no sin and are redeemed to celestial life. Furthermore, others who have no understanding of the law because of their mental incapacities are redeemed by Jesus Christ.

Judgment: The Terrestrial Kingdom

Those who are admitted into the terrestrial kingdom are (1) those people who rejected the gospel of Jesus Christ in mortality but later accepted it in the spirit world, (2) honorable and good people who were blinded by the craftiness of men so they never accepted the gospel of Jesus Christ, and (3) those who followed the doctrine of Christ and made covenants with the Lord but did not remain faithful to those covenants. I have often asked myself: Am I honorable (terrestrial) or valiant (celestial)?

We often hear the testimonial, "I know Jesus is the Christ" or "I know this Church is true." Those are not significant statements. Even the devils can say that. The Three Witnesses to the Book of Mormon never denied their testimonies, yet they spent much of the latter part of their lives outside the Church. Knowing, loving, and appreciating all the programs of the Church is not the essential element of our salvation.

President Benson said, "Not to be valiant in one's testimony is a tragedy of eternal consequence. These are members who know that this latter-day work is true but who fail to endure to the end. Some may even hold temple recommends, but they do not magnify their callings in the Church."[61]

The parable of the ten virgins found in Matthew 25 also refers to the Latter-day Saints. Some of the membership of the Church will not be prepared when they meet the Savior. All ten of the virgins had their lamp of testimony, but only five had the oil of conversion acquired through daily valiant faith and obedience. Some of the members of the Church will not have their lamps filled with the oil of faith and obedience. They will not have the power to abide His presence.

God wants our very best! Why? Because He gave His very best every day. Because that is how we can become like Him! If we desire to become like Him, we must sacrifice "me and my wants"—just like the Savior did—and devote our best energies to Him.

We must not be tempted to think that in the final analysis, God will beat us with a few stripes and then welcome us into His presence (see 2 Nephi 28:8). We need to remember that God is not only a God of mercy but also bound by the laws of justice: "I desire that ye should deny the justice of God no more. Do not endeavor to excuse yourself in the least point because of your sins, by denying the justice of God" (Alma 42:30). God is a God of justice as well as a God of mercy. He is God because He has always followed the same laws that He is encouraging us to follow.

---

61. *Teachings of Presidents of the Church: Ezra Taft Benson* (2014), 392–93.

Those assigned to the terrestrial kingdom will never see Father in Heaven again after the Judgment Day. However, they will rejoice as Jesus will visit them according to His timetable (see Doctrine and Covenants 76:70–79).

Judgment: The Telestial Kingdom

Those who are admitted into the telestial kingdom are those people who lived after the manner of the world. They preferred the ways of the world over the ways of the Lord. After suffering the pains of hell, they will be redeemed by the Savior. Because they rejected living a life patterned after Jesus Christ, they will not enjoy the presence of the Father or of the Son after the Judgment Day (see Doctrine and Covenants 76:80–86).

The rewards we receive at Judgment Day will wholly reflect the law of restoration. We will reap what we have sown. Alma taught, "The meaning of the word restoration is to bring back again evil for evil, or carnal for carnal, or devilish for devilish—good for that which is good; righteous for that which is righteous; just for that which is just; merciful for that which is merciful" (Alma 41:13). "The resurrection is a restoration, both a restoration of body and spirit, and restoration to the individual of the same mental and spiritual acquirements and attitudes he had in this life."[62]

Moroni taught, "Do ye suppose that ye could be happy to dwell with that holy Being, when your souls are racked with a consciousness of guilt that ye have ever abused his laws? Behold, I say unto you that ye would be more miserable to dwell with a holy and just God, under a consciousness of your filthiness before him, than ye would to dwell with the damned souls in hell" (Mormon 9:3–4). Following Moroni's teachings to their rightful conclusion, the Lord will place every one of us in the kingdom and mansion that will maximize our happiness! If a person is placed in any mansion found in the terrestrial or telestial kingdom, it will be because they will find greater happiness there! He or she will live among peers with similar values and motivations, as reflected by their decisions both in mortality and in the spirit world.

---

62. Bruce R. McConkie, *Mormon Doctrine*, 2nd ed. (1966), 641.

We will be restored to who we were and will be happy to such a degree that we never expected. We will call the Lord blessed and merciful.

I am convinced that no matter in what mansion one is placed, that individual will be happy in their sphere and will glorify God for receiving (in their mind) more than they deserve (see Doctrine and Covenants 88). No matter one's status or position in life, no matter one's faith, Judgment Day will be a revelatory, transformative experience for all. That day, all will bend the knee and confess with the tongue that Jesus indeed is the Christ. Such is the majesty of Jesus Christ!

Judgment: No Redemption by Christ

There is one other judgment: those who had a firm knowledge of Jesus Christ and of His power but then later chose to align themselves with Satan. They loved Satan more than God (see Moses 5:18, 28). They will not be redeemed by the Savior in any way. They will not inherit any kingdom of glory; they will dwell with Satan and his angels. They will be known as the sons of perdition. Again, they are restored to a place and environment that they followed during their probationary period. The Lord does not punish. He places all people in a kingdom that reflects who they have become.

That marvelous revelation reveals that with very few exceptions (i.e., the sons of perdition), Jesus Christ has rescued all of us from the clutches of Satan. How majestic is His grace! In that sense, almost all people will be saved. That is why the Prophet Joseph wrote:

> What has Jesus said? All sin, and all blasphemies, and every transgression, except one, that man can be guilty of, may be forgiven; and there is a salvation for all men, either in this world or the world to come. . . . Hence God hath made a provision that every spirit in the eternal world can be ferreted out and saved. . . . God has wrought out a salvation for all men. Hence the salvation of Jesus Christ was wrought out for all men, in order to triumph over the devil; for if it did not catch him in one place, it would in another; for he stood up as a Savior.[63]

63. *Teachings of the Prophet Joseph Smith*, sel. Joseph Fielding Smith (1976), 356–57.

What Kind of Body Will One Have After the Resurrection?

Those who come forth in the morning of the First Resurrection will rise from the dead with celestial bodies. Those who come forth in the afternoon of the First Resurrection will rise from the dead with terrestrial bodies. Those who participate in the Second Resurrection will rise from the dead with telestial bodies. The glory of a celestial body has been compared to the brightness of the sun, the glory of a terrestrial body has been compared to the brightness of the moon, and the glory of a telestial body has been compared to the brightness of the stars (see Doctrine and Covenants 76:70, 78, 81). Yet we also learn that the glory of the telestial kingdom surpasses all understanding. The glory of the terrestrial kingdom exceeds the glory of the telestial kingdom in all things. The glory of the celestial kingdom exceeds the glory of the terrestrial kingdom in all things, where God the Father reigns upon His throne (see Doctrine and Covenants 76:89–92).

When the Resurrection does happen, what will one's resurrected body be like? One of my young granddaughters said she didn't want to get old because then when she was resurrected, she would be old forever! As noted previously, Amulek taught that the body will be in its "perfect form." Likewise, Alma taught that "all things shall be restored to their proper and perfect frame" (Alma 40:23). But the body experiences no growth in the grave. When the Resurrection occurs, the body will come forth as it was put in the grave. Then, in the twinkling of an eye, it will be rejuvenated into a perfect body. What about those with disabilities, both physical and mental? Gone—those are just mortal conditions. What about one's poor heart health? obesity? cancer? high blood pressure? All gone, for they are mortal conditions. What about a body bowed down with old age? Gone—the aging process is a mortal condition. All bodily deformities and imperfections will be removed, and the body will conform to the likeness of the spirit.

What about those who die as infants? Their bodies never had a chance to grow to maturity in mortality. Their adult spirits want adult bodies. President Joseph F. Smith writes, "The body will come forth as it is laid to rest, for there is no growth or development in the grave.

As it is laid down, so will it arise, and changes to perfection will come by the law of restitution."[64] He further taught, "Joseph Smith declared that the mother who laid down her little child, being deprived of the privilege, the joy, and the satisfaction of bringing it up to manhood or womanhood in this world, would, after the resurrection, have all the joy, satisfaction, and pleasure, and even more than it would have been possible to have had in mortality, in seeing her child grow to the full measure of the stature of its spirit. . . . When she does it there, it will be with the certain knowledge that the results will be without failure."[65]

Moroni beautifully summarized the Resurrection and Final Judgment of God that will come to all men:

> And because of the redemption of man, which came by Jesus Christ, they are brought back into the presence of the Lord; yea, this is wherein all men are redeemed, because the death of Christ bringeth to pass the resurrection, which bringeth to pass a redemption from an endless sleep, from which sleep all men shall be awakened by the power of God . . . and they shall come forth, both small and great, and all shall stand before his bar, being redeemed and loosed from this eternal band of death, which death is a temporal death. (Mormon 9:13)

All men, no matter who they are, will have the glorious experience of being reunited with their Father in Heaven and with our eldest brother, Jesus Christ, at the judgment bar! What a magnificent experience it will be, and we will fully understand the majesty of Jesus Christ! How long one stays in Their presence will be determined by the judgment they receive. That judgment will reflect who they have become.

---

64. *Gospel Doctrine*, 449.

65. *Gospel Doctrine*, 453–54.

The Majesty of Christ's Way

"Jesus saith unto him, I am the way, the truth, and the life; no man cometh unto the Father, but by me" (John 14:6). "There shall be no other name given nor any other way nor means whereby salvation can come unto the children of men, only in and through the name of Christ, the Lord Omnipotent" (Mosiah 3:17).

With very few exceptions, Christ will redeem all humankind from Satan, and all will dwell in peace and happiness within their sphere. But Jesus Christ wants all of us to experience His kind of joy. Jesus paid the ultimate price that gives all of us hope that we can return to our Father in Heaven and enjoy happiness with Them in celestial glory. That gives Jesus the right to define the way or path that we must follow to obtain celestial glory. He has defined His way as "strait," meaning narrow. It is not a wide path that accommodates every whim and notion that man can conjure. No other pursuit, no matter how worthy, is sufficient to bring one back to dwell with God. No other belief, no matter how sincere, is sufficient for celestial happiness. The way of Jesus Christ is the only way for one to enjoy celestial joy!

Elder Bruce R. McConkie stated, "Sincerity has almost nothing to do with gaining salvation. Men who slay the saints can be just as sincere as those who thus become martyrs. Men can believe so devoutly in falsehood that they will even lay down their own lives for it. What does it matter that those who killed the prophets, either ancient or modern, thought they did God service? The thing that counts is truth, pure God-given truth."[66] The way of Christ is truth.

So what is the way of Jesus Christ? Jesus has defined His way very specifically. The Book of Mormon teaches us the "doctrine of Christ." Latter-day prophets speak of the covenant path. They are not exclusionary. They go hand in hand.

The Savior taught the doctrine of Christ to the Nephites when He ministered among them following His Resurrection and Ascension to heaven. Nephi also expounded beautifully on the doctrine of Christ. The doctrine of Christ can be summarized as (1) faith in Jesus Christ, (2) repentance, (3) baptism by water by priesthood authority, (4) baptism by fire (the gift of the Holy Ghost), and (5) enduring to the end.

The covenant path focuses on the saving ordinances and covenants that a disciple of Christ must receive and honor in order to obtain celestial glory. Following the doctrine of Christ will always lead a disciple to all the gospel ordinances and covenants. The saving ordinances are (1) baptism by water and the Spirit, (2) the priesthood, (3) the endowment, and (4) celestial marriage. With each ordinance comes covenants.

A covenant is a promise between a person and God. The Lord's intent for every ordinance and covenant is for us to create a closer bond with Him, develop a stronger relationship with Him, and ultimately become like Him.

I like to think of a covenant as a contract between God and man. During my work career, I dealt with many different contracts. There were contracts with trustees, investment managers, insurance companies, administrators, suppliers, and vendors. Contracts establish the responsibilities of each party. Each contract, in essence, says that if Party A will do this, Party B will do that. In business terms, Party A usually performs some service, and Party B, in return, pays Party A some money.

I have learned that the value of a contract is no better than the parties to the contract. Neither Party A nor Party B has the *right* to ignore the terms of the contract, but both parties have the *agency* to break the contract. If a party uses their agency and breaks the terms of

---

66. Bruce R. McConkie, *The Mortal Messiah* (Deseret Book, 1981), 4:94.

the contract, the offended party may go to court and obtain relief or redress. A contract allows legal remedies but does not establish a good business relationship itself.

Because the parties have agency to break a contract, the most important elements in a business relationship are trust, honor, and integrity. Indeed, vast amounts of business are conducted without the dotted line being signed. A meeting of the minds is established, a handshake is given, and work proceeds based on trust. The contract may not be signed until some months later.

If a party does not perform certain services as spelled out in a contract, payment can be withheld. A contract usually specifies the quality of workmanship demanded. One would be justified in withholding payment to a general contractor who did not build your house in accordance with all the building codes. Slipshod work is not entitled to payment. Perhaps the contractor met all the codes but did not complete the project. Again, full payment would not be warranted.

The same holds true with our contracts with the Lord. If one does not keep the promises contained in those contracts, the Lord can withhold payment. One who haphazardly keeps the covenants as stated in those contracts is not entitled to the promises of the Lord. The promises we make in those contracts with the Lord are not for one, five, or even twenty years. The duration is for this lifetime and even beyond. Being diligent for a period of time but not enduring to the end is like building a house according to codes but not finishing the project. Non-endurance does not warrant full payment.

The Lord is the perfect business partner because He can be trusted in every way. The scriptures tell us that "none of them that trust in him shall be desolate" (Psalm 34:22) and urges us to "trust in the Lord with all [our] heart" (Proverbs 3:7). Furthermore, we know that God cannot lie (see Hebrews 6:18; Ether 3:12). He tells us, "I, the Lord, am bound when ye do what I say; but when ye do not what I say, ye have no promise" (Doctrine and Covenants 82:10). None of us have to worry about the Lord exercising His agency to break contracts or covenants with us.

The Doctrine of Christ: Faith in Jesus Christ

The first principle of the gospel is not just faith but faith in the Lord Jesus Christ. There is a difference. Faith in the Lord Jesus Christ does not merely mean one believes in His identity as the Son of God, although that is part of it. It means a person believes in Christ's power to save them from their sins. It means one has trust in Him, to do things in life His way—to follow Christ's path and not their own.

True faith will always impel one to action. By faith, Nephi was able to obtain the plates of brass (see 1 Nephi 4) and later build a ship (see 1 Nephi 18). By faith, Moses delivered the Israelites from bondage (see Exodus 5–14). By faith, Alma and Amulek caused the walls of the prison to tumble (see Alma 14). By faith, Ammon and his brothers caused thousands of the Lamanites to reject the traditions of their fathers, repent, and be baptized (see Alma 17–27). By faith, the brother of Jared moved a mountain (Ether 12:30). By faith, miracles occur.

The same is true with each of us. "The Lord is able to do all things according to his will, for the children of men, if it so be that they exercise faith in him. Wherefore, let us be faithful to him" (1 Nephi 7:12). Although faith is a gift of God, it will be given to those who show a humility of soul and a sincerity of disposition. Faith is an iterative process; it will grow as we culture it with righteousness and with continual good works. "Nevertheless they did fast and pray oft, and did wax stronger and stronger in their humility, and firmer and firmer in the faith of Christ, unto the filling their souls with joy and consolation, yea, even to the purifying and the sanctification of their hearts, which sanctification cometh because of their yielding their hearts unto God" (Helaman 3:35).

My spirit is touched every time I sing or hear the hymn "Lead, Kindly Light." In part, we sing: "Lead, kindly Light, amid th' encircling gloom; Lead thou me on. The night is dark, and I am far from home. Lead thou me on" (*Hymns*, no. 97).

This hymn is a powerful message regarding faith in the Lord Jesus Christ and in His power to deliver us from darkness and walk in the light that comes from Him. It first struck a responsive chord in my heart when I was a young missionary. I was serving in the northern part of Finland, about a hundred miles south of the Arctic Circle. It was December. At that time, the sun peaked above the horizon at around 11 a.m., then sunset occurred thirty minutes later. There was some residual light in the sky for about ninety minutes, and the rest of the day was literally black. The stars gave little light, and at times we'd get a little light from the northern lights.

Now combine the physical darkness of the location with the unmistakable fact that missionary work was difficult, seeing as most Finns had no interest in any religion. Secularism guided most people. I still struggled with the language and the ability to communicate with people. I was discouraged. A zone conference began with that hymn. As I started to sing, the words penetrated deep in my heart: "Amid the encircling gloom . . . the night is dark . . . I am far from home." All of that was true. But then I heard the Lord speak to me, saying, "Let Me lead you—trust in Me. You can't do it alone. I will deliver you." I couldn't continue singing; my heart swelled and the tears came. As I humbled myself and applied myself to the work, the Lord was able to accomplish His purposes through me.

At one time or another, all of us may find ourselves in places of darkness. We may wander into spiritual blackness when we make foolish choices, use harmful substances, or turn away from the light of the gospel to embrace the ways of the world. As we journey away from the Light, it may seem harmless at first. Before long, however, we are left in darkness, alone. Even during those dark times, if we exercise faith and call upon the Lord for deliverance, He will hear our cry. No matter where we are, He will rescue us. The Savior has promised, "He that followeth me shall not walk in darkness" (John 8:12). But it will require faith on our part.

In his classic sermon on faith, found in Alma 32, Alma gave us a directive to choose. He used the words *awake, arouse, experiment, exercise, desire, seek,* and *plant*. All those words require a choice of action. There is much I do not know. But because I have chosen to have faith, I know some of the most important things in life. I know the reality of God. I know that Jesus is my Savior. I know the Savior's way. I know that Joseph Smith was called by God to restore truths that had been lost and to build up His Church. I know that prophets lead the Church today. I know the Book of Mormon is true. All these truths compel me to action—to do things that most people would not do.

But doing those things brings me happiness and peace. My pioneer ancestry never left a heritage of stocks, bonds, and worldly wealth. Neither did my parents. But they left me a heritage of faith that I try to emulate. That faith impels me to obedience.

The Doctrine of Christ: Repentance

Alma tells us that we should exercise faith unto repentance (see Alma 34:17). At roughly the same time I was called and ordained to be a bishop, Elder Theodore M. Burton gave a powerful talk on repentance. I kept his talk in the bishop's office and referred to it often. In part, Elder Burton taught:

> It is easier for me to tell you what repentance is *not* than to tell you what repentance *is.* My present assignment as a General Authority is to assist the First Presidency. I prepare information for them to use in considering applications to readmit transgressors in the Church and to restore priesthood blessings. Many times, a bishop will write: 'I feel he has suffered enough!' But suffering is not repentance. Suffering comes from lack of complete repentance. A stake president will write: "I feel he has been punished enough!" But punishment is not repentance. Punishment follows disobedience and precedes repentance. A husband will write: "My wife has confessed everything!" But confession is not repentance. A wife will write: "My husband is filled with remorse!" But remorse is not repentance. Remorse and sorrow continue because a person has not yet fully repented. People must somehow be made to realize that the true meaning of repentance is to change their lives so they can escape eternal punishment.[67]

What is genuine repentance? Genuine repentance is best explained by some Book of Mormon scriptures. Lehi taught, "Behold, he offereth himself a sacrifice for sin, to answer the ends of the law, unto all those who have a broken heart and a contrite spirit; and unto none else can the ends of the law be answered" (2 Nephi 2:7). What does it mean to have a broken heart and contrite spirit? It means that one is truly sorrowful for their sins and will exert every effort to change, or repent.

---

67. Theodore M. Burton, "Meaning of Repentance" (Brigham Young University devotional, March 26, 1985), 2, speeches.byu.edu.

How is true repentance exemplified? There are two trademark signs. First, one will "have no more disposition to do evil, but to do good continually" (Mosiah 5:2). Second, one will "shake at the appearance of sin" (2 Nephi 4:31). Even when we reach the state that we have no more disposition to do evil, and even shake at the appearance of sin, we will still sin in this fallen world. But rather than throwing our hands up in the air and quitting, we are to "press forward with a steadfastness in Christ, having a perfect brightness of hope" (2 Nephi 31:20). We just keep doing our best each and every day and repent every day.

Speaking of Christ on the cross, Elder John H. Groberg said:

> I feel that as he hung upon the cross and looked out over the dark scene, he saw more than mocking soldiers and cruel taunters. He saw more than crying women and fearful friends. He remembered and saw even more than women at wells or crowds on hills or throngs by seashores. He was more, much more. He, who knows all and has all power, saw through the stream of time. His huge, magnanimous, loving soul encompassed all eternity and took in all people and all times and all sins and all forgiveness and all everything. Yes, he saw down to you and to me and provided us an all-encompassing opportunity to escape the terrible consequences of death and sin.
>
> And even as he suffered for all of us, he voiced that most beautiful of all requests, "Father, forgive them" (Luke 23:34). We must do our part and cry with full fervor of soul, "Father, forgive me through the merits of thy Beloved Son. Please, Father, through Him forgive me! Help me to do better." All life as we know it comes about through the joining of two separate elements—each necessary. The Savior, through his infinite atonement, provides that vital element for us. He asks us to provide the other element—even a broken heart and contrite spirit—for he will not force us.[68]

True repentance means that we are continually striving to cast off the natural man (see Mosiah 3:17). Casting off the natural man is no easy task. Repentance is an iterative process. We avoid sinful behavior while pursuing good behavior and attributes—and we do this over and over again.

---

68. John H. Groberg, "The Beauty and Importance of the Sacrament," *Ensign*, May 1989, 39–40.

The Doctrine of Christ: Baptism

A truly repentant soul will desire baptism. Symbolically, one buries their old sinful self and comes forth as a new person, one whose heart is contrite and who desires to do good continually. They are born again. Jesus taught, "Except a man be born of water and of the Spirit, he cannot enter into the kingdom of God" (John 3:5). Thus, baptism is a saving ordinance; it must be performed in order to be saved. It is the gate to the celestial kingdom. Baptism places one on the strait and narrow path that leads to eternal life.

Nephi made a persuasive case for baptism with the reasoning that "if the Lamb of God, he being holy, should have need to be baptized by water, to fulfil all righteousness, O then, how much more need have we, being unholy, to be baptized" (2 Nephi 31:5). In this act of submission and humility, Jesus demonstrated His desire to "fulfill all righteousness." It was this ordinance of baptism—by immersion and under the hand of one authorized to perform the ordinance, even John the Baptist—that Christ "showeth unto the children of men the straitness of the path, and the narrowness of the gate, by which they should enter, he having set the example before them" (2 Nephi 31:9). Only as we are immersed in the waters of baptism can mortals "take upon [us] the name of Christ . . . yea, by following [our] Lord and [our] Savior down into the water" (2 Nephi 31:13).

Just as baptism is a requirement to enter the kingdom of heaven, it is also required to be admitted into the Church of Jesus Christ. "All those who humble themselves before God, and desire to be baptized, and come forth with broken hearts and contrite spirits, and witness before the church that they have truly repented of all their sins, and are willing to take upon them the name of Jesus Christ, having a determination to serve him to the end, and truly manifest by their works that they have received of the Spirit of Christ unto the remission of their sins, shall be received by baptism into his church" (Doctrine and Covenants 20:37).

Contrary to popular tradition, the waters of baptism do not make one spiritually clean; the baptismal waters have no miracle cleansing agent that washes away one's sins. Sins are washed away by Jesus Christ, through the power of His Atonement! Some scriptures teach that Jesus Christ uses the Holy Ghost as the cleansing agent: "For the gate by which ye should enter is repentance and baptism by water; *and then cometh a remission of your sins by fire and by the Holy Ghost*" (2 Nephi 31:17; emphasis added). But in order for that cleansing power to work, one must repent and be baptized. By being baptized, a person is showing the Lord their faith, their desire to be righteous, and their desire to follow the Savior. Then because of their faith and desire for righteousness, the Savior cleanses them from sin.

The Covenant of Baptism: Obedience

In the covenant of baptism, the promise we make is to take upon ourselves the name of Christ and keep the commandments. Alma tells us that the baptismal covenant includes being "willing to mourn with those that mourn; yea, and comfort those that stand in need of comfort" (Mosiah 18:9), but one could argue that those injunctions fall under the umbrella of keeping the commandments. To all the Saints of God, the Lord gives this charge: "Keep my commandments" (Doctrine and Covenants 11:6). Obedience to God is the first law under heaven.

When Adam was cast out of the Garden of Eden, he was given the law of sacrifice. After many days, an angel appeared unto him and asked why he was performing sacrifices. Adam's reply reflects an attitude that we all should have: "I know not, save the Lord commanded me" (Moses 5:6). Adam didn't have to know the reasons, the "whys," or the benefits of the law. Just knowing that it was the Lord's will was good enough for Adam.

We are familiar with the commandment the Lord gave to Abraham: to sacrifice his son, Isaac. Abraham didn't understand the commandment; he didn't understand what good would come from that law or how his seed would become as numerous as the sands of the sea. Yet he was willing to obey!

When Nephi was attempting to obtain the brass plates from Laban in accordance with the Lord's commandment, he ventured forth, "not knowing beforehand the things which [he] should do" (1 Nephi 4:6). He found Laban in a drunken state on the streets of Jerusalem. He heard the still, small voice of the Spirit command him to slay Laban. This commandment went against every conviction and feeling he had, yet he had learned through obedience to accept the "living voice" over the written word. Nephi obeyed without complete understanding.

Do we likewise obey without knowing all the reasons and justifications for a commandment? Or do we obey only when we understand, when we see the benefits of the law, or when it's convenient? Are we courageous and humble enough to listen to the living voice of our prophet?

We do not need to understand the nuances of a law to live according to the law and be blessed by the law. For example, we all enjoy the advantages of electricity, but how many of us understand how it works? We enjoy driving a car, but how many of us really understand the mechanics that make it run? We enjoy the wonders of TV, radio, and the internet, but how many of us understand the laws that make them work?

The person who is a true disciple of Jesus Christ keeps the commandments in the worst of times. They pay tithing when struggling financially. They are honorable in their dealings when underhanded methods could work to their advantage. They extol and defend virtue when it isn't popular.

We read, "Be diligent in keeping all my commandments, lest . . . your faith fail you, and your enemies triumph over you" (Doctrine and Covenants 136:42). Obedience to commandments will strengthen our faith. The commandments are not an arbitrary set of rules to make us jump through hoops in order to please God. Every single commandment is given to bless us, increase our faith, and make us better. Breaking any law is serious because it weakens one's spiritual shield against the buffetings of Satan. It weakens one's spiritual sensitivities, making it difficult to hear the whisperings of the Spirit.

The Doctrine of Christ: The Holy Ghost

Shortly after baptism, one will receive the gift of the Holy Ghost. This gift is a manifestation of the love God has for His children who have entered the covenant of baptism. The Holy Ghost is absolutely essential for a person to become a better disciple of Christ. Much more will be written later when we probe all the things our majestic Savior has given us to overcome the natural man, the world, and Satan.

The Doctrine of Christ: Enduring to the End

The final element constituting the doctrine of Christ is to endure to the end. "He that endureth to the end, the same shall be saved. I know . . . that unless a man shall endure to the end, in following the example of the Son of the living God, he cannot be saved. Wherefore, ye must press forward with a steadfastness in Christ, having a perfect brightness of hope, and a love of God and of all men. Wherefore, if ye shall press forward . . . and endure to the end, behold, thus saith the Father: Ye shall have eternal life" (2 Nephi 31:15–16, 20).

For some, "enduring to the end" conjures up images of crawling through desert sands, and if they can just endure long enough, they will find an oasis of water and vegetation. But the Lord's definition of endurance is more positive and growth-oriented. Enduring helps us in becoming. This is because the Lord's ways are designed to develop the individual to their full potential. What we are is more important than what we know or what we do. The Savior did not say "*Know* ye therefore perfect" or "*Do* ye therefore perfect"; He said, "*Be* ye therefore perfect" (Matthew 5:48).

Enduring Well Leads to the Priesthood

Enduring faithfully on the gospel path will lead one to more sacred covenants. The first covenant (or contract) one must enter after baptism is the oath and covenant of the priesthood.

It is the Lord's intent that members of the Church receive many spiritual and temporal blessings through the power of the priesthood. All ordinances of the gospel are performed by the power and authority of the priesthood. Some ordinances are absolutely essential to our salvation and exaltation; hence, they are called saving ordinances. They include baptism, confirmation, ordination to the Melchizedek Priesthood, the temple endowment, and the marriage sealing.

Other ordinances, such as naming and blessing children, giving special blessings to spouses and children, consecrating oil, administering to the sick and afflicted, and patriarchal blessings are also performed by priesthood authority. While they are not essential to our salvation, they are important for our comfort, guidance, and encouragement.

The Covenant of the Priesthood: Obedience and Service

One makes covenants with the Lord when the Melchizedek Priesthood is conferred upon him. As with the ordinance of baptism, a man covenants to be obedient to "every word that proceedeth forth from the mouth of God" (Doctrine and Covenants 84:44). He also covenants to magnify the priesthood. How does one magnify the priesthood? By forgetting self and serving others.

The lay ministry of this Church is designed for a special purpose: to have the Saints experience service as they magnify callings. "If God loved only one person in a ward and wanted only one person to grow toward perfection, only that one would be invited to pray, preach, sing, usher, and handle other necessary assignments. However, such is not the case. God cares about you and me and all of his children; he wants everyone to develop talents and to grow through Church service. Because he loves us and trusts us and wants us to become more like him, he extends us callings through his authorized representatives."[69]

In the economy of God, only men are ordained to priesthood offices. But women, while performing duties assigned by priesthood keys, operate with the same priesthood authority. President Dallin H. Oaks taught, "We are not accustomed to speaking of women having the authority of the priesthood in their Church callings, but what other authority can it be?"[70] Hence, women have the same obligation to honor and magnify their priesthood authority.

The very essence of our discipleship is to serve our brothers and sisters. We can never begin to appreciate Christ's infinite Atonement until we place our own infinitesimal offering upon the altar by lifting another fellow being. No one can catch the slightest intimation of Jesus's profound love for humanity without becoming involved in service to others—service rendered without a hint of recognition or recompense. So I have asked myself, "How am I doing? Am I doing enough?" As we study the lives of great disciples in the scriptures, great disciples in the early

---

69. Carlos E. Asay, *Family Pecan Trees: Planting a Legacy of Faith at Home* (Deseret Book, 1991), 179.

70. Dallin H. Oaks, "The Keys and Authority of the Priesthood," *Ensign* or *Liahona*, May 2014, 51.

days of this dispensation, and great disciples in our day, we discover a common denominator: Service is not always easy or convenient. In the midst of our service, there will be problems to overcome.

The Lord expects our full energies in serving. "Let every man learn his duty, and to act . . . in all diligence. He that is slothful shall not be counted worthy to stand" (Doctrine and Covenants 107:99–100). Again, we read, "O ye that embark in the service of God, see that ye serve him with all your heart, might, mind and strength, that ye may stand blameless before God at the last day" (Doctrine and Covenants 4:2). "We should waste and wear out our lives" (Doctrine and Covenants 123:13) as disciples of Jesus Christ.

President Monson gave this challenge: "I am confident it is the *intention* of each member of the Church to serve and to help those in need. How many times has your heart been touched as you have witnessed the need of another? How often have you *intended* to be the one to help? And yet how often has day-to-day living interfered and you've left it for others to help?" He continued, "We become so caught up in the busyness of our lives. Were we to step back, however, and take a good look at what we're doing, we may find that we have immersed ourselves in the 'thick of thin things.' In other words, too often we spend most of our time taking care of the things which do not really matter much at all in the grand scheme of things, neglecting those more important issues."[71]

Patricia Holland wrote, "God wants so much for us to bless others, to find our lives by losing them, that he frequently and purposefully answers our own prayers, as well as those of others through our acts of caring and comfort. Many times, I have heard people say, 'I was praying for someone to come, and God sent you. I was lonely, and you walked in the door. I was down until you said "hi." I was blue and you wrote me that note. I was fearful until you took my hand.'"[72]

---

71. Thomas S. Monson, "What Have I Done for Someone Today?," *Ensign* or *Liahona*, Nov. 2009, 85.

72. Jeffrey R. and Patricia T. Holland, *On Earth as It Is in Heaven* (Deseret Book, 1989), 36–37.

The Covenant of the Priesthood: Sustaining the Prophets

Another covenant associated with the Melchizedek Priesthood is to honor, sustain, and follow Church leaders. "The day cometh that they who will not hear the voice of the Lord, neither the voice of his servants, neither give heed to the words of the prophets and apostles, shall be cut off from among the people. What I the Lord have spoken, I have spoken, and I excuse not myself; and . . . my word shall not pass away, but shall all be fulfilled, whether by mine own voice or by the voice of my servants [prophets and apostles], it is the same" (Doctrine and Covenants 1:14, 38).

The Prophet Joseph said, "I will give you one of the keys of the mysteries of the Kingdom. It is an eternal principle: that man who rises up to condemn others, finding fault with the Church, saying that they are out of the way, while he himself is righteous, then know assuredly, that that man is in the high road to apostasy; and if he does not repent, will apostatize, as God lives."[73]

George Q. Cannon taught, "No man, however strong he may be in the faith, however high in the Priesthood, can speak evil of the Lord's anointed and find fault with God's authority on the earth without incurring His displeasure. The Holy Spirit will withdraw itself from such a man."[74] Similarly, President Boyd K. Packer taught, "The man who will not sustain the bishop of his ward and the president of his stake will not sustain the Brethren."[75]

In return for keeping the covenants associated with the priesthood, the Lord promises that people will be sanctified by the Spirit unto the renewing of their bodies. There are so many ways this promise can be manifested. I relate just one experience wherein my body was renewed. When I was serving as a bishop, often my Sundays would start early in the morning, and my service would continue until late evening. On any weekday, I would not have lasted without food, but on

---

73. *Teachings of the Prophet Joseph Smith*, sel. Joseph Fielding Smith (1976), 156.

74. *Gospel Truth: Discourses and Writings of President George Q. Cannon,* com. Jerreld L. Newquist, (Deseret Book, 1974), 1:278.

75. Boyd K. Packer, "Follow The Brethren" (Brigham Young University devotional, Mar. 23, 1965), speeches.byu.edu.

those busy Sundays, I never felt hungry while I was serving. However, as soon as I locked the doors to the church, I was instantly famished. So long as I was serving the Lord, food was not necessary as my body was renewed by the Spirit.

The Lord also promises that one will become the elect of God and will receive all that the Father has; in other words, one will be given eternal life (see Doctrine and Covenants 84:34–38). Even after giving our best efforts, we are still considered "unprofitable servants" (Mosiah 2:21). Yet the Lord graciously and majestically gives us everything He has.

Enduring Well Will Lead to the Endowment

Enduring on the gospel path will lead a disciple to another sacred ordinance: the endowment. The endowment provides instruction and blessings that offer power and protection in our lives. The endowment is intended to deepen our relationship with the Lord. President Russell M. Nelson has promised, "The ordinances of the temple and the covenants you make there are key to strengthening your life, your marriage and family, and your ability to resist the attacks of the adversary. Your worship in the temple and your service there for your ancestors will bless you with increased personal revelation and peace and will fortify your commitment to stay on the covenant path."[76]

President Brigham Young taught, "Your endowment is to receive all those ordinances in the house of the Lord, which are necessary for you, after you have departed this life, to enable you to walk back to the presence of the Father, passing the angels who stand as sentinels, being enabled to give them the key words, the signs and tokens, pertaining to the holy priesthood, and gain your eternal exaltation."[77]

The Endowment Covenant: Obedience and Sacrifice

Some of the covenants we make in the endowment are the same as previously made with other ordinances. First, one covenants to obey the Lord. (So important is obedience that it is found in every covenant associated with every saving ordinance.) There is a special emphasis on

76. "As We Go Forward Together," *Ensign* or *Liahona*, April 2018, 7.

77. *Discourses of Brigham Young*, sel. John A. Widtsoe (1954), 416.

obeying the law of chastity, defined as sexual relations only between a man and woman legally married by the Lord's law. Second, one covenants to live the law of the gospel, which is synonymous with the doctrine of Christ.

Some of the covenants are unique. We covenant to live the law of sacrifice. Adam and Eve were taught the law of sacrifice and were commanded to practice it by giving offerings. These included two emblems: the firstlings of the flock and the first fruits of the field. They obeyed without questioning (see Moses 5:5–6). Those who sought to worship the Lord were asked to sacrifice the best part of their source of life. It was a real test of Adam and Eve's faith, and they obeyed.

After His mortal ministry, Christ elevated the law of sacrifice to a new level. In describing how the law would continue, Jesus told His Nephite Apostles that He would no longer accept burnt offerings but that His disciples should offer "a broken heart and a contrite spirit" (3 Nephi 9:19–20; see also Doctrine and Covenants 59:8, 12). Instead of the Lord requiring our animals or first fruits, now He wants us to give up all that is ungodly. This higher practice of the law of sacrifice reaches into the inner soul of a person. Elder Neal A. Maxwell said, "Real, personal sacrifice never was placing an animal on the altar. Instead, it is a willingness to put the animal in us upon the altar and letting it be consumed."[78]

President Russell M. Nelson has taught, "We are still commanded to sacrifice, but not by shedding blood of animals. Our highest sense of sacrifice is achieved as we make ourselves more sacred or holy. This we do by our obedience to the commandments of God. Thus, the laws of obedience and sacrifice are indelibly intertwined. As we comply with these and other commandments, something wonderful happens to us. We become more sacred and holy—[more] like our Lord!"[79] In fact, the word sacrifice means literally "to make sacred" or "to render sacred."

The Prophet Joseph taught:

---

78. Neal A. Maxwell, "Deny Yourselves of All Ungodliness," *Ensign*, May 1995, 68.

79. Russell M. Nelson, "Lessons from Eve," *Ensign*, Nov. 1987, 88.

> A religion that does not require the sacrifice of all things never has power sufficient to produce the faith necessary unto life and salvation. . . . It is through the medium of the sacrifice of all earthly things that men do actually know that they are doing the things that are well pleasing in the sight of God. When a man has offered in sacrifice all that he has for the truth's sake, not even withholding his life, and believing before God that he has been called to make this sacrifice because he seeks to do his will, he does know, most assuredly, that God does and will accept his sacrifice and offering, and that he has not, nor will not seek his face in vain. Under these circumstances, then, he can obtain the faith necessary for him to lay hold on eternal life.[80]

Listen to the language of the scriptures as they describe the level of sacrifice the Lord requires of us: "Offer your whole souls as an offering unto [God]" (Omni 1:26; Mosiah 2:24). "Present your bodies a living sacrifice, holy, acceptable unto God" (Romans 12:1). In our day, the Lord said we should keep our "covenants by sacrifice—yea, every sacrifice which I, the Lord, shall command" (Doctrine and Covenants 97:8). The sacrifice the Lord asks of us is to wholly rid ourselves of the "natural man" and all the ungodliness associated with it.

Elder M. Russell Ballard has said:

> If I have a fear, it is that the principle of sacrifice may be slipping away from us. This principle is a law of God. We are obliged to understand it and practice it. If being a member of this Church becomes too easy, testimonies will become shallow, and the roots of testimony will not go down into the soil of faith as they did with our pioneer forefathers. May God grant each of us an understanding of the law of sacrifice and a conviction that it is necessary today. It is vitally important that we understand this law and live it.[81]

The Endowment Covenant: Consecration

The other unique covenant we make in the temple is to live the law of consecration—to be *willing* to give all our time, talents, and everything we have been given or will be given for the kingdom of

80. *Lectures on Faith* (1985), 69.

81. M. Russell Ballard, "The Law of Sacrifice," *Ensign*, Oct. 1998, 13.

God on earth, and for the establishment of Zion. Too many are willing to give up everything to advance their career or to obtain power or money. The Lord wants our dedicated devotion to be fixed on Him and establishing Zion.

My family lived in the Palmyra, New York, area for several years. We delighted in seeing various structures restored, such as the Smith Log Home and the Grandin Building, where the Book of Mormon was published. We helped rebuild the rock fence that served as the northern boundary for the Smith farm. We were inspired as we attended the Palmyra Temple groundbreaking and saw the Palmyra Temple built. We fulfilled various assignments related to the temple and attended its dedication. Our testimonies were greatly strengthened by many spiritual events in the cradle of the Restoration. Through it all, we had many occasions to reflect upon the consecration of the early Saints.

Almost all the early Saints lived in abject poverty. Yet they were willing to give that which they needed in order to build temples. It may be difficult for us today, in an era of easy dollars and high costs, to appreciate the magnitude of the Kirtland Temple. It cost $60,000. In today's dollars, that would be $2.1 million. The Saints consecrated that huge amount of money when they were short on cash. The Church itself had little money. There were few rich men, and they couldn't totally endow the project.

Though later temples have been more elegant and more costly, it is doubtful that any required greater consecration and total involvement than what the Kirtland Temple required. Not only were dollars scarce and members few, but the temple was erected during a period of great persecution. The Zion's Camp expedition, which was attempting to assist the Saints in Jackson County, Missouri, took many of the most able-bodied men who had been working on the temple.

The law of consecration encompasses much more than the consecration of money. It entails the consecration of one's time and dedicated service to the Lord—to build the Lord's kingdom and establish Zion. In 1838, Governor Boggs of Missouri issued his infamous extermination order of the Mormons. That order legalized the murder of any Latter-day Saint in the state of Missouri; killing a Mormon would be viewed no differently, legally, than killing a mad dog. Shortly thereafter, the Hawn's Mill Massacre occurred.

It must have taken great courage for Jehu Cox and his wife to be baptized in the state of Missouri in that same year. Like the other Saints, they left their home and moved to Illinois. In May 1846, they again left their home and began the long, grueling trek out West. They buried a newborn son just north of Winter Quarters. They said a tearful goodbye to their sixteen-year-old son, Henderson, who joined the Mormon Battalion. In May 1848, the family began the final trek to the Salt Lake Valley. Just a month later, tragedy struck as their five-year-old daughter fell out of the wagon and was run over, killing her. It was the first recorded death for that vanguard company. When they reached the valley, they learned that they would never see Henderson again; acting as a scout for a group of the disbanded Mormon Battalion, he was killed by Indians while crossing the Sierra Nevada range. Jehu served in three bishoprics and was a vice president of an established United Order. Jehu, my great-great-great grandfather, consecrated almost all he had for the cause of Zion.

Why did those Saints consecrate so much when they themselves were in such want? The early Saints left good farms and comfortable homes, often with no compensation for those assets, to follow the prophet. Studies indicate that one of every ten or eleven Saints who made the dangerous trek to Utah died along the way. Many more would suffer terrible deprivations. Yet in spite of the odds and difficulties, they continued to come. Why? What drove them? They had a vision of building Zion or the kingdom of God and were willing to consecrate what they had in order to be part of that righteous endeavor.

"Creating Zion was the burden of the prayers of the early Saints. They yearned for it, carried it like a fire in their hearts, longed for that society away from the oppressions of the world where a celestial order prevails. It was a heavenly homesickness they carried with them. So new converts left their fields and fortunes and bade farewell to all they had known to gather. They were willing to shoulder their part to make [Zion] happen even if they left a heartbreaking string of graves across the prairies and their backs were bowed under the weight of what they had given up."[82] My pioneer ancestors and all the other Mormon

82. Maurine Jensen Proctor and Scot Facer Proctor, *The Gathering: Mormon Pioneers on the Trail to Zion* (Deseret Book, 1996), 11.

pioneers were not merely escaping persecution; they were involved in a monumental effort to build Zion.

I've often asked myself the question, "Why didn't the Lord make it easier for the pioneers?" For example, it seems the Saints were being driven out of their homes in the dead of winter. Why didn't the Lord cause it to be in the summer? The Lord could have tempered the weather when the Saints crossed Iowa, but instead it was the wettest spring on record, which caused them to get bogged in the mud and made the trek most tiring and slow. It was terribly difficult and inconvenient to build a temple when most were living in abject poverty.

The Lord didn't make it easy or convenient for those Saints—and He won't make it easy for us—because He is in the business of making a Zion people:

> The promised land is reached only after a tedious and difficult journey, and the heart is transformed in the process. Priorities became clear to converts who shed every precious keepsake along the trail, who dragged on when their bodies cried out in utter exhaustion. They came to know the Lord when human strength was gone and He was there to compensate, when their faith, like gold, was seven times purified. They learned to give freely to each other and bear one another's burdens in the furnace of affliction. These are Zion lessons that the world cannot offer. Though it didn't always succeed, the gathering trail to the West was to strip Babylon from the heart of one who wanted to build Zion.[83]

We are now in the process of building Zion, not by gathering to Utah but by building up the stakes of Zion. The Lord has called for the elders of His Church to be sent forth across the world to gather Israel into the stakes of Zion: "Go ye forth unto the land of Zion, that the borders of my people may be enlarged, and that her stakes may be strengthened, and that Zion may go forth unto the regions round about" (Doctrine and Covenants 133:9). President Gordon B. Hinckley said:

> As great things were expected of them, so are they of us. We note what they did with what they had. We have so much more, with an overwhelming challenge to go on and build the kingdom of

---

83. Proctor and Proctor, *The Gathering*, 12–15.

> God. With so great an inheritance, we can do no less than our very best. Those who have gone before expect this of us. We have a mandate from the Lord. The great pioneering movement of more than a century ago [must go] forward with latter-day pioneers. It's the essence of our courage to face modern-day mountains and our commitment to carry on.[84]

Today, in practice, Church members are being asked to consecrate only a small portion of their means, talents, and time for the kingdom of God. Many of the principles that are foundational for the law of consecration are still binding, however. The intent of the law of consecration is to root out those traits and attributes that are not in harmony with celestial law. "Zion cannot be built up unless it is by the principles of the law of the celestial kingdom" (Doctrine and Covenants 105:5). It's obvious to state that a person cannot live the higher law of consecration until they are able to live a lower law. A person cannot consecrate *all* their resources, time, and talents unless they first are willing to consecrate *some* of their resources, time, and talents.

The law of tithing is a lesser law to prepare oneself to live the law of consecration. The law of the fast offering provides us an opportunity to live the law of consecration. When I was a bishop, Church headquarters financed 96 percent of the budgetary needs of the ward. So I needed to ask ward members to make contributions to the ward budget. It was enlightening to see the differing levels of faith by the ward members in making those contributions.

My wife and I have had the privilege and pleasure of working daily with two mission presidents and their wonderful wives as we served in the mission office of the England London Mission. They wholly committed their time and talents to the missionaries and to the Lord. We were not as busy as them, but we can honestly say that our missions gave us the opportunity to live the law of consecration more fully. My wife and I believe the Lord blessed our family because of our consecrated missionary work.

---

84. Gordon B. Hinckley, "True to the Faith," *Ensign*, May 1997, 64, 67.

Enduring Well Will Lead to Celestial Marriage

The supreme ordinance given by Jesus Christ is the sealing of a marriage performed in a temple. "If a man marry a wife by my word, which is my law, and by the new and everlasting covenant, and it is sealed unto them by the Holy Spirit of promise . . . [it] shall be of full force when they are out of the world" (Doctrine and Covenants 132:19). For a marriage to be eternal, two elements must be in place. First, it must be done by the Lord's word and authority, as part of the new and everlasting gospel covenant. That authority was restored to the Prophet Joseph Smith in 1836 by Elias and Elijah. That authority has continued in the hands of the Apostles ever since.

The second element necessary for an eternal marriage is that the marriage must be verified to be worthy to last throughout the eternities by the Holy Spirit of Promise, which is the Holy Ghost. In this life, certain important legal documents must be notarized by one who has been given that authority by the State. If not notarized, the document is not considered complete or legal. Similarly, a celestial marriage is not everlasting through all eternity unless the Holy Ghost verifies or notarizes to the Lord that the couple has kept the marriage and gospel covenants. Only when the Holy Ghost seals that marriage will the marriage continue through eternity.

Because of the overarching importance of an eternal family and the sacredness of the priesthood keys that make it possible, the Lord has designated that such a marriage be done only in His temples. That sealing authority is delegated to those who preside over temples. Because a marriage, meant to last throughout eternities, is done in temples, it is often called a temple marriage. It is also called celestial marriage. It is also known as the Abrahamic covenant.

Abraham was given three specific blessings when he made a covenant with the Lord. First, he was promised that Christ would come through his lineage. Obviously, that blessing does not pertain to us. That was an individual-specific promise.

Second, Abraham was promised that he and his posterity would receive certain lands of inheritance. We too are promised a land of inheritance. What will be our land of inheritance? The Prophet Joseph taught, "This earth will be rolled back into the presence of God, and crowned with celestial glory."[85] President Joseph Fielding Smith wrote, "This earth on which we dwell is destined to become a celestial sphere and the righteous shall inherit it forever. After it has filled the measure of its mortal creation, it shall be crowned with glory, even with the presence of God the Father. Like man, the earth also shall die, but it also shall be quickened again, and shall abide the power by which it is quickened, to continue throughout eternity as the celestial abode of man."[86] Our land of inheritance, as part of the Abrahamic blessings given to us, will be an inheritance on this earth when it becomes the celestial kingdom.

Third, Abraham was promised that his posterity would be more than the sands of the sea or the stars of the sky. We only see a portion of the universe from our place in the Northern Hemisphere. One sees a different universe in the Southern Hemisphere, as I discovered some years ago when I was in Chile and Ecuador. Truly, the number of stars and creations goes beyond our numbering system.

The same is true for the sands of the sea. How many granules of sand would fill a small bucket? Multiply that by the number of buckets all the beaches in the world could fill. Again, the number is staggering and goes beyond our numbering system and our ability to comprehend. This promise can and will be given to us—that our posterity will be more numerous than the stars of the sky or the sands of the sea. How is such possible? It can only happen as we are privileged to live forever, with the potential to have children forever.

The Abrahamic covenant was not given in a random location. Abraham received those blessings in the form of an ordinance, accompanied by an oath and covenant. Abraham and Sarah received the blessings of Abraham when they received the ordinance of celestial marriage! One cannot have a forever family without the ordinance of celestial marriage. One cannot have children more numerous than the stars of the sky without the ordinance of celestial marriage. One cannot have the quality of life enjoyed by our Father in Heaven without the ordinance of celestial marriage. In a very real sense, we left the presence of God to come to this earth in order to go to the temple and

---

85. *Teachings of the Prophet Joseph Smith*, 181.

86. *Doctrines of Salvation*, comp. Bruce R. McConkie (1955), 3:26–27.

receive the ordinance of celestial marriage. The majesty of Jesus Christ makes that possible!

During the early hours of a chilly April morning in 1975, as I was kneeling with my bride at the altar in one of the sealing rooms of the Manti Temple, I heard the blessings of "thrones, kingdoms, principalities, . . . powers, [and] dominions" (Doctrine and Covenants 132:19) pronounced upon us. For a brief moment, I saw a glimpse of eternity. I was receiving those same blessings promised to Abraham 4,000 years ago when he received the same temple ordinance!

The great promise of celestial marriage is the power to beget spirit children. We read that those whose marriages are eternal "shall pass by the angels, and the gods . . . to their exaltation and glory in all things . . . which glory shall be a fulness and a continuation of the seeds forever and ever" (Doctrine and Covenants 132:19). The great glory that we will enjoy in our exaltation will be eternal family relationships. Rebekah was promised that she would be the mother of "thousands of millions" (Genesis 24:60). That is an eternal marriage! Those who enter lower degrees of the celestial kingdom or the other kingdoms will not have children (see Doctrine and Covenants 131:4).

When Adam and Eve were married by God, they were commanded to multiply and replenish the earth. That same command is given to every couple who enters marriage. In eternity, they will multiply in order to populate worlds! For this reason, one can understand why God only accepts a marriage between a man and a woman.

The Church builds temples so we can receive the ordinance that will allow us to have eternal families—the kind of life we saw our Father in Heaven have when we lived with Him as spirits in the premortal world. Forming an eternal family for each of us was and is the purpose of all creation. Forming an eternal family for each of us is the purpose of Christ's Atonement. We must choose to go to the temple to receive that sealing ordinance. We then must choose to be faithful to the commandments and covenants that we have made to the best of our abilities. If we are faithful, we will be blessed with eternal life, which by definition means the kind of life God now enjoys. At the center of eternal life is family.

The temple, then, isn't just a nice place to marry. When we kneel across the altar in a holy temple, we receive the priesthood ordinance that gives us the power to become eternal parents conditioned on our enduring faithfulness! The plan of salvation never intended that we remain as children. Its intent was for us to become joint heirs with Jesus Christ and be mothers and fathers throughout eternity!

Just as baptism is the gate to salvation in the celestial kingdom, celestial marriage is the gate to exaltation found in the highest degree of the celestial kingdom. "In the celestial glory there are three heavens or degrees; And in order to obtain the highest, a man must enter into this order of the priesthood [meaning the new and everlasting covenant of marriage]; And if he does not, he cannot obtain it" (Doctrine and Covenants 131:1–3).

Those who attain this highest degree of the celestial kingdom will be heirs to all that God has and become like Him. And we know it is not just a theoretical possibility. We know that Abraham, Isaac, and Jacob, because they were obedient to all these same covenants, have already been resurrected, been awarded the highest degree of the celestial kingdom, and are now gods, doing the same work as our Father in Heaven (see Doctrine and Covenants 132:37). That is simply majestic!

Only the valiant will be trusted with the sacred responsibility of being eternal parents. Only those who sacrifice and consecrate their all to know Jesus Christ can enjoy family relationships in the eternities. Why? Because God will only allow godlike or Zion-like righteousness to be perpetuated forever. All others, the honorable and the dishonorable, will live as single persons.

Over the years, my wife and I have witnessed our children be married in the temples of the Lord. As we have been in the temple witnessing those sacred events, with full and joyful hearts, the Spirit has confirmed to us that this life is all about that celestial sealing experience in the temple.

Elder Bruce R. McConkie said:

> From the moment of birth into mortality to the time we are married in the temple, everything we have in the whole gospel system is to prepare and qualify us to enter that holy order of matrimony which makes us husband and wife in this life and in the world to come. Then from the moment we are sealed together . . . everything connected with revealed religion is designed to help us keep the

> terms and conditions of our marriage covenant, so that this covenant will have efficacy, virtue, and force in the life to come. . . . There is nothing in this world as important as the creation and perfection of family units of the kind contemplated in the gospel of Jesus Christ.[87]

President Spencer W. Kimball said that "any of you would go around the world for the sealing ordinance if you knew its importance, if you realized how great it is. No distance, no shortage of funds, no situation would ever keep you from being married in the holy temple of the Lord."[88]

Eternal Relationships Are a Privilege, Not a Right

Satan desires that we be miserable like him (see 2 Nephi 2:18). Perhaps much of his misery stems from the fact that he will never be a husband or a father. He will do everything he can to prevent and destroy celestial marriages. Satan can prevent us from realizing the blessing of eternal family relationships if he can keep us comfortably honorable, pretty good people, but not really valiant in our testimonies. Honorable but not valiant people will inherit the terrestrial kingdom where there are no marriage or family relationships.

There will be many marriages solemnized in temples that will not last throughout the eternities. Sadly, the number of temple marriages that end in divorce is increasing. Other marriages are just limping along, the spouses simply tolerating each other. Death will not suddenly change the relationship. The blessing of having family and children throughout eternity will be extended only to those who have been true and faithful to each other and to gospel covenants.

While I was a bishop, I worked with a couple, encouraging them to become worthy to enter the temple in order to be sealed. I couldn't understand their lack of enthusiasm over that prospect. Finally, they told me that they didn't want a temple marriage because they didn't want to be together forever! Recently, I learned of a brother who wanted his records removed from the Church in order to break the sealing ordinance with his family. How truly sad! But I'm sure those two

---

87. *Improvement Era,* June 1970, 43–44.

88. Spencer W. Kimball, "The Importance of Celestial Marriage," *Ensign*, Oct. 1979, 4–5.

situations can be multiplied many times over. It reflects a sad misunderstanding of sealings. The Lord will never force individuals to live in a relationship that they don't want, regardless of any sealing ordinance. The Holy Ghost simply won't place His stamp of approval on that sealing. That is true for spouses and for children. Jesus Christ's love, omniscience, and mercy are so expansive that He will arrange relationships that make everyone happy—so long as they have kept all the temple covenants.

What about those couples who truly love each other but choose not to follow the covenant path? The scriptures are clear on one thing: They will not be in a marriage relationship. I have heard some claim that God would never separate families. True, God wants all families to be together forever. But an eternal family is a privilege, not a right. Only those who have faithfully followed the doctrine of Christ and walked the covenant path can be trusted with eternal relations. Again, the Lord will follow the law of restoration. A married couple will harvest what they have sown. If they have sown disobedience—if they have not sacrificed, not consecrated, not endured—then they will not reap an eternal marriage. Eternal marriage will be reserved only for those who have shown a commitment to keep all commandments no matter the cost, to serve others, to forget self, to sacrifice and consecrate, to show love and compassion, and to repent. Only they can be trusted to be heavenly parents to billions.

The scriptures are silent in describing the kind of relationship, if any, experienced by those who didn't keep the doctrine of Christ and didn't walk the covenant path. It is consistent with the mercy, grace, and love of Christ that they will be allowed to at least enjoy the same association and sociality with each other (see Doctrine and Covenants 130:2). However, that association will be less than a marriage relationship.

What about couples where only one partner is keeping covenants and the other is not? The faithful spouse will enjoy all the blessings of exaltation, including marriage, but the unfaithful spouse will not. The faithful spouse will not be limited in his or her eternal blessings based on the choices of the unfaithful spouse. Such is the majesty of Jesus Christ!

To summarize, the way of Jesus Christ is strait and narrow, but it will enable us to become who we wanted to become while in premortality. His way requires us to:

1. Have faith in Jesus Christ—faith that He is our Savior. Such faith will drive us to our knees in acknowledgment that we are dependent on the Lord.
2. Repent—to forsake the ways of the world, to cultivate a broken heart and contrite spirit, and to strive daily to cast off the natural man.
3. Be baptized by priesthood authority as a witness of our commitment to follow the Lord.
4. Be confirmed a member of the Lord's Church and receive the gift of the Holy Ghost.
5. Obey all the commandments, as each one is designed to purify us and make us holy.
6. For men, receive the Melchizedek Priesthood and magnify it by forgetting self, serving others, and sustaining the Lord's prophets.
7. Receive the ordinance of the endowment and honor the covenants to sacrifice all worldly ways and consecrate our resources, time, and talents for the building up of the kingdom of God on earth and for the establishment of Zion.
8. Receive the ordinance of celestial marriage and establish a holy relationship with our spouse and with God.
9. Endure to the end by keeping the gospel covenants each and every day.

There is absolute truth. One absolute truth is Jesus Christ is the Savior of the world. Hence, His way is absolute truth. He has only one gospel and one Church to provide the saving ordinances and covenants. The majesty of Jesus Christ is manifested throughout our lives as we make and keep gospel covenants. His Way is glorious, far more satisfying than the world, and with majestic, delicious fruit to be enjoyed throughout the eternities.

The Majesty of Christ in Our Lives

Christ is on our side. He suffered and died so that we might have eternal joy! Once, in the distant past, we joined with Christ and defeated Satan. The War in Heaven continues, and Satan remembers. That fact alone should cause us to shudder; it should summon our constant vigilance to "watch and pray always lest [we] enter into temptation; for Satan desireth to have [us]" (3 Nephi 18:18). We do not face a typical enemy; even the worst tyrants who have ever lived are tame compared with the master tyrant who taught and controlled them. Peter tells us that Satan and his followers "walketh about [the earth] . . . as a roaring lion . . . seeking whom he may devour" (1 Peter 5:8). He knows that without the power of the Savior, he would easily overcome us in this life, as he would make each of us sin to some degree.

"Behold, at that day shall [the devil] rage in the hearts of the children of men, and stir them up to anger against that which is good" (2 Nephi 28:20). In our day, that which is good is now called evil, and that which is evil is not only tolerated but also celebrated and considered good. That which is darkness is now considered enlightenment, and that which is light is now viewed as old-fashioned (see Isaiah 5:20). "And then shall many be offended, and shall betray one another, and shall hate one another" (Joseph Smith—Matthew 1:8). It seems that all-encompassing evil, not random and occasional evil, will be the challenge.

Enoch saw our day in a grand vision. He saw that our day would be defined by gross wickedness. He also "beheld Satan; and he had a great chain in his hand, and it veiled the whole face of the earth with darkness; and he looked up and laughed, and his angels rejoiced" (Moses 7:26). Satan's chains put men in bondage. The bondages of sin and addiction are real and very difficult to break. In fact, the only sure way to break such bondage is by the power of Christ's Atonement.

Satan laughs and rejoices as he has persuaded the world to follow him to lower levels of depravity. We read the whole earth will be in commotion (see Doctrine and Covenants 45:26–27; 88:91). The commotion will go beyond the elements of the earth; it will include a dramatic swing from traditional moral values. We read that "the powers of darkness prevail upon the earth" (Doctrine and Covenants 38:11). The powers of darkness are exhibited by every sexual deviancy and by many other acts not in accordance with the Lord's moral code. The powers of darkness are exhibited by the loss of respect for the law, crudeness, corruption in high places, secret works of darkness, the lack of civility in the public square, and the lack of respect for human life, born or unborn.

Can we defeat the formidable evil forces of Satan? Left to our own devices, we simply cannot. But Jesus Christ can and does deliver us! If we join forces with Christ as we did in premortality, we can defeat Satan again! We are assured by Jesus Christ, "Be of good cheer; I have overcome the world" (John 16:33). We are promised a successful outcome. Why? Because He has already accomplished the outcome! He knows! Such is His majesty! We just need to be on His side.

The majesty of Jesus Christ is manifested in all the ways He helps us in mortality. I would like to focus on six wonderful gifts He has given us to overcome Satan: (1) the Light of Christ, (2) the word of God, (3) prayer, (4) His Church and His prophets, (5) the Holy Ghost, and (6) His temples.

The Light of Christ

First, Jesus has given every man and woman the Light of Christ in order to "know good from evil" (Moroni 7:16). The Light of Christ is manifested by a conscience. It will whisper to each of us to help us know good from evil, and it gently beckons men to do good. If one will hearken to its whisperings, one will be directed by God to paths of righteousness (see Moroni 7:16–17; Doctrine and Covenants 88:11). Most men and women sense an "inner feeling" that guides them. Those feelings can disappear, however, when one constantly chooses to sin.

People have little comprehension of the full magnitude that the Light of Christ has upon all creations. We read:

> He comprehended all things, that he might be in all and through all things, the light of truth; Which truth shineth. This is the light of Christ. And the light which shineth, which giveth you light, is through him who enlighteneth your eyes, which is the same light that quickeneth your understandings; Which light proceedeth forth from the presence of God to fill the immensity of space—The light which is in all things, which giveth life to all things, which is the law by which all things are governed, even the power of God who sitteth upon his throne, who is in the bosom of eternity, who is in the midst of all things. (Doctrine and Covenants 88:6–13)

Jesus Christ is the light of the world and all other creations because as the Creator, He is the source of all light, physical and spiritual.

The Word of God

We are taught that "out of small things proceedeth that which is great" (Doctrine and Covenants 64:33). One simple principle that will help us overcome Satan is stated as follows: "Feast upon the words of Christ: for behold, the words of Christ will tell you all things what ye should do" (2 Nephi 32:3). Earlier, Nephi gave us this wonderful promise regarding the word of God: "Whoso would hearken unto the word of God, and would hold fast unto it, they would never perish; neither could the temptations and the fiery darts of the adversary overpower them" (1 Nephi 15:24). There is great power as we daily feast upon the scriptures. Never has any people in any dispensation had so much scripture to feed them and guide them as we do today.

Prayer

Nephi gives us another second simple principle to help us overcome Satan: "If ye would hearken unto the Spirit which teacheth a man to pray, ye would know that ye must pray; for the evil spirit teacheth not a man to pray, but teacheth him that he must not pray. But behold, I say unto you that ye must pray always, and not faint; that ye must not perform any thing unto the Lord save in the first place ye shall pray unto the Father in the name of Christ, that he will consecrate thy performance unto thee, that thy performance may be for the welfare of thy soul" (2 Nephi 32:8–9). Great power will come into each of our lives as we pray daily. Reading the scriptures and praying are so fundamental yet so simple.

Elder Richard G. Scott taught:

> Prayer is a supernal gift of our Father in Heaven to every soul. Think of it: the absolute Supreme Being, the most all-knowing, all-seeing, all-powerful personage, encourages you and me, as insignificant as we are, to converse with Him as our Father. It matters not our circumstance, be we humble or arrogant, poor or rich, free or enslaved, learned or ignorant, loved or forsaken, we can address Him. We need no appointment. Our supplication can be brief or can occupy all the time needed. It can be an extended expression of love and gratitude or an urgent plea for help. He has created numberless cosmos and populated them with worlds, yet you and I can talk with Him personally, and He will ever answer.[89]

I know many people have felt the power of prayer in their lives. Sadly, others feel like the heavens are closed and that God doesn't hear their prayers. Books and many general conference talks have addressed prayer. The focus of this book is not on prayer, but I wish to address two issues.

First is the issue of faith and works. I believe Brigham Young once said something to the effect that a person should pray as though

89. Richard G. Scott, "Using the Supernal Gift of Prayer," *Ensign* or *Liahona*, May 2007, 8.

everything depended upon the Lord and then work as though everything depended upon themself. The Lord follows the law of the harvest: you reap what you sow. If effort doesn't follow prayer, then one will reap something less than that which they prayed for.

Second, at times, one may pray for what he or she wants without considering what the Lord wants. Early in my career, I really wanted to find a job near family in Utah. So I prayed that I could find a job in Utah. That went on for months and months. I was not successful and was full of disappointment. A wise leader counseled me that I should pray to go where the Lord wants me. So I changed my attitude and opened my heart to other possibilities. I sincerely prayed "with real intent" to go where He would have me go. A short time later I was given a good job offer—but not in Utah.

His Church and His Prophets

Another resource Jesus Christ has given us to defeat Satan is His Church, even The Church of Jesus Christ of Latter-day Saints. In a revelation given in 1838, Jesus proclaimed "that the gathering together upon the land of Zion, and upon her stakes, may be for a defense, and for a refuge from the storm, and from wrath when it shall be poured out without mixture upon the whole earth" (Doctrine and Covenants 115:6).

The protection of the Church comes from living prophets and apostles who teach us truth and the ways of the Lord. It comes from inspired priesthood leaders located throughout the world. On the day the Church was organized on April 6, 1830, the Lord gave a revelation with this commandment: "Thou shalt give heed unto all his words [speaking of the prophet] which he shall give unto you as he receiveth them. . . . For his word ye shall receive, as if from mine own mouth, in all patience and faith" (Doctrine and Covenants 21:4–5). Almost a year later, the Lord gave another revelation wherein He proclaimed that the prophet of the Church, and no other, was appointed to receive commandments and revelations for the Saints (see Doctrine and Covenants 43:2–7). Years later, President Wilford Woodruff told the Saints, "The Lord will never permit me or any other man who stands as President of this Church to lead you astray" (Official Declaration 1).

The Church constitutes the whole armor of God. Paul exhorts, "Put on the whole armour of God, that ye may be able to stand against the wiles of the devil. Stand therefore, having your loins girt about with truth, and having on the breastplate of righteousness; And your feet shod with the preparation of the gospel of peace; Above all, taking the shield of faith, wherewith ye shall be able to quench all the fiery darts of the wicked. And take the helmet of salvation, and the sword of the Spirit, which is the word of God: Praying always" (Ephesians 6:11–18).

Paul tells us that truth can be a protection. Pure truth is found in Christ's Church. Surely one receives great protection when one remembers who they are—a son or daughter of God. Knowing from whence one has come, the purpose of life, and one's eternal possibilities are truths that will give one great power. Too many just think of themselves as mere mortals trying to find some spiritual experiences. In reality, we are immortal spiritual beings who have come from God's presence to have a short, temporary mortal experience. Knowing the plan of salvation will give one power against the enemy. Knowing that Jesus Christ will give us all the necessary power in any difficult situation can be enabling and uplifting!

A breastplate protects vital organs such as the heart. The Lord's Church will help us develop a broken heart, one that desires to be obedient and lead a person to repent when they make mistakes. Satan attempts to harden a heart, one that is flippant about Christ, about obedience, and has an "eat, drink, and be merry" attitude. Righteousness will develop a broken heart and will protect the core of one's spiritual life.

One's feet represent the direction in which one is going. The gospel of Jesus Christ will place a person on the path that leads back to God and will give them wisdom to avoid worldly paths. One's feet should be swift in following Christ and avoiding spiritual danger.

A shield is the most effective means of defense in battle. A shield of faith will defend against all the arsenal thrown at us. Christ's Church will help us develop faith as we are obedient to commandments, repent, show reverence for God, and honor His prophets and apostles.

A helmet protects the head from fatal blows. Christ's Church helps us keep our minds focused on Jesus Christ. Our minds need to be single to God (see Doctrine and Covenants 88:68). The Church will help us determine what the Lord wants us to do and then to do His will. Our minds need to be free from unclean thoughts: "Let virtue garnish thy thoughts unceasingly; then shall thy confidence wax strong in the presence of God" (Doctrine and Covenants 121:45).

A sword is the most effective offensive weapon to destroy the enemy. The word of God represents the sword. Alma taught that the word of God "had had more powerful effect upon the minds of the people than the sword, or anything else, which had happened unto them" (Alma 31:5). In our dispensation, the Lord declared, "Give heed to my word, which is quick and powerful, sharper than a two-edged sword, to the dividing asunder of both joints and marrow; therefore give heed unto my word" (Doctrine and Covenants 11:2). With one's testimony, coupled with the word of God, one can strike against and conquer the enemy.

The Holy Ghost

Another resource Jesus has given us is the Holy Ghost. Nephi tells us the Holy Ghost "will show unto you all things what ye should do" (2 Nephi 32:5). Whereas the scriptures will *tell* us what to do, the Holy Ghost will *show* us what to do. In our quest to be like the Savior, we can only succeed to the degree that we have the guidance of the Holy Ghost. We learn from the Doctrine and Covenants 11 that the Spirit is the key "to do good—yea, to do justly, to walk humbly, to judge righteously" and that the Spirit "shall enlighten your mind, which shall fill your soul with joy; And then shall ye know . . . all things . . . which are pertaining unto things of righteousness" (Doctrine and Covenants 11:12–14).

Elder Neal A. Maxwell said, "More than any other way, the Holy Ghost can reveal to us how we can connect the doctrines with our personal discipleship."[90]

After the death of the Prophet Joseph Smith, Brigham Young had a dream in which Joseph appeared to him with the following advice:

---

90. Church News Archives, "Receive Revelation to Lead," *Church News*, Jan. 18, 2023, https://www.thechurchnews.com/2003/1/18/23240977/receive-revelation-to-lead/.

"Tell the brethren to keep their hearts open to conviction, so that when the Holy Ghost comes to them, their hearts will be ready to receive it. It will whisper peace and joy to their souls, it will take malice, hatred, strife and all evil from their hearts; and their whole desire will be to do good, bring forth righteousness and build up the kingdom of God. Tell the brethren if they will follow the spirit of the Lord they will go right. Be sure to tell the people to keep the Spirit."[91]

The Holy Ghost is critical to change who we are and to become more like Christ. I have heard people say, "I can't help how I feel," or "That's just the way I am!" These assertions are wrong. Feelings can change. We can change. That's the whole essence of the gospel of Jesus Christ. President George Q. Cannon taught, "No man ought to say, 'Oh, I cannot help this; it is my nature.' He is not justified in it, for the reason that God has promised to give strength to correct these things, and to give gifts that will eradicate them. If a man lack wisdom, it is his duty to ask God for wisdom. The same with everything else. He wants His Saints to be perfected in the truth."[92]

Whatever changes need to be made in our character for us to become like Jesus Christ can only be done in a lasting way by the power of the Holy Ghost. Behavior modification programs are not enough. Dogged determination is not enough. Time management and goal-setting programs are not enough. Gritting our teeth and holding on in white-knuckled fashion is not the answer. As helpful as certain human plans and procedures may be—and as important as it is that we do all in our power to bring about meaningful change in our natures—it is our Redeemer that re-creates men and women by the influence of the Holy Ghost. He who commanded us to become like Him knew that we could only do so as we looked to Him in great faith, repented of our sins, and kept his commandments in the best way possible so we could have the Holy Ghost as our constant companion.

Some years ago, I participated in a management team-building exercise. The objective for each of us was to drive a Formula 3 racing

91. *Manuscript History of Brigham Young: 1846–1847*, ed. Elden J. Watson (Elden Jay Watson, 1971), 529; 23 February 1847.

92. Dallin H. Oaks, *Pure In Heart* (Deseret Book, 1988), 151.

car safely at high speeds on a racetrack. We had a track with eight different curves.

Our trainers were all professional race car drivers. We were first given class instruction regarding the dynamics and physics of acceleration, braking, and curving. Those dynamics are much greater at high speeds. We then spent considerable time driving a regular sedan through obstacle courses or around the track itself. We learned through these exercises that one can turn safely at much higher speeds than we normally do on the road. Through it all, a professional driver was sitting in the front seat giving valuable instruction and feedback. We learned that there was a proper way to negotiate a curve and a wrong way. If done properly, the car handled smoothly, and one could begin accelerating during the latter part of the curve and be at top speed at the straight-away. If done incorrectly, one would run off the track, or one had to brake sharply and fight the car through the curve and lose valuable time in the race. Generally, given no mechanical failure, the ultimate winner in a race is the one who makes the fewest mistakes in the curves.

To help us negotiate the curves correctly, cones were placed at the beginning of the curve, in the deepest part of the curve, and at the outer edge of the curve. The cones were a standard to the driver that showed them when to brake, when to turn, and the path to take through the curve. Many racetracks have indicators (either cones or lights) before a curve to help the drivers. During preliminary rounds, the drivers test their ability to go correctly through the curve at varying speeds by using these cones or lights. The driver who can maintain top speed until the last cone and still negotiate the curve properly has the edge in the race.

As we go through the race of life, we quickly learn that there are difficult and tough turns. But our loving Father in Heaven and our Savior, Jesus Christ, have given us cones (commandments, prophets, scriptures) to help us navigate properly the curves of life. We may want to move those cones for our convenience, but that will only get us in trouble; we will run off the track that leads us back to Heavenly Father.

At last, I was firmly strapped in a Formula 3—a car with no room for a companion. I was expected to drive the car and negotiate the track in accordance with the instructions I previously received. But a Formula 3 is different from a car sedan. First, it can go much, much faster—190 mph. Second, it rides close to the ground, which gives you a greater sensation of speed. Third, it has a firmer suspension; that, coupled with its low ride, gives it an ability to round curves faster. The professional drivers, aware of these differences, aware of our limited experience, and knowing that we wanted to test the car's speed, gave us something most valuable: a pace car to drive along with us. The pace car was a Ferrari, which could go 135 mph. It was their way of directly showing us on the track the speed they felt we could safely drive the Formula 3.

As I drove directly behind the pace car, my objective was to precisely follow that car and not lose space between it and me. The most important learning occurred during that time. I put my tires right on the pace car's tracks. I hit every curve at the speed it did. I turned at the precise points it did. I accelerated in the curve when it did. I sped to 135 mph when it did. Following that pace car, I developed the feel of driving a precision-powered racing car. Eventually, I didn't lose any space between it and me, and I became comfortable.

It has struck me that the Lord's plan to bring each one of us back to His home is much like my experience with the Formula 3. First, He gives us parents, teachers, and other loved ones to give us classroom training and then to provide feedback and instruction as we sit side by side with them during our early run through life. As our experience grows, we become less dependent on them for feedback and instruction, and we eventually become physically separated from them. But the Lord gives us a pace car—the gift of the Holy Ghost.

The Holy Ghost will first teach and show us what's right and what to do. If we precisely follow its instructions and teachings (its tire tracks, if you will), we will negotiate the track of life successfully. As our obedience grows, we will not lose space between Him and us. As our humility and obedience stay true, our ability to go faster and faster around the track and through the curves—to do more things for the Lord—will increase.

I had fun and was free of accidents as I followed the pace car. Then for the last few hours of the school, the instructors parked the pace car and told us to go it alone. For the first couple of rounds, I was nervous, but then I gained confidence and circled around the track admirably. So I pushed harder, especially through the curves, and ended up pushing too hard. Coincidentally, a magazine crew was there to write an article on the school, and they captured the moment in this way: "In a heart-stopping incident, one driver went into a 360-degree spin, sliding completely off the track backward into the trackside gravel in a cloud of dust."[93]

Without the guidance of the pace car, I ultimately spun out of control. It didn't happen immediately, but it happened nevertheless. Without the Holy Ghost, the difference in our lives may not be noticeable at first, but eventually we will lose our way, we will lose guidance, and we will spin out of control and lose our eternal reward. But unlike the instructors who removed the pace car, there is only one person who can cause the guidance of the Holy Ghost to be lost in your personal life: you! A person will cause the Holy Ghost to leave through sin, pride, or indifference.

The Holy Ghost is the third member of the Godhead. He performs many functions, but I simply want to emphasize that He will come and be one's companion as one is clean and worthy of His presence. The Holy Ghost can't guide someone through each day if they can't hear His voice. His voice or impressions are almost always quiet and subtle. It is often described as a still, small voice. Sin will prevent a person from hearing His voice. External noise and busyness will muffle His voice.

Sometime after I was called and ordained as a patriarch, a bishop called and asked me to speak to a combined youth fireside at 4 p.m. on a subsequent Sunday. I duly noted my speaking obligation in my appointment book. The Sunday that I was to speak happened to be my birthday, and all my children and grandchildren were at the house to celebrate my birthday. There was considerable joyous noise in the house. A few minutes before 3 p.m., I excused myself and went to my office to regather my thoughts about what I would say to the youth. I no sooner sat down in my office chair when I felt a very strong prompting of the Spirit; I almost heard an audible voice. The prompting gave me a feeling in the pit of my stomach that I was going to disappoint the youth, the bishop, and the Lord if I didn't leave for the

---

93. *Morning Calm*, June 1997, 35.

fireside at that very moment. Panicked, I reached for my appointment book to verify the appointment time. But the Spirit stopped me and basically told me to trust Him—that I needed to go now! I ran out the door. My wife chased after me to see if there was something wrong. I told her I just needed to go to the fireside right then and there.

As I was speeding down the highway to the church's location, my wife called me. She had just received a phone call from that bishop. His call was to let me know that he needed me not at 4 o'clock as he had previously communicated but at 3 o'clock! I walked into the fireside just after an opening hymn and prayer were completed. I was so relieved that I was there on time for my part of the fireside.

I wondered why the Spirit waited until just a few minutes before 3 p.m. to warn me that I was going to be late. Why didn't the Spirit tell me earlier? The answer came immediately from the Spirit. He had tried to communicate with me, but I couldn't hear Him because of all the noise and commotion surrounding my birthday party! I wasn't doing anything bad, but it was just too loud and noisy for the Spirit to communicate. The lesson to be learned: Each of us needs to have quiet, reflective time each day. It is during those times that the Lord can speak to us through the Spirit.

Temples

Jesus has given us temples to help us conquer Satan. We go to temples to receive saving ordinances and covenants. But there is even more power in temples. When I was a teenager attending seminary, I was required to memorize all thirteen temples: Salt Lake, Manti, St. George, Logan, Idaho Falls, Cardston, Mesa, Los Angeles, Oakland, Hawaii, Switzerland, London, and New Zealand! Obviously, only those living in those thirteen locations could regularly attend the temple. In 1998, Elder Ben Banks of the Seventy informed our stake presidency that it was the Church's intent to have a temple within a two-hour drive of every member of the Church. That is almost a reality today. Under the inspired leadership of Presidents Hinckley, Monson, and Nelson, there are now over 300 temples either dedicated, being constructed, or being planned throughout the world. The Lord wants to strengthen the Saints by providing temples for them.

The temple is more than a place to go to receive our saving ordinances and to do the same glorifying work for those who have gone on before us. The dedicatory prayer of the Kirtland Temple reveals the blessings that await those who go to the temple with proper preparation: "Grant, Holy Father, that all those who shall worship in this house may be taught words of wisdom . . . And that they may grow up in thee, and receive a fulness of the Holy Ghost . . . that thy servants may go forth from this house armed with thy power, and that thy name may be upon them, and thy glory be round about them, and thine angels have charge over them" (Doctrine and Covenants 109:14–15, 22).

Three great promises are mentioned in that wonderful scripture: (1) a fulness of the Holy Ghost, (2) great power, and (3) protection by holy angels. A promise of having the fulness of the Holy Ghost implies that we may go through life without the fulness—that we may just have a portion of the Holy Ghost. It is only by regular temple attendance—coupled with proper preparation—that we can receive the fulness of the Holy Ghost.

We are promised great power as we attend the temple with proper preparation. This is an offensive weapon as we battle against the forces of Lucifer. This is the power to recognize evil and sin and overcome them. This is the power to say, "Get thee hence, Satan" (Matthew 4:10). This is the power to be an instrument in God's hands in helping others recognize truth. This is the power to build Zion. This is the power to overcome individual weaknesses and shortcomings. The covenants and ordinances will fill us with faith as a living fire.

The third promise for temple attendance is protection, safety, and refuge. Since we live in a world full of temptations, stress, and subject to the laws of the jungle, we may often feel beat down and utterly exhausted. We may become discouraged and begin to lose hope. The Lord has established His temples among us. We would do well to go frequently to His temples to increase our faith and learning.

I love this scripture: "And there shall be a tabernacle for a shadow in the daytime from the heat, and for a place of refuge, and for a covert from storm and from rain" (Isaiah 4:6). Isaiah speaks of the tabernacle or temple. He gives three images to describe what the temple will do for us. The temple is a "shadow in the daytime from the heat." The summer sun and heat would exhaust me while I was working on my dad's farm. I would seek some relief by finding shade under a large tree. When the world's heat becomes oppressive, the Lord beckons us to come into the shade of His house to be refreshed.

Isaiah calls the temple a "place of refuge." We fight daily against the forces of Satan. When we feel wounded by life's struggles, the Lord tells us to come into His temple for refuge. It is no coincidence that the walls of the pioneer temples are crowned with battlements. Satan and his forces cannot enter the temple. In the temple, our wounds can be healed, and we can then return to life's battle with the full armor of God.

Isaiah calls the temple a "covert from the storm and from rain." More than once, I have become drenched by a downpour while being in the open with no shelter. Life's storms also beat upon us. The Lord invites us to dry off while being warmed by the spiritual fire found in His temples. When we are comforted by His temple, the storm will not seem so black.

Speaking to Manti Temple workers in April 1987, Elder Vaughn J. Featherstone made this statement:

> As the evil night darkens upon this generation, we must come to the temple for light and safety. In our temples we find quiet, sacred havens where the storm cannot penetrate to us. Before the Savior comes, the world will darken. There will come a period of time where even the elect will lose hope if they do not come to the temples. The world will be so filled with evil that the righteous will only feel secure within these walls. The Saints will come here not only to do vicarious work, but to find a haven of peace. They will long to bring their children here for safety sake.
>
> The season of the world before us will be like no other in the history of humankind. Satan has unleashed every evil, every scheme, every blatant, vile perversion ever known to man in any generation. Just as this is the dispensation of the fullness of times, so it is also the dispensation of the fullness of evil. There is no safety in the world; wealth cannot provide it, enforcement agencies cannot assure it, membership in this Church alone cannot bring it.
>
> Our garments worn as instructed will clothe us in a manner as protective as temple walls. The covenants and ordinances will fill us with faith as a living fire. In a day of desolating sickness, scorched earth, barren wastes, sickening plagues, disease, destruction, and

> death, we as a people will rest in the shade of trees, we will drink from the cooling fountains. We will aide in places of refuge from the storm, we will mount up as on eagles' wings, we will be lifted out of an insane and evil world. We will be as fair as the sun and clear as the moon.[94]

Why is the temple such a protective force? Why is it such a purifying power? I believe the answer is simple yet profound. The temple gives us a deeper insight into who we are and our eternal potential. Fifty years ago, I knelt on an altar of the Lord's temple across from my bride. As I listened to one who had the sealing power of the priesthood promise us kingdoms, thrones, principalities, and dominions based on our faithfulness, I saw briefly a vision of the eternities and was awed and overcome by it. I think it is significant and revealing of the Lord's character that we must do so little to be able to receive so much.

With such a vision of eternity, how can one leave the temple and go home and be unkind to one's spouse and children? How can one deal unjustly with their neighbor? How can one be unforgiving of others? With such a vision of one's eternal identity, how can one put popularity and fashion first in their life? How can one put power and prestige first in their life? How can one not pay tithing? How can one be impure? With such a vision of eternity, the things of this world become less desirable. With such a vision of eternity, it becomes easier to withstand the powers and temptations of Satan.

In short, temple worship has the power to produce a new and different kind of person who knows the path of principles followed by the Savior and gives them application in his or her personal life. Temple worship gives us a purifying spirit that will enable us to practice love and charity, to do the will of the Lord, to be loyal to wholesome standards, and to seek first the kingdom of God.

Some years ago, we lived in the Atlanta Temple district, but it was a six-hour drive from our home. My wife and I would leave early in the morning and spend that afternoon, evening, and the next day in the temple before returning home. Obviously, we needed someone we

---

94. Trevor Holyoak, "Vaughn J. Featherstone's Atlanta Temple Letter," FAIR, June 13, 2020, https://www.fairlatterdaysaints.org/blog/2020/06/13/vaughn-j-featherstones-atlanta-temple-letter.

could trust who would be willing to watch our children during our absence. One particular time, we were having difficulty finding a suitable babysitter. Over the dinner table, we told our kids our dilemma and that we might have to cancel our plans to go to the temple. Our oldest son pleaded for us to try harder to find a sitter, saying, "Dad, you come back a better dad after being in the temple." He was right, and we did find a sitter.

A primary purpose of the temples is to bless the here and now—you and me. The sacred proxy work that is done blesses our ancestors, but we are just scratching the surface of what is needed. That work is primarily for a future day when we will not be as tempted, for Satan will be bound. But while Satan reigns on the earth, the temples are here to bless us. Each of us needs to be worthy of the temple and to receive a revelatory experience when we are there. We must drink deeply from its fountains frequently. As we do so, we will become strengthened and become more like our Savior.

President Henry B. Eyring recently taught, "Qualifying to receive sacred covenants is not a one-time effort but a lifetime pattern. Frequent participation in the ordinances of the temple can create a pattern of devotion to the Lord. You will come to know that every covenant with God is an opportunity to draw closer to Him, which will then create a desire in your heart to keep temple covenants."[95]

Christ Is Involved in the Details of Our Lives

At times, Christ will be intimately involved in the details of our lives. That doesn't take away our agency, and that does not imply predestination. He knows what we will do because He knows who we are and how we will act in every situation.

Isaiah writes, "He hath made my mouth like a sharp sword; in the shadow of his hand hath he hid me, and made me a polished shaft; in his quiver hath he hid me" (1 Nephi 21:2). After we have been polished and properly prepared, the Lord then says to us, "Thou art my servant . . . in whom I will be glorified" (1 Nephi 21:3). The key is to

---

95. Henry B. Eyring, "All Will Be Well Because of Temple Covenants," *Liahona*, May 2024, 26.

not lose sight of who we are as we go through the mundaneness and difficulties of life.

We largely go through life unaware of what the Lord is making of us. If we are humble, however, the Lord will polish us in the shadow of His hand. To the world, our worth may be invisible. Notice, however, that this situation is meant to be temporary. In time, the Lord will retrieve us from His sheath as though we were a sharp sword or a polished shaft in His quiver. He has been preparing us to become His secret weapon!

Who can forget Joseph who was betrayed by his brothers and sold as a slave into Egypt where he was cast into prison? Without family or friends, languishing in captivity in a hostile land, Joseph was stripped of everything except his covenant and his God. But he remembered who he was! He was being polished, and when deliverance finally came—*and it always comes*—Joseph was snatched out and exalted. He went from prisoner to prince.

Joseph Smith Sr. suffered through three straight years of crop disaster in Vermont. I'm sure he and Lucy Smith wondered why things weren't going well for them when they were doing their best in all things. But those disasters were necessary to get them thinking about relocating to the location that God had picked for them: the Palmyra, New York, area. Shortly after their relocation, Jesus began restoring gospel truths via the Book of Mormon—plates that had been buried in the area by the prophet Moroni around AD 400—and establishing His Church!

I know that the heavens guided a girl from New Jersey to California. She then met my best friend at a California wedding. He, in turn, introduced her to me, and she later became my wife. Those were not circumstantial events; the Lord's hand was clearly evident in putting us together.

The Lord directed my wife and I to go east from Utah rather than west to California, which was our desire. Eventually, He placed us in the Palmyra area where we had significant experiences. He directed us to the Austin, Texas, area when it would have been so easy to go elsewhere. So I know that the Lord does care about where we live. I know He will guide us in the daily pursuits of life if we truly listen and are willing to leave our comfort zone.

The Hope of Christ During Our Trials

Speaking of our time in mortality, God in the premortal world said, "We will prove them herewith, to see if they will do all things whatsoever the Lord their God shall command them" (Abraham 3:25). It is necessary for man to learn by actual experience rather than from some textbook. There will be opposition in all things (see 2 Nephi 2:11). When a person tastes the bitter, it enables them to appreciate the sweet. A person must comprehend the effects of sin before they can enjoy the peace promised to the faithful and obedient.

This is truly a time for us to prove ourselves. Who will be our master—God or Satan? As in premortality, we have been given the precious gift of agency. We read that people have the power to "act for themselves and not to be acted upon, save it be by the punishment of the law at the great and last day, according to the commandments which God hath given" (2 Nephi 2:26–27). We are our own agents. We can't blame anyone for our failures.

There is another connotation to proving ourselves. In simplistic terms, steel is made by combining carbon, iron, and oxygen at very high temperatures. If one wants to make steel fireproof, another heating process is involved. But after all the heat, the elements become more valuable: steel. Similarly, we prove ourselves by experiencing opposition in all things. The opposition in all things is the Lord's heat; it is meant for us to become better.

While in the premortal world, we knew that trials in mortality were necessary in our journey to become like God. Mentally we knew that mortal life would not be easy, but we had no experience to judge how difficult it really would be. How ironic—we came to earth to experience trials and opposition, yet we complain as we go through those trials and opposition. This opposition in all things engulfs all of mortality. We are to learn from our opposition and be tempered much like steel. Opposition is what gives us pleasure and pain, health and sickness, and success and failure and what causes righteousness or sin. It's why bad things happen to good people. It's why worldly riches are often given to bad people. The really important proving ground is whether we will follow God or follow Satan and the world's ways. It is why agency is so important.

President Thomas S. Monson taught, "Our mortal life, however, was never meant to be easy or consistently pleasant. Our Heavenly Father knows that we learn and grow and become refined through hard challenges, heartbreaking sorrows, and difficult choices. Each one of us experiences dark days when our loved ones pass away, painful times when our health is lost, and feelings of being forsaken when those we love seem to have abandoned us. These and other trials present us with the real test of our ability to endure."[96]

A trial or affliction is not an indication of the Lord's displeasure. It should never be an occasion when one asks, "Why is the Lord punishing me?" The Lord is never in the punishment business. I am rescued by the reassuring reality that "He doeth not anything save it be for the benefit of the world [insert your name]; for he loveth the world [insert your name], even that he layeth down his own life that he may draw all men [insert your name] unto him" (2 Nephi 26:24). Some of our best soul-stretching experiences occur when we endure well the sufferings and afflictions of life. The key to enduring such afflictions is to "press forward with a steadfastness in Christ" (2 Nephi 31:20).

96. Thomas S. Monson, "Joy in the Journey" (address given at the BYU Women's Conference, May 2, 2008), womensconference.ce.byu.edu.

Jesus gave instruction regarding tragedies and other vicissitudes of life that each of us encounters. It was the prevailing belief of the time, and still exists today, that punishments and tribulations received by an individual were merited because of that individual's sins and disobedience. We know that Job's friends asked him what great sin he had committed to warrant such severe trials. Some of the multitude spoke to Jesus regarding a tragic event that had taken place inside the temple walls. A number of Galileans had been slain by Roman soldiers at the base of the altar so that their blood had mingled with that of the sacrificial animals. Jesus used that event and then referred to another catastrophe—the death of eighteen people when the tower of Siloam collapsed—to teach that the victims of both of those events should not be considered greater sinners than the rest of us. He taught, "Except ye repent, ye shall all likewise perish" (Luke 13:1–5).

The Lord carefully designed the laws of this mortal schoolhouse to be consistent with His proving purposes. If disaster struck each time sin was committed, sin would soon cease for fear of punishment. "True virtue would [be] impossible. A sun that shines and a rain which falls equally on the evil and on the good, are essential to morality."[97]

President Spencer W. Kimball, a man well acquainted with trials and afflictions, gave this counsel:

> Was it the Lord who directed the plane into the mountain to snuff out the lives of its occupants, or were there mechanical faults or human errors? Did our Father in heaven cause the collision of the cars that took six people into eternity, or was it the error of the driver who ignored safety rules? Did God take the life of the young mother or prompt the child to toddle into the canal or guide the other child into the path of the oncoming car? Did the Lord cause the man to suffer a heart attack? Was the death of the missionary untimely? Answer, if you can. I cannot, for though I know God has a major role in our lives, I do not know how much he causes to happen and how much he merely permits. . . .
>
> If all the sick for whom we pray were healed, if all the righteous were protected and the wicked destroyed, the whole program of the Father would be annulled and the basic principle of the gospel, free

97. Neal A. Maxwell, "Thanks Be to God," *Ensign*, July 1982, 52.

> agency, would be ended. No man would have to live by faith. If joy and peace and rewards were instantaneously given the doer of good, there could be no evil—all would do good but not because of the rightness of doing good. There would be no test of strength, no development of character, no growth of powers, no free agency, only satanic controls. Should all prayers be immediately answered according to our selfish desires and our limited understanding, then there would be little or no suffering, sorrow, disappointment, or even death, and if these were not, there would also be no joy, success, resurrection, nor eternal life and godhood. Being human, we would expel from our lives physical pain and mental anguish and assure ourselves of continual ease and comfort but if we were to close the doors upon sorrow and distress, we might be excluding our greatest friends and benefactors. Suffering can make saints of people as they learn patience, long-suffering, and self-mastery.[98]

As the Prophet Joseph languished in the Liberty Jail, the Lord told him that his jail experience—and all other trials and afflictions that he had endured and would continue to be asked to endure in patience—"shall give thee experience, and shall be for thy good." Then the Lord gave this stunning observation: "The Son of Man hath descended below them all. Art thou greater than he?" (Doctrine and Covenants 122:7–8).

Granted, while one is in the midst of adversity and suffering, it can be very difficult. We, like the Prophet Joseph, may cry out, "O God, where art thou?" (Doctrine and Covenants 121:1). In Gethsemane, when it seemed like His burdens were too heavy to bear, our Savior prayed more earnestly and asked if His trial could be removed. For a while, He received no satisfactory answer. Only when the purposes of the Lord had been fulfilled did relief come. We too may have to patiently suffer until the Lord's timing and purposes are fulfilled.

The Lord has declared to our generation, "They must needs be chastened and tried, even as Abraham" (Doctrine and Covenants 101:4). "I will prove you in all things, whether you will abide in my covenant, even unto death, that you may be found worthy" (Doctrine and Covenants 98:14). "My people must be tried in all things, that they may be prepared to receive the glory that I have for them, even

98. *Teachings of Presidents of the Church: Spencer W. Kimball* (2011), 14–15.

the glory of Zion; and he that will not bear chastisement is not worthy of my kingdom" (Doctrine and Covenants 136:31).

In the face of affliction, it is sad to see many curse God and turn away from Him. They use their agency to change a would-be blessing from God into a self-imposed curse. Why do they get mad at God? Perhaps because they believe that God should have conformed to their desires! The purpose of mortality is to learn to conform our will to God's desires.

Jesus Christ Heals Us and Gives Us Hope

Moroni recognized that hope in Christ would become the "anchor to the souls of men, which would make them sure and steadfast" (Ether 12:4). This hope does not allow for wavering or hesitation. In fact, once we have an "unshaken faith in him, relying wholly upon the merits of him who is mighty to save," then it is necessary that we "press forward with a steadfastness in Christ, having a perfect brightness of hope" (2 Nephi 31:19–20).

This hope in Christ strengthens us through our trials and tribulations. It is the hope that allows us to be "patient in tribulation" (Doctrine and Covenants 54:10). In all that comes into our lives, such brightness of hope allows the growth and development of the soul.

Elder Neal A. Maxwell once said, "What are a few fingers of scorn now anyway when the faithful can eventually know what it is like to be 'clasped in the arms of Jesus'? What are mocking words now, if later we hear those glorious words, 'Well done, thou good and faithful servant'?"[99]

With a perspective firmly grounded in the gospel of Jesus Christ, we can see the Lord's hand in blessing our lives through the trials He sends or allows to come our way. We can find joy regardless of what is happening in our lives. My wife and I have suffered the stress and worries of unemployment. We know how unjust and unfair life can be. We have had financial setbacks. We have had to deal with the loss of a child.

We rejoiced in the birth of our fifth child. She was born in October. We decided to spend the Christmas holidays with my parents and

---

99. Neal A. Maxwell, "Plow in Hope," *Ensign*, May 2001, 59.

extended family in Utah. The trip across the country was rather routine and uneventful. We arrived at my parents' home on the evening of December 23. Some of my siblings were also there. We enjoyed showing off our baby girl and then put her to bed. She never woke up. An autopsy indicated that she died of SIDS, or "crib death" as it's commonly called. You can well imagine our grief. We buried her in a small cemetery in my hometown the day after Christmas. The next day, we attended the Manti Temple and spent quiet time in the celestial room and also in the room in which we were sealed. At that time, the Lord taught me a lesson through an experience I had had at the Salt Lake airport some years ago.

I was flying home from my mission. In those days, people disembarked the plane on the open tarmac. Friends and relatives could wait at the gate. As I started walking toward the gate, my mother saw me. No barrier could stop her as she came running onto the tarmac to greet me with a big hug and kiss. I then greeted my siblings and friends. At the end of the line was my father, patiently waiting. His love and handshake let me know that he was proud of my willingness to serve a mission but that he was also happy I was home.

In the Manti Temple, a vision came to my mind. I saw my daughter having the same kind of experience I had at the Salt Lake airport. The Lord has not seen fit to give much detail as to what exactly happens when we die and pass on to the other side. But who can deny that at some point in time, her heavenly parents will rush to her with open arms? Surely, she will be greeted by her many family members and friends who will welcome her back after her short ten-week absence. Who can doubt that she will at last be greeted by her Elder Brother and her Heavenly Father? That same experience can be had by all of us.

As we left Utah to return home, my thoughts turned to my ancestors. It occurred to me that the loss of our daughter—indeed, all our trials that we may ever face—likely had been faced by our ancestors. History was simply repeating itself with minor variations. The one common element through it all could be captured by the words "this is a test." We are more likely to pass the test if we have an eternal perspective and have gratitude in our hearts for what the Lord has given us.

We like to say that time heals the bitterness of life. I don't think that's true. Bitterness often festers and becomes worse. The only thing that heals is the Atonement of Jesus Christ! If we humbly and faithfully turn to Him and ask Him to give us a changed heart, He will do so. It matters not the situation or circumstances. If we need help to cultivate gratitude, or humility, or patience, or any other attribute, we need to put our faith in our Savior. At our petition, in His time, He will heal.

It's so important to maintain a gospel perspective. One billion years from now, how will we remember the trials and tribulations of life? One billion years from now, surrounded by all our loved ones, will we even remember the grief we felt when one of our loved ones died and left us alone for a small season? Will we remember our physical deformities? Will we remember our other mortal afflictions? Will we remember our feelings of being forgotten or forsaken? One billion years from now, we may experience regret if in this brief mortal life, we choose to have trials and afflictions change our eternal perspective and lose sight of who we really are. Whatever regret we may feel then will most likely be a result of the lack of perspective and gratitude we feel now! Our attitude of gratitude could very well be the means of escaping the clutches of our eternal enemy who wants us to be miserable.

Conclusion

Some years ago, I addressed an area conference of single adults. They had asked me to speak on making Christ our friend. It's a catchy sentiment. However, I may have disappointed them, as I basically taught that such a premise was ill-advised. What kind of relationship do we have or should we have with Jesus Christ? Should He be our friend? I go golfing with friends. I go to dinner with friends. I do fun things with friends. Is it proper to develop a casual, friendly relationship with Jesus Christ? Is Christ to be our friend in this sense?

We learn from the scriptures that Christ is known by many titles. Each of those titles gives us a glimpse into who He is and the kind of relationship we should develop with Him. Jesus Christ is the Almighty God, the Lord Omnipotent, the Son of God, the Redeemer of all humankind. He is Jehovah, the God of Abraham, Isaac, and Jacob. He is our Savior. He is the Captain of the Lord's Host. He is the Holy One of Israel. He is the King of kings. He is the Light of the World. He is the Resurrection and the Life. He is the Good Shepherd, the Prince of Peace, our Advocate with the Father. He is the Creator, the Judge of the world, the Bread of Life, the Rock of our Salvation, our great Exemplar. He is the Lamb of God, our Mediator, the promised Messiah. There are many more. None of these titles suggest that

Jesus should be our buddy or friend. Such casualness makes mockery of who He is and diminishes His majesty.

Those who knew Jesus best during His mortal ministry never referred to Him as a friend. Peter and others called Him Lord. Many called Him Master. On the morn of His Resurrection, He first appeared to Mary. With soul-filled exuberance, she cried, "Rabboni" which means "Master" (see John 20:16). She didn't call Him "friend." Shortly afterward, the Lord appeared to other favored women, and "they came and held him by the feet, and worshipped him" (Matthew 28:9–10).

When the resurrected Christ appeared on the American continent, He invited all to come and touch the wounds in his feet, hands, and side. Afterward, they "did cry out with one accord, saying: Hosanna! Blessed be the name of the Most High God! And they did fall down at the feet of Jesus, and did worship him" (3 Nephi 11:16–17).

As these scriptural stories suggest, our attitude toward Jesus Christ should be one of worshipful adoration. Christ condescended below all things to come to this world to save you and me. There have been too many miracles, too much pain, too much cost for Him to be our casual friend. Though He is our Elder Brother, we are not His equals.

So what is to be our relationship with Christ? As we study the scriptures, we learn that those who choose to serve the Lord and who keep his commandments are called His *servants*. We read, "For unto me the children of Israel are servants" (Leviticus 25:55). Also, "Surely the Lord God will do nothing, but he revealeth his secret unto his servants the prophets" (Amos 3:7). At the last day, all of us hope to hear the words, "Well done, thou good and faithful servant; thou hast been faithful over a few things, I will make thee ruler over many things: enter thou into the joy of thy lord" (Matthew 25:21). In his great discourse on service, King Benjamin teaches us that "if ye should serve him with all your whole souls yet ye would be unprofitable servants" (Mosiah 2:21).

When John the Baptist appeared to Joseph Smith and Oliver Cowdery on May 15, 1829, to restore the Aaronic Priesthood, he laid his hands upon their heads and began his blessing with these words: "Upon you my fellow servants" (Doctrine and Covenants 13:1).

Simply stated, the scriptures teach that we are servants to our Master, our Lord, our God, Jesus Christ.

Now in mortality, Jesus had the same social needs as any of us. Jesus called Lazarus His friend (see John 11:11). One can only assume that He called Lazarus's sisters, Mary and Martha, His friends. On the night of His betrayal, He called Judas His friend (see Matthew 26:50). That is why in our dispensation, Jesus said He was "wounded in the house of my friends" (Doctrine and Covenants 45:52). But nowhere in scripture do we find Jesus's friends calling Him anything other than some reverential name such as Lord or Master.

Near the end of His life, Jesus said, "Ye are my friends, if ye do whatsoever I command you" (John 15:14). Attaching this condition does not indicate conditional love for us since we are loved perfectly by Him. Rather, it describes the condition—keeping His commandments—we must fulfill in order to eventually earn a friendship with Him. Jesus reserves the right to call someone His friend. But Jesus, not you or I, makes the decision to change the relationship from servant to friend.

In our dispensation, Jesus called Joseph Smith, Sidney Rigdon, and other leading brethren His friends (see Doctrine and Covenants 84:63, 77; 94:1; 100:1). But those brethren didn't call Jesus their friend. As mortals, though Jesus may call us friends, we must always reverence Him as Savior, Redeemer, and God.

According to John, the difference between a friend and a servant is that a friend knows the Lord's doings (see John 15:15). That happens only when one is doing the same things as the Lord. That is precisely what Jesus Christ asks us to do (see 3 Nephi 27:27; Luke 10:37). As we do the things that Christ does, as we become the kind of person He is, then we will begin to *know* Christ (see John 17:3) and He will call us His friends. As we prove our discipleship, He will make us His friends as He takes us into His kingdom (see Doctrine and Covenants 93:45). I'm confident that if we ever make it into His presence, our appreciation for what He did for us will be so deep that we will forever have a worshipful attitude toward Him. He will always be our Lord, our Savior, and our Redeemer.

Even more importantly, as His friends, we will receive the adoption of sonship. Speaking of those who will be redeemed, Paul teaches,

"Wherefore thou art no more a servant, but a son; and if a son, then an heir of God through Christ" (Galatians 4:7). In Ether, we read, "I am Jesus Christ. In me shall all mankind have life, and that eternally, even they who shall believe on my name; and they shall become my sons and my daughters" (Ether 3:14). Furthermore, He tells us "that as many as receive me, to them will I give power to become the sons of God, even to them that believe on my name" (Doctrine and Covenants 11:30). Thus, those who are faithful servants here in this life will gain exaltation hereafter. In that sphere, we will not only be Christ's friends but also His sons and daughters.

Interestingly, those who do not choose to serve the Lord, who do not keep His commandments, and who do not receive the ordinances of the gospel shall be servants through all eternity (see Doctrine and Covenants 76:112). They did not choose to be His servants here, and so He will require ministering servitude from them in eternity. We read that they will be "ministering servants, to minister for those who are worthy of a far more, and an exceeding, and an eternal weight of glory" (Doctrine and Covenants 132:16–17, 25).

Jesus Christ, He who was born in Nazareth, is the Son of God, the Savior of the world, the promised Messiah. That is absolute truth. Revealed knowledge that comes from God is the source of absolute truth. Books may facilitate the necessary revelation as one ponders and prays over truths that are contained in books. Personal revelation, by the power of the Holy Ghost, will reveal absolute truth to the mind and heart of any seeker. Those who follow the scientific method of learning, or the analytical method of learning, or the academic method of learning may discover many truths. But they are not sufficient to discover absolute spiritual truth. Many who are sincere will claim that revelation does not exist today. They deny the very process by which absolute spiritual truths are discovered!

Jesus Christ was and is the Lord God Omnipotent, the great Creator. As the Creator, He is also the source of life and light in all things. Then the source of all light teaches us, "That which is of God is light; and he that receiveth light, and continueth in God, receiveth more light; and that light groweth brighter and brighter until the perfect day" (Doctrine and Covenants 50:24). When I realize that all the good natures of all men are simply a reflection of the Light of Christ,

I am in awe of His majesty. When I realize that the beauty of all the animal and plant kingdoms in this world is a reflection of the Light of Christ, I am in awe of His majesty.

Jesus Christ is the Creator of this world, and I am grateful for the beauty of this earth. I love the great rivers and small streams. I love the mountains and the oceans. I love the beauty of flowers; I love the beauty of green pastures or of golden grain. The beauty of this "lone and dreary world" is amazing; I can only imagine how much more glorious will be the future kingdoms in which we find ourselves!

There is beauty in all peoples and in all cultures. Life has given me the opportunity and pleasure to visit most states as well as many foreign countries in the Americas, Europe, and Asia. Although I have not visited Africa, I have had the pleasure of doing gospel service with people from that continent. I have delighted in the beauty of people no matter what continent they call home. All people have great capacity for good because all of them are sons and daughters of God.

As the Son of God, Christ had powers and intelligence that no human has ever had before or since. He majestically used those powers and intelligence to always bless others. His miracles were many. The deaf were made to hear. The blind were made to see. The dumb were made to speak. The lame were made to walk. The lepers were healed. Those who were sick, diseased, or maimed were healed. The unclean and evil spirits were cast out. Three individuals we know of were raised from the dead. His miracles continue even today, especially as He changes hearts through His agent, the Holy Ghost.

I am in awe of His ministry that He performed while walking the roads of Palestine. His ministry continues today through His chosen prophets, apostles, and other men and women throughout the world who are willingly sacrificing and consecrating their efforts to establish Zion. I marvel at how He is gathering Israel on both sides of the veil. I am in awe at the temples being built in all parts of the Lord's vineyard that will enable men and women to become more Zion-like.

I am in awe of the meekness and lowliness of heart shown by Jesus Christ throughout His life. Jesus submitted to His Father's will in all circumstances; He never deviated.

I am in awe of His love for you and me. The words of the hymn "I Stand All Amazed" captures my feelings beautifully:

> I stand all amazed at the love Jesus offers me,
> Confused at the grace that so fully he proffers me.
> I tremble to know that for me he was crucified,
> That for me, a sinner, he suffered, he bled and died.
>
> I marvel that he would descend from his throne divine
> To rescue a soul so rebellious and proud as mine,
> That he should extend his great love unto such as I,
> Sufficient to own, to redeem, and to justify.
>
> I think of his hands pierced and bleeding to pay the debt!
> Such mercy, such love and devotion can I forget?
> No, no, I will praise and adore at the mercy seat,
> Until at the glorified throne I kneel at his feet.
>
> Oh, it is wonderful that he should care for me
> Enough to die for me!
> Oh, it is wonderful, wonderful to me! (*Hymns*, no. 193)

I am in awe that He accomplished the Atonement, which was made possible because Elohim is His biological father and because He lived a sinless life. His Atonement will give me the power to rise from the dead with an immortal body. His grace will forgive me of my sins so long as I sacrifice the natural man upon the altar and daily repent. His grace enables me to do things far beyond my normal capacity. His mercy and grace will one day make me perfect if I faithfully follow the covenant path.

Perhaps, more majestically, to those who are humble and lowly in heart, Jesus gives hope. Jesus purifies their hearts. Jesus shows them a better way—a way of faith, hope, and charity. Jesus gives them His gospel and Church, which will enable them to return to His presence. He shows us how to forsake the world and keep our priorities in perspective. He shows us how to rise above petty weaknesses and to demonstrate affection, love, and charity.

Elder Patrick Kearon recently said:

> The intent of the Father's great plan of happiness is your *happiness*, right here, right now, and in the eternities. It is not to prevent your happiness and cause you instead worry and fear.

> The intent of the Father's plan of redemption is in fact your *redemption*, your being rescued through the sufferings and death of Jesus Christ, freed from the captivity of sin and death. It is not to leave you as you are.
>
> The intent of the Father's plan of mercy is to *extend mercy* as you turn back to Him and honor your covenant of fidelity to Him. It is not to deny mercy and inflict pain and sorrow.
>
> The intent of the Father's plan of salvation is in fact your *salvation* in the celestial kingdom of glory as you receive 'the testimony of Jesus' and offer your whole soul to Him. It is not to keep you out.[100]

In this dispensation, Jesus gave us this counsel: "Lift up your hearts and be glad, for I am in your midst, and am your advocate with the Father; and it is his good will to give you the kingdom" (Doctrine and Covenants 29:5). Jesus Christ is not piling on trials to see if our knees will buckle. The Lord's good will is to give us the kingdom. He wants us to have it. He's on our side. The Savior loves us. He promises us joy and rejoicing. He doesn't want us to beat up on ourselves, to feel guilty, or to wallow in discouragement. The message of Jesus Christ isn't that we're miserable sinners. It's that we are unique and beloved children of our Father in Heaven and that we can be recipients of His redeeming love, which will allow us to be happy and cheerful in this life and in the world to come.

I am in awe at the majesty of Jesus Christ. His majesty allows me to have faith in Him, to have confidence in Him, to have hope in my eternal destiny through Him, and to receive strength from Him to overcome the world.

So that we might enjoy eternal blessings, Moroni pleaded to all of us, "Come unto Christ, and be perfected in him, and deny yourselves of all ungodliness; and if ye shall deny yourselves of all ungodliness, and love God with all your might, mind and strength, then is his grace sufficient for you, that by his grace ye may be perfect in Christ; and if by the grace of God ye are perfect in Christ . . . then are ye sanctified in Christ by the grace of God, through the shedding of the blood of

100. Patrick Kearon, "God's Intent Is to Bring You Home," *Liahona*, May 2024, 87–88.

Christ, which is in the covenant of the Father unto the remission of your sins, that ye become holy, without spot" (Moroni 10:32–33).

I rejoice in the majesty of Jesus Christ!

About the Author

Burke Rees has been a teacher of the gospel to both adults and youth throughout his life in a number of capacities. He has been a patriarch since 2011 and has served in that capacity in three different stakes in Texas and Utah. He has also served as a counselor in a stake presidency, bishop, high councilor, ward mission leader, high priests group leader, and Young Men president, and he loved being an early-morning seminary teacher.

He and his wife served two years in the mission office in the England London Mission. As a young man, he served a full-time mission in the Finland Helsinki Mission. He and his wife just celebrated their fiftieth wedding anniversary, and they currently have five children and fifteen grandchildren.

Brother Rees obtained a bachelor's degree in business management from Brigham Young University and an MBA degree from Indiana University. He worked in the corporate world in various management positions before becoming an entrepreneur.